— HMS INTREPID —

FEARLESS AND INTREPID
1965 – 2002

The Royal Navy's First Purpose-Built Assault Ships

Neil McCart

FOREWORD BY COMMODORE A .J. S. TAYLOR CBE, ROYAL NAVY

To the memory of those who lost their lives in the Falkland Islands 1982, and to all those who have served in HM Ships *Fearless* and *Intrepid* between 1965 and 2002.

Front Cover: A magnificent photograph of *Fearless* courtesy of Derek Fox, Southsea, Hampshire.

Cover Design by Louise McCart
© Neil McCart/FAN PUBLICATIONS 2003
ISBN: 1 901225 07 0

Typesetting By: Highlight Type Bureau Ltd,
Clifton House, 2 Clifton Villas, Bradford,
West Yorkshire BD8 7BY

Printing By: The Amadeus Press, Ezra House,
West 26 Business Park, Cleckheaton,
West Yorkshire BD19 4TQ

All Rights Reserved. No part of this publication may be reproduced, stored in a retrieval system, or transmitted in any form by any electronic or mechanical means without the prior permission of the publisher.

Published By FAN PUBLICATIONS
17 Wymans Lane, Cheltenham, GL51 9QA, England.
Fax & Tel: 01242 580290
Email: info@fan-publications.i12.com

A dramatic photograph of *Intrepid* in Norwegian waters during amphibious operations in 1997.
(Official, courtesy Commodore A.J.S. Taylor)

Contents

Page No.

Foreword by Commodore A.J.S. Taylor CBE RN. 6

Prologue . . . . .The Two New Assault Ships 7

Part One: HMS *Fearless*

Chapter One . . . . .HMS *Fearless* - First Commission 1965-1967 10

Chapter Two . . . . .HMS *Fearless* - Second Commission 1968-1970 23

Chapter Three . . . . . . .HMS *Fearless* - Third Commission 1970-1972 32

Chapter Four . . . . .HMS *Fearless* - Dartmouth Training 1973-1978 42

Chapter Five . . . . .HMS *Fearless* - War In The South Atlantic 1979-1982 58

Chapter Six . . . . .HMS *Fearless* - Return To Training 1982-1985 75

Chapter Seven . . . . . . .HMS *Fearless* - A Royal Review 1988-1995 82

Chapter Eight . . . . . . .HMS *Fearless* - Return To The Middle East 1995-2002 94

Part Two: HMS *Intrepid*

Chapter Nine . . . . .HMS *Intrepid* - First Commission 1967-1968 110

Chapter Ten . . . . .HMS *Intrepid* - Withdrawal From The Far East 1968-1972 125

Chapter Eleven . . . . . .HMS *Intrepid* - Redundancy 1972-1981 .134

Chapter Twelve . . . . . .HMS *Intrepid* - An Unexpected Reprieve 1981-1991 155

Acknowledgements 176

Foreword
by Commodore A. J. S. Taylor CBE, Royal Navy

I was delighted to be asked to contribute the Foreword to this excellent record of two very capable and happy ships particularly as my own naval career almost completely matches the service life of the LPDs in the Royal Navy. Furthermore, I had the very great pleasure and privilege of serving in both of these ships - as Executive Officer of *Intrepid* in 1987 and 1988 and again as Captain of *Fearless* from 1993 to 1995. This detailed and thought-provoking book reminds us of the fascinating and historically important roles played by both ships, in all parts of the world, during their busy and active lives.

As Neil McCart mentions, in their earlier days there was a friendly but quite definite rivalry between the ships' companies of both *Intrepid* and *Fearless*. In later years, with only one ship in commission at any time, this rivalry was replaced with a feeling of very real pride in serving in the Amphibious Flagship, and taking part in something that was completely different from the rest of the Service. Over many years a deep-rooted LPD family spirit was established, and was readily obvious in the ships. In my time, going from *Intrepid* to *Fearless* with a gap of five years, it was reassuring to be able to serve again with more than half of the ship's company. Serving in these ships became much requested as many of the ship's company went from one LPD to a shore billet, then to the other ship, and then back again and so on for years and it led to a very professional, experienced and happy ship's company that maintained unique skills.

These amphibious skills and expertise that had been developed with the introduction into service of the LPDs in the 1960s were very nearly lost with John Nott's much criticised Defence Review of 1981. As the author clearly explains, the outstanding contribution made by both ships during the Falklands campaign was enough to ensure the retention of this singular capability and over the years that followed, demonstrate time and again, the utility of operating offshore to meet political requirements and timescales before acting militarily and decisively by landing Royal Marines and supporting elements across the beach by landing craft and helicopter. In the uncertainties of the post Cold War era, the need for these skills has never been more important and has indeed led to a new direction for the Royal Navy with the introduction of a wholly modern and amphibious force of an LPH, two new LPDs, LSD (A)s to replace the LSLs and a number of specialized Ro-Ro vessels.

The activities of the ship were not limited simply to the mechanics of undertaking amphibious operations. The key to their vital role was the necessary communications and control capability which provided a dedicated command platform where the planning function and execution of amphibious operations could be conducted. Within the Assault Operations Room (AOR), staffs from Commodore Amphibious Warfare, 3 Commando Brigade, the embarked force, as well as ship's own staff, planned, rehearsed and executed all the various details of this complicated facet of military endeavour. The activities of the AOR were essential to the success of amphibious operations and as the ships remained longer in service, all manner of the most modern communications and command and control equipment was installed.

During amphibious operations, the ship bristled with all sorts of additional equipment and aerials were run wherever space could be found. In the early stages of amphibious operations the ship hummed, the AOR was a hive of activity, the tank decks were packed, the messdecks and accommodation were filled to capacity. On occasions even this capacity was exceeded with embarked troops being found space throughout the ship. The chefs provided miracles, and apparently unlimited, hot and cold food to meet all tastes. When operations began with the ship ballasted, troops, vehicles and stores moved from the tank deck to the landing craft or flight deck. The flight deck itself was the centre of constant air activity with a mixed bag of ship's and visiting helicopters of all sorts using the facilities.

In this most readable book, the author does not forget the secondary training role conducted by both ships after the demise of the Dartmouth Training Squadron and young officers from across the world had their first taste of the rigours of life at sea. The ships had a well merited reputation for rolling in a seaway, no doubt as a result of the flat-bottomed nature of the design. This together with messdeck accommodation that had received little in the way of modernization since first built gave a most abiding memory of their early days.

For more than thirty years the ships led a busy and active life but it was in the Falklands campaign that they established their true amphibious credentials. These lessons have not been forgotten and in the uncertainties of today's world there remains a full recognition of the need for the Royal Navy to retain a highly mobile and professional amphibious warfare capability. This is the real legacy of these two excellent and long-lived ships.

Prologue

The story of the Royal Navy's first two purpose-built assault ships goes back to the late 1950s when the search was on for two ships which, when in service, would replace the assorted landing ships of the Amphibious Warfare Squadron, most of which dated back to the Second World War. The two ships had to be able to land all the assault elements of a brigade group of 1,400 men, together with armoured fighting vehicles, self-propelled guns and other 'soft-skinned' transport. In September 1959 there was a lively debate within the Ship Characteristics Committee of the Admiralty regarding the title by which the two ships would be known. Among those considered was 'Landing Ship Dock', which it was decided could lead to confusion as it was already in use to describe ships which had no troop transport function. Another title, 'Amphibious Transport Dock', was put forward, but it was decided that ships' companies would be 'happier and prouder to serve in a ship rather than a dock'. When the title 'Trans-Ocean Assault Transport' was suggested the First Sea Lord understandably turned it down and noted alongside it, 'no comment'. In the event, although the official title was 'Landing Platform Dock' the simple term 'Assault Ship' was selected to describe them as it struck just the right 'fighting' note. Throughout this book both *Fearless* and *Intrepid* are referred to as assault ships.

Eight shipbuilding companies were asked to tender for the first contract and, at £7,925,575, Harland & Wolff of Belfast provided the lowest bid*, the only one below the £8 million requested from Parliament in the Navy Estimates of 1961-62.

In the immediate post-war years Britain became involved in local 'bushfire' wars, often in support of newly independent Commonwealth countries, as the withdrawal from Empire in Africa and South-East Asia got under way. It was important that these local conflicts should not be allowed to develop into full-scale wars, so military power had to be deployed quickly and effectively to contain them. This was the task of the Royal Navy. Ideally troops, together with their heavy equipment, had to be escorted to the scene of action and landed ashore. Following these initial landings it would be necessary to provide them with support and air cover until bases could be established. The new assault ships would also function as a fire brigade and, unaided, avert or extinguish small conflagrations.

The new ships would carry up to four assault landing craft, which were designated as Landing Craft Mechanized, known as LCMs. The original Mark I version was 45 feet long, displaced 36 tons fully loaded and was driven by two, six horsepower Chrysler diesel engines. It had a range of 56 miles at seven-and-a-half knots, was armed with two Lewis guns and carried a crew of six Royal Marines, commanded by a Colour Sergeant. Each LCM could carry up to 100 fully equipped men, or a combination of two battle tanks, trucks or specialist beach equipment. By flooding special compartments the assault ships could be ballasted down by some nine feet to a deep condition, allowing the LCMs to be floated in or out of an internal dock, via a massive 45-ton stern gate, which gave them direct access to three vehicle decks. The main vehicle deck, known appropriately as the tank deck, was capable of housing main Centurion battle tanks. At the apron, where the dock met the tank deck, the LCMs could load vehicles which would be driven from any of the vehicle decks, or from the flight deck to the apron, via a system of ramps. The vehicle decks occupied a large volume of space in the centre of the ship and movements in and out were controlled by a team of Royal Marines. As well as being approached by ramps from the flight deck or apron, they could also be entered through air-lock doors from the 'walls' of the ships, where the embarked force mess decks were situated, and from where the troops could easily be got ashore by sea or by air. A typical load might include tanks, four-ton trucks, armoured cars, self-propelled guns and snow vehicles. There was also an armoured recovery vehicle and two track-laying vehicles which were permanently available for use by the Beach Unit; helicopters could also be housed in these decks.

The two vessels would also carry four smaller landing craft which were designated as LCVPs (Landing Craft Vehicle and Personnel), each of which could transport 30 fully equipped men or two Land Rovers. These craft were stowed in davits on both sides of the ship and were usually lowered into the water after loading. This way, during combined operations with the Royal Marines and the Army, an embarked force, together with tanks, vehicles and ammunition, could be landed. The two assault ships would also be able to act as Command Ships for transit

---

* The other tenders were: John Brown & Co, £8,005,360: Hawthorn Leslie & Co, £8,452,600: Swan Hunter & Co, £8,489,375: Cammell Laird & Co, £8,130,995: Fairfield Shipbuilding & Engineering, £8,549,425. Scotts Shipbuilding and Vickers Armstrong both declined to tender, stating their shipyards were too busy.

operations, and as Headquarters Ships in the assault area. The Operations Room was built specially for the Commodore Amphibious Forces and his staff, together with a Brigade Headquarters. Another very valuable feature was a helicopter flight deck, which doubled as the deckhead of the internal dock from which the LCMs would be floated out, but the lack of a hangar area meant that the two vessels rarely carried their own ship's flight, usually 'borrowing' them from the Fleet Air Arm, the Royal Marines, the RAF or the Army. In order to operate the flight deck in an assault role and to maintain the equipment, the ships would carry a small number of Fleet Air Arm ratings, headed by the Aviation Officer, who formed part of the ship's company. The new ships would have a unique hull form which would combine features of both an escort aircraft carrier and a troop transport, with the basic lines of the dock landing ships of the Second World War. They would be similar in design to the US Navy's Raleigh-class dock landing ships, but their unique appearance would ensure that they were instantly recognizable the world over.

With an overall length of 520 feet, a beam of 80 feet and a draught of 20ft - 6in (32 feet when flooded down), the two assault ships would be almost identical in appearance. With their tall midships superstructure, twin funnels staggered across the beam, long plated mainmast and the after part of their hulls given over to the flight deck and docking bays, they could not be said to be handsome ships, but they were practical and their design stood the test of time. Both vessels had a standard displacement of 11,600 tons and a full load displacement of 12,120 tons, which increased to 16,950 when their docks were flooded. Despite the fact that they were large and valuable units their armament was light; initially they were each armed with four quadruple launchers for Seacat CWS 20 anti-aircraft missiles, which were situated on either beam forward of the superstructure abaft the port funnel and forward of the starboard funnel. Immediately forward of the bridge, and on both port and starboard sides were mounted two 40mm Mk 7 Bofors guns. Both ships could operate four Wessex helicopters. During the design stage the First Sea Lord had expressed some concern at the absence of gun armament, but he was assured that during hostilities the ships would be unlikely to operate without an escort capable of dealing with a surface threat.

The two assault ships would carry a complement which averaged 35 officers and 600 men, including 85 members of the flight deck personnel and the Royal Marines Assault Squadron. The Assault Squadron formed an integral part of the ship's company, and provided crews for all the landing craft. Its Beach Unit was specially trained to land and recover vehicles from most terrains, and the drivers, mechanics and signallers ensured its complete autonomy. When operational in the amphibious role these numbers would be increased by another 400 officers and men of the embarked force and, should the need arise, they could be increased further to 700, with the vehicle decks and passageways being used as temporary accommodation. It had been determined that when 700 or more troops were embarked an 'austerity standard' of 15 square feet per man would be acceptable although not surprisingly this 'overload' situation was unpopular with the ships' companies as it increased the queues for all facilities. The ships' companies themselves enjoyed accommodation fitted to 'modern' standards with all mess decks being air-conditioned, clear of main passageways and fitted with 'standee' three-tiered bunks. There were separate dining spaces for the embarked troops and for both senior and junior rates. The largest mess deck was the Royal Marines barracks which was situated right forward, being the only one which covered the full width of the ship. Next to it was the capstan flat which gave access to the canteen and, until 1970, the all-important rum issue. Although few officers or men who served in the two vessels remember them as being comfortable, most recall the fact that they were happy ships.

Part One

HMS *Fearless* 1965-2002

Chapter One

HMS *Fearless* - First Commission 1965-1967

The order for the first of the two assault ships was placed with the Belfast shipbuilders Harland & Wolff Ltd in December 1961 and seven months later, on 25 July 1962, the first keel plates were laid. By the final quarter of 1963 the ship was ready to be launched and to emphasize the fact that she would spearhead combined operations by all three armed services, her sponsor was Lady Antoinette Mary Hull, the wife of the Chief of the Imperial General Staff, General Sir Richard Hull GCB DSO. The launching ceremony took place on 19 December 1963 and after naming the ship *Fearless,* the seventh unit of the Royal Navy to bear the name, Lady Hull pulled the lever which broke a bottle of wine over the bow and sent the new assault ship down the slipway and into the waters of the River Lagan, from where she was towed to the Musgrave Channel for fitting out at the Thompson Wharf.

In March 1964 the first naval personnel, led by Commander (E) A. J. R. Smith RN, travelled to Belfast to stand by *Fearless* as she was fitted out. Fifteen months later, on 30 June 1965, her first commanding officer, Captain H. A. Corbett DSO DSC RN, a wartime destroyer captain, joined the ship. Shortly after this on 5 July, flying the Red Ensign, *Fearless* left Belfast for the first time under her own steam to carry out her builder's trials and Staff Sea Checks. Within a week, however, she was back in Belfast alongside her fitting-out berth. In early November 1965 the main body of the ship's company and the Royal Marines Detachment all joined her. Most of them arrived in the shipyard on a dull, wet morning, in the pouring rain to find that work on their accommodation was not quite completed and they had to spend a day at the nearby Holywood Barracks. It was not long, however, before the embarkation was completed and everyone was able to settle in to their new home. During the early forenoon of Wednesday 24 November, whilst preparations for the Commissioning Ceremony were finalized, *Fearless* was shifted from Thompson Wharf to the Airport Wharf, close to Sydenham Railway Station. Next morning the Portsmouth Command Royal Marines Band boarded the ship, to be followed during the forenoon by a company of Irish pipers. At 12.30 the VIPs, including Lady Hull the ship's sponsor, began arriving. Also in attendance were camera crews and correspondents from the BBC and Independent Television Companies, but unfortunately their efforts that day were only broadcast to viewers in Northern Ireland. The ceremony began at 14.30, with the Royal Marines providing a very smart honour guard, and by 15.30 it was over, with the VIPs leaving the ship. The event did not receive a great deal of publicity, for just a few days earlier in Southern Africa, Ian Smith, the Prime Minister of Rhodesia's white minority government, announced his country's Unilateral Declaration of Independence. With the United Nations having imposed trade

Shipyard workers look down from the forecastle as Lady Hull is about to pull the lever which will send *Fearless* thundering down the slipway and into the water for the first time.
(Royal Marines Museum, Eastney, No 14/2/10 - 4)

sanctions on the breakaway state, most newspapers concentrated on this story in which *Fearless* herself would also play an important role.

During the 42 hours which followed the Commissioning Ceremony enormous quantities of stores, together with 15 cars, were embarked but finally, at 09.30 on Saturday 27 November, *Fearless* left Belfast and steamed out into Bangor Bay where, two hours later, the engineers began working the main engines up to full power. During the remainder of the forenoon and for most of the afternoon watch the assault ship pounded at full speed down the Irish Sea before returning to Bangor Bay where, at 15.50, she anchored and the builder's trials party were able to disembark. Just over four hours later *Fearless* weighed anchor to spend the night at sea in Force 8 gales, carrying out consumption trials, but early next morning she anchored in Bangor Bay once again. That evening, at 19.45, she left Irish waters and, in the continuing stormy weather, she set course for Portland. For five days, in heavy seas and high winds, the first phase of the flying trials was carried out using Wessex, Scout and Sioux helicopters, on conclusion of which clearance was obtained for Wessex helicopters to make day or night deck landings. During one short break in the inclement weather conditions *Fearless* steamed round to Poole to pick up her four LCVPs, which were hoisted at the davits, and two of her LCMs, both of which made perfect entries into the ship's dock. So intensive were the flying trials that during the forenoon of 3 December a Wessex helicopter with Captain Corbett on board made the 100th deck landing in just four flying days. It had been intended to embark the band of the King's Shropshire Light Infantry in Weymouth Bay that evening, but after heavy seas put paid to their attempt to embark by MFV, they were flown on by helicopter the following forenoon after the ship had anchored in Plymouth Sound. After two hours in the Sound waiting for some fine weather, *Fearless'* first ceremonial entry into Devonport Dockyard was made during the afternoon of 4 December and as she passed Mount Wise, despite the torrential rain, the KSLI band was able to play 'Rule Britannia'. The first time, it was thought, that an Army band had played one of HM Ships alongside.

For most members of the ship's company Christmas leave came and went far too quickly, and on their return to Devonport they found *Fearless* docked down and swarming with visitors, from senior Staff Officers to visiting Army units. For those remaining on board there was the testing and tuning of the communications and radar equipment to be undertaken, and a third LCM joined the ship. By 11 January 1966, however, *Fearless* was back alongside the sea wall, ready to resume her trials, and six days later she put to sea and steamed into the Channel. Three days later she returned to Devonport Dockyard where, once again, an array of senior officers, including the C-in-C Plymouth and the Army's GOC Southern Command, visited the ship. On Tuesday 8 February the ship's first sizeable embarked force, in the form of the 1st Battalion King's Own Borderers and the 1st Battalion Royal Irish Fusiliers, boarded the ship to take passage to Belfast. Next day, at just after 08.00, *Fearless* slipped her moorings to set course for her birthplace where, during the afternoon of 10 February, she secured alongside the city's Musgrave Wharf. She had returned to Harland & Wolff's shipyard to have some outstanding work completed by the builders, and once alongside the troops disembarked to make room for the shipyard workers. During the ten days alongside the Belfast Corporation laid on a ship's dance and many members of the ship's company voted it the 'best ever' run ashore. When *Fearless* left Belfast on 20 February to begin her work-up, there were many sad hearts and many more empty wallets.

During the period spent alongside in Devonport considerable experience had been gained in dock operations and the handling of large loads, but it had all been carried out in calm conditions. The ship's company needed to discover the limiting conditions of working the dock in the open sea, and over the weeks which followed they gained valuable experience as weather conditions ranged from the ideal to the impossible. On 21 February, with the ship at anchor in Plymouth Sound, a military force was embarked, and an amphibious assault was carried out at Saunton Sands in Barnstaple Bay. Although the weather conditions were poor, for the first time a landing was made using both LCMs and Wessex helicopters, with the former ferrying just about every type of vehicle which the Army possessed. With the exercise completed the ship sailed for Southampton where, during the forenoon of 26 February, she secured alongside 101 berth of the city's Western Docks, close to Mayflower Park and the Royal Pier. Over the weekend all sorts of Army vehicles were embarked from the Army depot at Marchwood, and on 2 March the ship steamed into the Solent where she anchored off Lee-on-Solent to carry out an amphibious exercise in the spotlight of the world's press. The National Press Day ensured some good publicity for the ship, and trials with hovercraft proved that there would be no problem handling these craft in the ship's dock. On 3 March *Fearless* sailed for Portland where, next day, she secured alongside and the work-up teams streamed on board. The month of March was to be a very busy period.

With the ship's company having to work itself and the ship up to a high state of operational and material efficiency, which would enable them to face with confidence the duties and obligations which may arise during a commission, the weeks spent at Portland were hard. As well as testing all the systems and procedures on board, there were 'presidents' and 'royalty' to receive, as well as long and complicated damage control exercises.

Stern first *Fearless* enters the waters of the River Lagan. *(Laurence Nolan)*

With the launch having been successfully completed *Fearless* is prepared for a tow to her fitting-out berth.
(Royal Marines Museum, Eastney, No 14/2/10 - 8)

Ashore, landing parties maintained calm before a 'rioting mob' and the village of 'Campo de Portlando' was twice weekly damaged by 'earthquakes'. The sailors and marines cheerfully tackled all the problems associated with setting up field kitchens to feed a starving population, rescuing injured people, dealing with the press and sterilizing water supplies, whilst not being bothered overmuch by 'looters' or outbreaks of 'bubonic plague'. During the final week of evolutions, 43 Commando, Royal Marines, was embarked for 'Exercise Morning Glory', which involved landing them successfully on the Dorset coast. At the end of the work-up, with everyone on their toes, the Flag Officer Sea Training and his staff embarked for the day. *Fearless* left Portland in a war state and, after a very full and exciting day, she returned having passed all the exercises and evolutions which had been set. On Thursday 31 March the ship made a ceremonial entry into Portsmouth Harbour, where she secured alongside Pitch House Jetty and the first long leave parties left for their homes.

During the period alongside at Portsmouth, men, stores and equipment of the King's Shropshire Light Infantry, together with the armoured cars and tanks of the 16/5th Queen's Royal Lancers, were embarked ready for the first of a series of amphibious exercises. On Saturday 16 April there was a special Visitors' Day, when the ship was opened to 'old *Fearless* hands', amongst whom were some who had served in the old coal-fired, four-funnelled, light cruiser, including 72-year-old Mr H. B. Gill, who had been a Writer on board. Others had served in the F-class destroyer which, in 1941, had been lost to enemy air attack; among them was Captain K. L. Harkness CBE DSC RN, who had commanded the vessel. After lunching on board and touring the ship, the guests were given mementoes of their very successful visit. Two days later *Fearless* left Portsmouth Harbour to anchor at Spithead from where the infantry battalions and the tank squadron, much to the surprise of the local residents of Cromwell and Henderson Roads, assaulted the beach at Eastney in what were described as 'Normandy style landings'. There was also a visit to the ship by Admiral of the Fleet Lord Mountbatten who came to watch the first Hovercraft trials, when it was found that with two LCMs removed it was possible to fit four SRN 5 hovercraft in the dock.

Although *Fearless* had no resident aircraft of her own, the Wessex V helicopters of 845 Squadron operated from her flight deck and, during the commission, they spent a great deal of time with her. On 19 April, with the troops and tanks now ashore, *Fearless* returned to Pitch House Jetty where, over the next two days, the infantrymen of the KSLI and the Armour of the 16/5th Lancers were re-embarked. This time the assault ship was due to take part in a major combined exercise in South Wales, and when she left Portsmouth during the afternoon of 22 April she set course for Plymouth Sound and the Bristol Channel. Code-named 'Lifeline', the exercise involved the Army and RAF, as well as units of the Italian Army who were in the UK for training. During the early hours of Sunday 24 April, with her screen of escort ships, *Fearless* anchored off Milford Haven and, to the scream of Buccaneers and Sea Vixens overhead, she began landing her troops. Soon

13

On 25 November 1965 *Fearless* was commissioned at Belfast, with the ceremony taking place on the tank deck.
(Laurence Nolan)

afterwards the blunt-nosed landing craft surged through a 50-yard gap in the reef at Angle Bay where, after wheeling spectacularly in the angry Atlantic surf, they grounded on the beach to put tractors and a recovery tank ashore. While Royal Marines marked the approaches and organized the beach, Sappers laid a flexible roadway. As their waterproofed vehicles drove bonnet-deep up to the firm sand, soldiers of the KSLI were ferried ashore to Pembroke Dock, or flown from *Fearless*' flight deck to the beachhead. The landings were 'opposed' by troops of the 3rd Battalion, Parachute Regiment, and the Italian 8th Regiment of Bersaglieri. The Commodore Amphibious Forces controlled the assault from the Assault Operations Room, and this first use of the ship's HQ facilities was a resounding success, despite heavy rain, strong winds and low temperatures.

On 25 April, after leaving Milford Haven, *Fearless* returned to Portsmouth where it took two days to embark the men and equipment of the 38th Regiment, Royal Engineers, for a logistics exercise in Scotland. When on 29 April *Fearless* left Portsmouth, she was carrying most of the equipment required to build a temporary airfield, for which she had now become literally a floating stores dump. After leaving the Nab behind she set course up Channel and that afternoon she passed Dover. Next day, at 11.07, the assault ship anchored in the Firth of Tay, off the landing area at Barry Budden, and some ten miles from Dundee. The next 48 hours saw intense activity as all the stores and equipment were unloaded, which at one stage involved the towing of a fuel pipeline from the ship to shore. Once this task had been completed the Royal Engineers were left to build their operational airfield and *Fearless* steamed south for Plymouth Sound. From there, flying the flag of the C-in-C Plymouth, Admiral Sir Fitzroy Talbot, she made a four-day visit to Brest for a VE-Day parade in the French city. On her return to Plymouth she spent a week at anchor in the Sound, venturing to sea for only a few hours, and on 17 May she steamed up harbour to secure alongside No 8 wharf in Devonport Dockyard. Six days later Field Marshal Lord Hull visited the ship and soon afterwards *Fearless* was shifted to the North Lock dry dock for an intermediate docking period.

On Thursday 30 June *Fearless* was moved back to the sea wall, and originally it had been planned that she would sail east of Suez for the 'foreign' leg of her commission. However, due to delays in the fitting out and completion of *Intrepid*, the programme was changed and the ship's company found themselves remaining closer to home waters for an additional two months. It was decided to occupy this time by carrying out 'first of class' noise ranging trials. These fell into three phases, the first of which entailed a visit to the Mediterranean where propeller viewing trials could be carried out in the clear water. Before this, however, *Fearless* left Plymouth Sound on 12 July with ship's company families and 50 members of the Plymouth Disabled Association on board for a day at sea. Despite inclement weather everyone enjoyed the excursion, during which the assault ship took them round Eddystone Light and put on a helicopter rescue display. For the more daring passengers there were even LCVP trips round Plymouth Sound. Next day *Fearless* arrived at Portland for a three-day mini work-up before sailing for Gibraltar at 14.00 on Friday 15 July. Four days later she anchored in Gibraltar Bay where B Company of the Royal Worcestershire Regiment was embarked. That same day she sailed for the North African coast where, for two days, the 'propeller viewing' was carried out. The exercise was concluded during the afternoon of 21 July when the embarked force went to assault stations, to be landed on the beaches at Gibraltar, and *Fearless* herself entered harbour. During her eight days at Gibraltar the ship went into dry dock for modifications to her propeller, then on 29 July she sailed for Loch Fyne, via Plymouth Sound, arriving at her destination five days later. Here there was a special range to record ships' machinery noises, and *Fearless* steamed up and down the beautiful highland loch as the engineers stopped and started the main and auxiliary machinery. During the early evening of 9 August, *Fearless* set course south to Portland

On a blustery winter's day in late November 1965, having disembarked the builder's trials party, *Fearless* steams out of Bangor Bay to begin a period of intensive training. *(Ulster Folk & Transport Museum, Holywood, No 24890)*

where the third and final stage of the trials would be carried out. This involved the assault ship running up and down the ranges for three days to test the effectiveness of the noise suppression arrangements. Following this she returned to Spithead on 19 August for another Families Day. The ship's company guests were ferried out to the ship in the LCMs and they spent most of the forenoon touring the ship, before being served lunch in the junior rates dining hall. During the afternoon the families 'fell in' on the after Seacat deck, whilst the ship's company fell in for a ceremonial entry into Portsmouth Harbour where, at 15.30, she secured alongside Pitch House Jetty. Once alongside the families left the ship, along with many of their hosts who were taking foreign service leave. During her stay in Portsmouth Dockyard *Fearless* took part in Navy Days and when she was opened to the public some 42,000 people took the opportunity to visit her.

Having been delayed for over seven hours by a mechanical fault, at 17.55 on Tuesday 13 September *Fearless* left Portsmouth to make a fast passage to Aden. She spent just over ten hours anchored in Gibraltar Bay and three days in Malta, making her transit of the Suez Canal on 25 September and arriving in Aden's outer harbour four days later. She had averaged 18 knots during the passage and her arrival in Aden coincided with tribal unrest in Oman, in the region of Dhofar (Zufar), about 500 miles east of Aden. The Sultan of Oman was experiencing a great deal of trouble from armed tribesmen there and he had called on British forces in the area for assistance. During the first two weeks of *Fearless'* stay in Aden, however, a lot of time was spent showing Army visitors round the ship and carrying out small exercises. One of these, on 11 October, involved the embarkation of a troop of scout cars which were landed 70 miles west of Aden State, to carry out a patrol into the interior. It was hoped that this unusual method of attack would surprise the rebel tribesmen. On her return to Aden *Fearless* spent two weeks in the harbour carrying out self-maintenance.

In late 1966 Aden was in the throes of a vicious terrorist campaign by two Nationalist organizations, FLOSY (Front for the Liberation of South Yemen) and the NLF (National Liberation Front of Occupied South Yemen), who were fighting each other as they jockeyed for power, while pressing the British Government for independence. The once busy shopkeepers of The Crescent at Steamer Point sat idle amid mountains of unwanted duty-free electrical goods, as the steady stream of passengers from liners at the port, and servicemen on leave, dried up. The British Government had announced that there would be a total withdrawal from the Crown Colony by 1968, but far from settling the unstable political situation, the two Nationalist groups intensified their private war and in both Steamer Point and Maalla British off-duty servicemen became prime targets for the gunmen. On board *Fearless,* which was now moored in Aden's inner harbour off military pier, armed sentries were posted round the ship and, with street curfews in force ashore, liberty men did not walk around alone. In effect shore leave was more or less restricted to the service clubs on the beaches in the Tarshyne area and, as had been the case since 1839 when Aden was captured by the British, no serviceman ever regretted leaving the colony which, at the best of times, was an uncomfortable and exhausting place. In the last week of October, when the assault ship prepared to sail, the sense of relief on board was shared by all. *Fearless'* departure from Aden was combined with 'Operation Fate', a cordon and search operation in a small coastal village near the Muscat border. The 1st Battalion Irish Guards was embarked and, after moving to the outer harbour, *Fearless* sailed on 26 October to land on five Wessex helicopters of 78 Squadron RAF. Two days later, at 09.30 on 28 October, she anchored off Dhofar Province, from where the troops were ferried and airlifted ashore. The military operation was carried out to implement a treaty with the Sultan of Oman and it had a temporary pacifying effect, demonstrating to the dissident rebels in the area that British forces were able to intervene when necessary. With 22 rebels having been captured, the infantrymen were withdrawn by helicopter and *Fearless* returned them to Aden before sailing for the more hospitable climes of Mombasa.

During the afternoon of Wednesday 2 November, as the assault ship steamed south, King Neptune introduced the uninitiated to his domain before, next day, *Fearless* arrived in Kilindini Harbour. For six days the ship's company was able to enjoy the bars of Kilindini Road, the beaches of Nyali or the game parks at Tsavo. It was a welcome break from the barren, hostile atmosphere of Aden, but on 9 November she sailed north once again to anchor in Aden's outer harbour four days later. *Fearless* had been scheduled to take on an embarked force for an exercise in the Persian Gulf, but three days later she was ordered to sea and soon after sailing she was directed to Durban to pick up the Royal Irish Fusiliers who had been carrying out internal security duties in Swaziland. After crossing the equator during the evening of 19 November, the assault ship secured alongside at Durban six days later. Despite the fact that the visit had received no advance publicity, the ship's company was overwhelmed by the generous hospitality of the local people, and on 29 November, after the embarkation of troops was completed, a large crowd turned out on a wet and windy day to wave goodbye. During the return passage to Aden there was a brief stop in the Mozambique Channel to carry out a mail transfer with the frigate *Falmouth* which was operating the Beira oil blockade of Rhodesia. As *Fearless* steamed north the ship's company was entertained by the pipes and drums of the Royal Irish Fusiliers, then on 7 December she secured to buoys in Aden Harbour and the troops were disembarked. To everyone's relief the stay in Aden was limited to three days and at just after midnight on 11 December the ship sailed for Singapore, arriving alongside the naval base during the forenoon of 21 December - in time for the Christmas festivities.

The first two weeks of January 1967 were spent carrying out self-maintenance at Singapore, but on Monday 16 January *Fearless* left the naval base to steam round to the island's south coast where she anchored in the Outer Roads, off Singapore city. For the next seven days senior officers from all three services received regular demonstrations of the assault ship's capabilities, then on 23 January she sailed for the island of Penang anchoring off Muka Head the following day. Once at anchor *Fearless* embarked the 2nd Greenjackets and their transport before sailing for Terendak, close to Malacca on Malaya's west coast, where a full-scale amphibious landing took place. On 27 January, after the troops had been re-embarked, *Fearless* returned to Penang where she anchored off George Town for a four-day visit to this pleasant green island. On the first day of February the assault ship returned to Singapore Naval Base, where a week was spent preparing for her first amphibious group exercise in Far Eastern waters. This was the first time that the newly formed east of Suez Combined Amphibious Force, which consisted of *Fearless, Bulwark* and the LSL *Sir Lancelot,* had worked together and *Fearless* embarked the 3rd Commando Brigade HQ, among whose attached sub-units was a Royal Marines Air Troop. The remainder of the force was embarked in the other major units and, together with the destroyer HMAS *Vendetta* and the frigates *Chichester* and *Loch Fada,* they all left Singapore on 8 February to set course for Hong Kong. Five days later they arrived in Hong Kong Harbour, and after refuelling they started a series of amphibious exercises, mainly in the Port Shelter area west of Kowloon Peak. During this period the 1st Battalion Welch Regiment was embarked and landed for a battalion exercise, and the LCMs proved their ability to land vehicles at night on narrow beaches which were inaccessible to the larger LCTs (Landing Craft Tanks). On 20 February, after a week of beach landings and re-embarking the units, *Fearless* steamed into harbour to secure alongside the West Arm of Hong Kong Dockyard for a week's 'rest and recreation'. For most members of the ship's company this was their first visit to Hong Kong and everyone was able to enjoy the 'delights' of Wanchai and Kowloon.

On the last day of February the Chief of the Defence Staff, Field Marshal Sir Richard Hull and Lady Hull, *Fearless'* sponsor, visited the ship and Lady Hull addressed the ship's company. That same afternoon, as soon as the visitors had left, the assault ship, in company with *Bulwark,* sailed for Singapore, arriving at the naval base four days later. After five days alongside, however, on 9 March *Fearless* sailed for the full-scale exercise FOTEX 67 with the Far East Fleet, which also included *Victorious, Bulwark, Triumph, Kent,* and the frigates *Brighton, Blackpool, Chichester, Falmouth, Llandaff* and *Londonderry*. *Fearless* carried out an amphibious landing of the 2/6th Gurkha Rifles on the Malayan mainland, with the helicopters of 845 Squadron operating from the flight deck, together with a flight of RAF Whirlwinds, although the most popular part of the exercise was probably the period spent at anchor of Pulau Langkowi. The exercise concluded on 17 March and that evening *Fearless* secured alongside

An excellent stern view of *Fearless* showing the massive 45-ton gate which, when lowered, allowed the LCMs to be floated in and out of the internal dock. *(Imperial War Museum, London, No HU 90939)*

Fearless lies alongside Portsmouth's Pitch House Jetty in early September 1966, shortly before leaving for service on the Far East Station. Her stern gate has been lowered, but she is not flooded down.
(Maritime Photo Library, Cromer, Norfolk, No 3546)

After operating off Aden and East Africa, on 21 December 1966 *Fearless* arrived alongside Singapore Naval Base.
(Royal Marines Museum, Eastney, No 14/2/10 - 30)

Singapore Naval Base. During her spell alongside, the fleet's sports meeting took place, in which the ship's teams acquitted themselves well.

On Monday 27 March *Fearless* left Singapore to set course for Okinawa and the first leg of her Japanese and Korean cruise. On 1 April, after a five-day passage, she secured alongside No 6 berth at Nahu Ku, the island's main town. On board the assault ship was a specially trained demonstration troop of 34 Royal Marines who gave static weapons and unarmed combat demonstrations to the 7,500 visitors who were queuing to look round the ship. Meanwhile, the ship's company was generously entertained by the American forces stationed there. The next port of call was Hiroshima where, during the forenoon of 6 April,

Fearless secured alongside the Foreign Trade Berth after a passage through the Inland Sea. Here a lot of interest was shown in the aftermath of the first atomic bomb which has been preserved as a monument in the city centre. Once again the ship was opened to visitors, with Miss Hiroshima, Seiko Miki, proving to be one of the most popular guests. During the forenoon of 11 April *Fearless* left Hiroshima for Inchon in Korea, where she anchored two days later. Once again the local US bases were very popular as they lavished hospitality on the ship's company. With the ship at anchor in the harbour she was opened to the public on only one occasion, but the Royal Marines were able to show off their drill and weaponry skills. After leaving Inchon during the afternoon of 17 April, *Fearless* arrived back in Singapore seven days later for docking and a six-week maintenance period in dockyard hands.

On 8 May, with the ship's company having moved into shore accommodation at HMS *Terror*, *Fearless* was shifted to the King George VI dry dock, where she remained until 27 May when she returned to the sea wall and everyone moved back on board. At this time many members of the ship's company had the opportunity to take some station leave in Kuala Lumpur, Penang, or at the Navy's leave centre at Fraser's Hill, up-country in Pahang State. On Tuesday 6 June came the first change of command when Captain M. W. B. Kerr DSC RN took over from Captain Corbett. The new commanding officer was soon able to remark that his ship's company, 'have been imbued with a spirit that matches the ship's capability, and they have welded *Fearless* into an operational unit which is second to none'. Four days after taking command, during the evening of 10 June, Captain Kerr took *Fearless* to sea for a short work-up, which saw her steaming up Malaya's east coast to Pulau Tioman and, whilst the Royal Marines Detachment took their craft and vehicles ashore, there was the opportunity for some banyan leave. By 16 June, however, the assault ship had returned to Singapore Naval Base to prepare for another operational exercise.

On 20 June, after embarking 42 Commando, *Fearless* sailed for an exercise in local waters, but next day she was recalled to Singapore where the marines were disembarked and 63 LAA Squadron of the RAF Regiment boarded the ship for passage to Hong Kong where the effects of the Chinese Cultural Revolution were being felt, with violent demonstrations in both Kowloon and Victoria. These disturbances had turned into riots, and bombs had been planted in built-up areas. As part of the security arrangements the RAF Regiment was being transferred to Hong Kong, and after two false starts, *Fearless* finally left Singapore on the last day of June for the South China Sea. In addition to the RAF Regiment, she also had on board men of 42 Commando and the Gurkha Rifles, together with their transport, and the passage was dubbed 'the overcrowding trials'. By the time she arrived in the colony on 4 July the civil unrest had quietened and everyone was able to enjoy the run ashore, but six days later the sojourn came to an end, and by 13 July the assault ship was back in Singapore Naval Base preparing for more amphibious exercises. During this period Ron Kelbrick who was an Electrical Officer on board recalls the young Gurkha soldiers who were always popular visitors: 'During my middle watch rounds I had to go into the troop accommodation where the Gurkhas were living. When I got to the bottom of the ladder I was confronted by a young Gurkha who was sitting cross-legged with his rifle across his knees. Although we were miles from land and in the middle of the night, they still had a sentry on watch which says it all for their vigilance.' He also recalls another amusing incident: 'During my morning watch I passed the ship's company galley and dining hall. The duty PO Ck was sitting outside having a smoke and with the words, "Come and have a look at this", he pointed to a young Gurkha in the dining hall. The soldier had gone along to the galley servery and had filled his plate to overflowing with fried eggs, scrambled eggs, bacon, sausage, tomatoes, baked beans and, to top it all off, a kipper.'

On Monday 17 July, having embarked the men of 3 Commando Brigade and all their equipment, *Fearless*, together with *Bulwark*, and the Army LSTs *Kittywake* and *Gannet*, sailed from Singapore into the South China Sea to head north along Malaya's east coast. The two ships were engaged on 'Exercise Firm Strike', the purpose of which was to demonstrate the capability of the Far East Amphibious Forces Group in landing and sustaining a brigade group. Next day, at 05.30, the force anchored off Tanjong Gelang, close to Kuantan, and shortly afterwards 'Assault Stations' was sounded. This was the signal for the amphibious and air assault to begin, and the troops were lifted ashore by either the Wessex helicopters of 845 Squadron, operating from *Bulwark*, or the assault ship's LCMs. During the first phase of the exercise *Fearless* was used in her role of Headquarters Ship, and by the end of the day almost 2,000 men had been put ashore. During the second phase, with the brigade operating in jungle terrain, a forward base was established ashore and the troops were supplied from *Bulwark* by the helicopters of 845 Squadron. Once the brigade HQ was ashore the naval element of the exercise left and on 21 July *Fearless* steamed back to Singapore where she anchored off Keppel Harbour to embark a squadron of tanks belonging to the 13/18th Hussars. Two days later she was heading north once again, this time to Kuala Marang on the coast of Trengganu State where, watched by the C-in-C Far East Station, the tanks were landed. Once this had been completed the assault ship returned to Kuantan to pick up part of the Commando Brigade to transport them to Singapore. The remainder of the month was spent operating between Pulau Tioman and Kuantan, but on 4 August, with the exercise over, *Fearless* returned to Singapore Naval Base to prepare for her annual inspection.

On 14 August, after a great deal of cleaning, polishing, painting and drilling, the ship was inspected by Rear-Admiral E. B. Ashmore, FO2 Far East Station and his verdict on *Fearless* was '...well run and in very good heart. *Fearless* can be relied on to produce a sound solution to any problem posed and I am confident that she would acquit herself creditably in any emergency.' Later that day *Fearless* sailed north to Marang to collect the 13/18th Hussars and their tanks for the return passage to Singapore. On 17 August the assault ship anchored off Horseborough Light in Singapore's Outer Roads, from where the tanks were ferried ashore, and by the afternoon *Fearless* herself was

In February 1967 *Fearless* visited Hong Kong for the first time.
(Imperial War Museum, London, No HU 90948)

On 4 March 1967, with her LCMs and LCVPs in formation, *Fearless* leads *Bulwark* into Singapore Naval Base.
(Fleet Air Arm Museum, Yeovilton)

Prewetting trials during 'Exercise FOTEX 67'.
(Imperial War Museum, London, No HU 90949)

Fearless in the foreground, with her sister *Intrepid* and the commando carrier *Albion* off Aden during the withdrawal in November 1967.
(Imperial War Museum, London, No A35117)

back in the naval base to begin a period of maintenance.

During the first week of September, whilst *Fearless* was completing her maintenance period, there was a sudden change to her schedule and she was ordered to sail for the Middle East. After hectic preparations and farewells, she left Singapore for Gan and Aden during the forenoon of Saturday 9 September, flying the flag of Rear-Admiral Ashmore, while a large crowd which had gathered at No 8 berth gave her a rousing send-off. With independence for the South Arabian Federation (Aden State and the surrounding Protectorates) set for midnight on Wednesday 29 November, *Fearless* was required to lift Army stores, heavy equipment and RAF helicopters from Aden to the British bases at Sharjah and Bahrain. After anchoring at Gan for fuel on 14 September, during which some limited recreational leave was granted, the assault ship set course for Aden where she arrived six days later. With the security situation having deteriorated still further since her previous visit, and with heavy fighting between FLOSY and the NLF in Dhala State, shore leave was out of the question and by the early evening, having embarked her first load, she sailed for Bahrain. Six days later, in temperatures of more then 125°F, she secured alongside Bahrain's deep water jetty and the unloading of equipment began. By 2 October *Fearless* was back at Aden and two days later she sailed fully loaded for her second passage to Bahrain. This time she was alongside for three days and so there was an opportunity for some shore leave, and on 10 October the

Ruler of Bahrain, accompanied by the royal falconer, visited the ship. *Fearless* made two more voyages between Aden and Bahrain, on one occasion stopping off at Muscat for the day when she received a visit from local Sheikhs, but by the forenoon of Tuesday 31 October she had anchored in Aden's Outer Harbour where she became part of Task Force 318, commanded by Rear-Admiral Ashmore, which was gathering for the final British withdrawal. Also present were the commando carrier *Albion, Ajax, Phoebe, London* and the aircraft carrier *Eagle,* which would provide air cover after the closure of RAF Khormaksar. With less than a month to go before independence, and with what amounted to a civil war raging ashore, all the ships remained at 3rd Degree of Readiness, with all ships' divers working round the clock to keep up continual searches of the underwater hulls. Even so, the ship's company on *Fearless* enjoyed some very limited swimming leave, with organized groups being escorted by the Army to the beaches at Tarshyne. Finally, however, came the day for which everyone in *Fearless* had been waiting when, having left Portsmouth on 19 October, *Intrepid* anchored in the Outer Harbour. Over the next four days large quantities of stores, as well as Admiral Ashmore and his staff, were transferred to *Intrepid* and on 21 November, to everyone's relief, *Fearless* left Aden bound for Durban and then Devonport.

After an eight-day passage south *Fearless* was welcomed into Durban by Perla Siedle, the 'Lady in White', who sang from the breakwater as the ship entered harbour to secure alongside Maydon Wharf for four days, where, at last, some overnight shore leave could be granted. By the forenoon of 3 December, however, she was back at sea and steaming for home with only a two-hour stop at Freetown for fuel. During the forenoon of 19 December the assault ship anchored of Roche's Point, outside Cork Harbour, to land the Irish leave parties, but by 13.00 she was under way again and at 06.50 the next morning she anchored in Plymouth Sound. By early afternoon, with Customs clearance having been obtained, *Fearless* was steaming up harbour and at 14.00 she secured alongside Devonport Dockyard's No 7 Wharf.

During the commission *Fearless* had carried out 134 LCVP and 294 LCM landings, she had carried 7,130 troops and 1,229 vehicles and over 2,700 officers and men of all three services had been given official conducted tours of the ship. On the flight deck some 2,200 deck landings had been made with nearly all types of helicopter from all three armed services, and for a ship with no aircraft of her own, it was a record of which the ship's small Air Department was justifiably proud.

On the day after her arrival at Devonport the main Christmas leave parties left the ship, and soon after this *Fearless* was taken over by the dockyard to begin a six-month refit. Her first commission was over.

With her paying-off pennant flying, and having been relieved by *Intrepid*, *Fearless* leaves Aden for the passage home and the end of her first commission. *(Royal Marines Museum, Eastney, No 14/2/10 - 93)*

Chapter Two

HMS *Fearless* - Second Commission 1968-1970

Fearless' refit officially began on 29 January 1968, but by the new year she was high and dry in Devonport Dockyard's No 8 dry dock where she remained until 20 April, when she was shifted back to the sea wall and alongside No 7 wharf. By the following month the ship's company had moved on board, and it was not long before the first conducted tours for Army units began, with the Royal Welch Fusiliers leading the way. During the second week of June the ship was closed down for 24 hours for fumigation, but once everyone was aboard again work continued to complete the refit and get the ship cleaned and tidied in preparation for her recommissioning. The ceremony itself took place at 11.00 on Friday 19 July 1968 on the tank deck, and the guest of honour was the ship's sponsor, Lady Hull, who was accompanied by her husband. The religious service was conducted by the Right Reverend E. J. K. Roberts, the Bishop of Ely, and the occasion was attended by many families and well-wishers from all three services. By the end of July, although *Fearless* remained alongside her berth, the main engines had been turned under steam, and a Wessex helicopter had landed on her flight deck. She was almost ready for sea.

On Wednesday 7 August 1968, just a few days before *Fearless* was due to sail, fires were discovered in the starboard ballast control room and in an adjoining fan room, which were extinguished by the dockyard fire service. Fortunately, damage was not serious, nor was sabotage suspected and five days later, during the forenoon of Monday 12 August, *Fearless* sailed on schedule for her post-refit acceptance trials. After four days of steaming at full power, and landing on Wessex helicopters, the assault ship returned to Devonport for machinery adjustments, during which time she was joined by a battalion of the Royal Welch Fusiliers. On 20 August, with the embarkation completed, the assault ship sailed for 'Exercise Calm Water', which was to be the first of a number of amphibious landing exercises carried out in the Portland area during a shakedown cruise. After returning to Devonport at the end of August for Navy Days, *Fearless* left harbour on 3 September to set course for Portland again and an extremely busy three weeks as she underwent her work-up period. This culminated in her Sea Inspection by the Flag Officer Sea Training on 4 October in company with *Ajax* and *Kent*. With the inspection successfully completed, she and *Kent* set course for Gibraltar where for almost a week she would be at the centre of world diplomatic events.

During late September and early October 1968 there had been growing speculation that a meeting between the Prime Minister, Harold Wilson, and the breakaway Rhodesian Prime Minister, Ian Smith, was imminent. It was generally agreed that any talks between the two would be a last chance to negotiate a settlement with the British Government and during the afternoon of 8 October, when *Fearless* arrived at 48 berth on Gibraltar's South Mole, with *Kent* secured alongside her, rumours of an impending meeting between the two leaders were rife. The last such meeting had taken place in December 1966 aboard the cruiser *Tiger,* which had put to sea for the event. *Fearless* had been chosen as the venue for the current talks and that same day, Ian Smith left Salisbury (Harare) in an RAF Britannia aircraft, bound for Gibraltar. Unlike the previous occasion, this time he was personally empowered to endorse any agreement reached and, although there were high hopes of a settlement, he had already made a radio broadcast in which he saw, 'no justification for wishful thinking'. Meanwhile Mr Wilson was also on his way to Gibraltar and he arrived on board *Fearless* at just before midnight that day. Instead of putting to sea *Fearless* and *Kent* (Captain R. Clayton RN) remained alongside, with the former playing host to Harold Wilson and his team, while Mr Smith and his staff were accommodated on board *Kent*.

Apart from a short press conference, which took place under an awning on *Fearless'* Seacat deck, Harold Wilson had the first day, 9 October, to himself and he took the opportunity to brief his delegation. The press were given a chance to examine in detail the 'conference citadel', which was in fact the assault ship's wardroom, and for most of the afternoon representatives from the world's leading newspapers and broadcasting companies filed into the compartment to view the wardroom table, which had been laid out for 12 negotiators on either side. The first full day of talks between Wilson and Smith began early on Thursday 10 October with a short private session in order to set out procedures, followed by nearly three hours in plenary with full delegations. After a break for lunch, during which Harold Wilson dined with the Governor of Rhodesia, Sir Humphrey Gibb, the delegations reconvened at 15.30 and continued until the early evening. Although the negotiations were described as 'affable', they were also said to be 'tough going', with the main point at issue being

23

Fearless and the destroyer *Kent* secured alongside Gibraltar's South Mole for the second Rhodesia summit meeting between Harold Wilson and Ian Smith. *(Imperial War Museum, London, No A35170)*

Laid out for the Prime Ministers and their diplomatic staff, the 'Conference Citadel' in *Fearless*' wardroom is ready for the start of negotiations. *(Imperial War Museum, London, A35155)*

how quickly the majority African population of Rhodesia should advance to government in a fully independent country. That evening Smith returned to *Fearless* to meet Wilson for a further session of informal talks. Next day the negotiations continued, with British sources already showing some pessimism about the chances of a successful settlement and on Sunday 13 October it appeared that the talks were close to collapse. The day started with a forenoon church service on the assault ship's flight deck, which was attended by Harold Wilson who also took the opportunity to meet members of the ship's company.

The conference was saved from complete collapse by Wilson who had ordered his delegation to work through the night to draw up a document outlining the way in which the British Government would be prepared to implement an agreement and grant independence to Rhodesia. Given the fact that Smith's breakaway regime had had three years' unqualified control of Rhodesia, during which time it had not been formally recognized by any other country, there were hopes that the conditions might be acceptable to the Rhodesian delegation. Having been told by Wilson that he could have as long as he liked to consider the document, and even return to Salisbury if necessary, Smith took the proposals back to *Kent* to discuss them with his negotiating team. At 16.35 there was another session of talks on board *Fearless*, which lasted well into the evening, and it was finally agreed that Smith would return to Rhodesia with the proposals. With that the conference was concluded. There was, however, little optimism regarding the outcome and, as anticipated, the British proposals were rejected. Rhodesia was to suffer 12 years of civil war, the tragic consequences of which are still being felt in the country, before, in 1980, the Smith regime finally surrendered to political realities and full elections handed power to a majority government.

Having bade farewell to *Fearless* and her ship's company, 'With very warm thanks for a job well done', Harold Wilson left the ship at 12.45 on Monday 14 October, to be flown back to Britain, and two and a half hours later the assault ship herself left Gibraltar to return to Devonport. She secured alongside No 7 wharf three days later but there was no rest for the ship's company for a battalion of troops was waiting to be embarked and two days later, with the embarkation completed, *Fearless* sailed for the Irish Sea and 'Exercise Swap' involving 6,000 servicemen, which was the largest peacetime military exercise ever carried out in Northern Ireland. The amphibious landing took place on the coast of County Down, then during the afternoon of 27 October, after an absence of eight days, *Fearless* returned to Devonport. Once again, however, her stay was limited to just a few days and on 4 November, after embarking the 1st Battalion Royal Welch Fusiliers and hoisting the flag of the C-in-C Plymouth, *Fearless* sailed for the Bristol Channel. Next day, at 08.30, the assault ship entered Cardiff's Queen Alexandra Dock to secure alongside for a 48-hour official visit to the city. After leaving Cardiff during the morning of 7 November, *Fearless* steamed up the Bristol Channel for Avonmouth and three hours later she secured alongside the King Alfred Dock, for the second of her visits to home ports. During her 72 hours in port the ship was opened to the public and various official visits were arranged between the C-in-C and Bristol's civic officials. On 10 November *Fearless* left Avonmouth to return to Devonport where, two weeks later, she embarked a battalion of the Royal Regiment of Fusiliers, hoisted the flag of the C-in-C Western Fleet and sailed for a visit to Bremerhaven. The visit to the German port, where the assault ship secured alongside Kaiser Hafen Island, lasted for five days and gave many members of the ship's company the chance to visit Berlin. During the return passage an amphibious exercise was carried out off the Dorset coast, and on 7 December *Fearless* secured alongside South Railway Jetty for a weekend break in Portsmouth.

With the officers and men fallen in on the flight deck, Prime Minister Harold Wilson addresses and thanks them for hosting his diplomatic conference. *(Imperial War Museum, London, No A35174)*

On 12 December, after a 24-hour passage, *Fearless* secured alongside her home base and Christmas leave began, as well as preparations for the ship's Mediterranean deployment which was intended to strengthen NATO's southern flank. During her period of maintenance at Devonport the redundant cruiser *Lion* was towed alongside *Fearless* so that the engineering department could raid her for spare parts. At 09.15 on 15 January 1969, however, with her leave periods over and with an embarked force on board, *Fearless* left Devonport for Gibraltar where she paused for fuel and mail before steaming on to Sardinia. Six days after leaving Plymouth the assault ship anchored off Cagliari to disembark her troops before returning to Gibraltar. On the last day of January *Fearless* left her berth alongside Gibraltar's South Mole to make visits to the Italian ports of Taranto and Genoa, where Italian army officers were given demonstrations of docking and berthing procedures when the ship was involved in amphibious operations. After leaving Genoa on 13 February *Fearless* set course for Cyprus and two days later she anchored off Dhekelia to begin preparations for her Operational Readiness Inspection, which was held at sea between Dhekelia and Limassol. On 3 March, with the inspection successfully completed, *Fearless* entered Malta's Grand Harbour to carry out a short maintenance period. Once again, however, African strife and politics were to thrust *Fearless* into the forefront of world events - this time it was to be the bloody civil war which was raging in the former British colony of Nigeria.

Having been a trading post for the British-owned Royal Niger Company, in 1900 the land which bordered the River Niger in West Africa was declared a British Protectorate. Unfortunately, Nigeria as it became known, had been acquired somewhat haphazardly by means of a military campaign, by treaties with local tribal chiefs and by settling borders with other European colonial powers with scant regard for existing tribal boundaries. The country was only held together by the colonial administration, and African resentment of the colonization by Britain was never far below the surface, with the result that civil strife, from riots to full-scale rebellions, was a feature of Britain's 60 years' rule over Nigeria. It was also apparent that should Britain, at some time in the future, leave Nigeria, it was likely that the mix of African tribes living in the country would then have difficulty maintaining a cohesive central government. In 1954 Britain formulated a federal constitution for Nigeria and five years later independence was promised. On 1 October 1960 Nigeria became Africa's most populous independent state and, under its first Prime Minister, Sir A. T. Balewa, it joined the Commonwealth. Three years later the country was declared a republic, and in August 1966 an army officer, and member of the Ibo tribe, Lieutenant-Colonel Yakabu Gowon, seized power in a military coup. Following this event it was only six months before the long-standing hostility between Nigeria's Moslem Hausas tribe in the north of the country and the Christian Ibos erupted into wholesale violence. Mutinous troops roamed the ancient

Following the Rhodesian Conference *Fearless* took part in 'Exercise Swap' off the coast of County Down, during which she operated Wessex helicopters of 845 Squadron. *(Fleet Air Arm Museum, Yeovilton)*

city of Kano shooting Ibo people on sight, and massacres between the two communities became commonplace. Finally, however, in May 1967, Colonel Ojukwa, the Ibo leader, announced the secession of the eastern region of Nigeria and proclaimed its independence as the Republic of Biafra. Gowon declared war on the breakaway region and government troops invaded oil-rich Biafra. For Britain, as the former colonial power and the largest single recipient of Nigeria's oil supplies, the war was particularly unwelcome and a great deal of diplomatic effort went into attempting to secure a ceasefire. There was little hope of compromise, however, and by March 1969 Biafra was on the point of collapse. The military situation was complicated by a Federal blockade of Biafra which led to a terrible famine in the region, with four million people facing starvation. In Europe there was deep concern about the situation, and in early March 1969, as *Fearless* was undergoing maintenance at Malta, rumours were circulating that she was once again to become a diplomatic conference centre, this time in West Africa.

On 15 March, when *Fearless* was ordered to cut short her refit and proceed to Lagos, via Gibraltar, the rumours became a reality and during the afternoon of Wednesday 26 March the assault ship secured to buoys in the Nigerian port. Once again *Fearless* was to play host to the Prime Minister, Harold Wilson, but this time with the security situation in Lagos so precarious, she would act mainly as a secure accommodation ship and a communications centre for Mr Wilson, his advisers and 20 other officials. The Prime Minister travelled to Nigeria in a VC10 of RAF Transport Command, and at 19.00 on 27 March he boarded the assault ship. Apart from press conferences and a small working dinner which was attended by British officials, the Prime Minister used the Admiral's quarters in *Fearless* as a safe haven after his diplomatic meetings with General Gowon were concluded. For the ship's company there was little opportunity to see anything of the troubled country for liberty men had to be back on board by 19.00 each evening, but few wished to venture far into the war-torn country in any case. As far as the diplomatic meetings

A close-up view of *Fearless'* midships superstructure as she arrives at Malta's Grand Harbour on 3 March 1969.
(Michael Cassar, Valletta, Malta)

Fearless at Grand Harbour in March 1969, when she carried out a short maintenance period.
(Michael Cassar, Valletta, Malta)

were concerned there was little Harold Wilson could accomplish, although he expressed his 'deep anxiety' at the suffering in Biafra. At 01.30 on the morning of Monday 31 March, after a tour of the Federal-held areas of the war zone, Wilson and his diplomatic party left *Fearless* to fly to Addis Ababa for talks on the Nigerian conflict with Emperor Haile Selassie, who was chairman of the Organization of African Unity. Twelve hours later, at 13.30, *Fearless* slipped her moorings and set course for Devonport. During the passage, when she was just north of Madeira, the assault ship passed astern of a Soviet Sverdlov-class cruiser, four Soviet submarines and a Riga-class destroyer, which called for a helicopter to be scrambled in order that photographs of the Soviet units could be taken.

On the morning of 10 April *Fearless* arrived in Plymouth Sound and by the afternoon she was alongside Devonport Dockyard's No 7 wharf, and the first long leave period had begun. As well as undergoing a dockyard assisted maintenance period there was also a change of command for the assault ship, when Captain J. R. S. Gerard-Pearse RN relieved Captain Kerr. During the seven-week refit *Fearless* spent four weeks in No 9 dry dock, but by the middle of May she had been refloated and two weeks later, on 28 May, she put to sea for trials and a mini-work-up. As soon as this was completed the ship was inspected by the Flag Officer Carriers and Amphibious Forces (FOCAS), and then during the forenoon of 4 June she left Devonport bound for Cape Town and the Far East Station. On 7 June Tenerife was sighted and four days later the Crossing the Line ceremony was held on the flight deck. With the Amphibious Detachment of Royal Marines acting as policemen most of the officers, including Captain Gerard-Pearse, were hauled into the barber's chair and ducked. Even after crossing the equator there were still ten days of steady steaming as *Fearless* headed south but finally, during the forenoon of 19 June, she secured alongside Cape Town's Duncan Dock. As always the ship's company received tremendous hospitality from the people of the city, and during the two afternoons she was opened to the public over 5,000 visitors came to look round the ship. The visit to South Africa was brief and all too soon, on 24 June, *Fearless* slipped her moorings and steamed out into the Indian Ocean bound for Farquhar Island, which is situated between Madagascar and the Seychelles, the island group to which it belongs. The afternoon of 30 June was spent at anchor off the island's Rose Point, but there were only limited opportunities for swimming and collecting coconuts from the unspoilt beaches. By the dog watches, however, *Fearless* was bound for the island of Gan where, during six hours spent alongside RFA *Wave Victor,* the ship's teams were able to beat RAF Gan's sides at soccer, hockey, rugby and basketball. By the evening of 4 July the assault ship was once again at sea, and bound for Singapore. Shortly before 10.30 on 10 July, *Fearless* arrived on station at Singapore Naval Base, where she secured alongside No 6 berth.

This was the second tour of duty in the Far East for *Fearless,* and it was not long before she was at sea and participating in her first major exercise. On 15 July, after embarking 42 Commando, Royal Marines, the assault ship left Singapore in company with *Sir Galahad* for the beaches of Marang on Malaya's north-east coast where, next morning, she anchored of Tanjong Penarck. Using both the LCMs and Wessex helicopters the men were landed and re-embarked, and by 19 July *Fearless* was back in Singapore Naval Base. Once again her stay alongside was brief and two days later she left to take part in 'Exercise Julex 69', which involved 23 units from Britain, Malaysia, Australia and New Zealand, and which kept her at sea for three days. Following her return to the naval base on 24 July *Fearless* underwent a short period of maintenance, during which she was visited by the C-in-C and FO2, Far East Station, Admirals Sir William O'Brien and Griffin respectively. On 8 August there was an unusual break when the assault ship steamed round to the south of the island to anchor in Singapore Roads, off Keppel Harbour, for the 150th anniversary of the founding of Singapore by Sir Stamford Raffles. Despite the fact that the British Government had announced that it was to withdraw from its military bases east of Suez by the end of 1971, the anniversary celebrations were held in an atmosphere of buoyant optimism and festivity. On board *Fearless* there were official receptions for Singapore's civic dignitaries and the ship was opened to the public on two days, with a hovercraft being put through its paces and demonstrating how it could dock in the assault ship's docking bay. On 13 August, with the celebrations over, *Fearless* weighed anchor and set course for Brunei and the small port of Seria, where she anchored during the morning of 16 August. Once at anchor a brigade of the Gurkha Rifles, their equipment and transport, were embarked for 'Exercise Happy Hunters', which took place in the Brunei area. On conclusion of the exercise *Fearless* returned to Singapore on 25 August to prepare for an official visit to Japan to coincide with 'British Week', which was being held in Tokyo.

At 07.30 on Thursday 11 September, following a short dockyard assisted maintenance period, *Fearless* left Singapore to steam into the South China Sea bound for Hong Kong, which was the first leg of her passage to Tokyo. On board she had 42 Commando's judo and basketball teams, the Duke of Wellington's Regimental Band and 3 Commando Brigade's Band. As well as these additional personnel she was also carrying four single-decker buses. During her crossing of the South China Sea the ship's company was entertained by the bands and the judo team as they rehearsed their displays, and on 15 September the ship secured alongside Hong Kong Dockyard's North Arm, for what to many on board was a very familiar run ashore. Some of the older hands, however, found that life was more expensive here now that the US Navy was using the colony as a rest centre for its forces engaged in the Vietnam War. As always the China Fleet Club proved an ideal starting point for liberty men, which usually led on to the 'attractions' of Wanchai. On 18 September, after leaving Hong Kong, *Fearless,* in company with RFA *Stromness,* steamed to Tokyo where, four days later, the two ships secured alongside Hanumi Pier. 'British Week' opened on 26 September and Captain Gerard-Pearse attended the ceremony on behalf of the ship's company. *Fearless* soon entered into the spirit of the occasion, with the ship being opened to the public on a number of afternoons. This proved to be very popular and at one stage *Fearless* was almost swamped with people crossing the gangway at the rate of 1,000 an hour. There were hovercraft demonstrations for Japanese officials and businessmen, while the ship's company could make the most of events as diverse as film premieres and visits to the Santori whisky distillery. *Fearless* left on 6 October to return to Hong Kong and on 26 October she embarked 902 Gurkhas for 'Exercise Sea Horse'. When the

Fearless in Nigeria's Lagos Harbour during March 1969 for Prime Minister Harold Wilson's efforts to broker peace during Nigeria's bitter civil war.
(Imperial War Museum, London, No HU 90947)

embarkation was completed the ship was crammed full of men, with barely enough room for sleeping and eating. The vehicle decks were used as temporary dormitories, with portable heads and showers being rigged up, and there were the inevitable long queues for all the facilities aboard. The 'assault' itself took place in nearby Mirs Bay, and *Fearless* remained at anchor offshore until 1 November when the Gurkhas were returned to Hong Kong Island.

On 8 November *Fearless* returned to Singapore for just two days before she left for the highlight of the commission, a ten-day visit to Fremantle. After seven days at sea, during the forenoon of 17 November the assault ship arrived alongside H berth of Victoria Quay in the West Australian port, at the start of what would be a very hectic visit. As always the people of Fremantle and Perth offered the ship's company tremendous hospitality and in return there was the usual children's party on board, together with two open days during which 7,000 people visited the ship. After leaving Fremantle on 27 November, *Fearless* returned to Singapore and many will still remember the warm tropical evenings, when speed was reduced to six knots and the ship's company was entertained to displays of traditional Nepalese dancing by the embarked force of Gurkhas. During early December there were more amphibious exercises off Malacca before, on 11 December, the assault ship returned to Singapore Naval Base for the Christmas and New Year festivities. Many members of the ship's company took advantage of station leave and enjoyed the cool and relaxed atmosphere some 4,500 feet up in the Cameron Highlands, whilst others went to the Sandycroft Leave Centre near Penang. Some were able to hitch lifts on RAF or RAAF flights to visit relatives in Australia and New Zealand, and a few hardy souls undertook gruelling expeditions in the rainforests of Malaya.

On 5 January 1970, having embarked a Royal Marines Band, *Fearless* left Singapore together with the frigate *Rothesay* for Penang where, next forenoon, she anchored off George Town for a three-day visit. From there she steamed south to Port Swettenham (Port Kelang) where, during the forenoon of 10 January, she and *Rothesay* entered harbour with full ceremony and secured alongside the North End Jetty. This was another three-day visit following which the two ships returned to Singapore Naval Base to prepare for a major fleet exercise. Beginning on Monday 19 January, 'Exercise Janex 70' in the South China Sea involved most units of the Far East Fleet, including *Andromeda, Duchess, Galatea, Lynx, Nubian, Rothesay* and *Yarmouth,* together with the depot ship *Forth. Fearless* was involved in an amphibious landing on Malaya's east coast, and on 24 January she returned to Singapore for 48 hours to embark the First Sea Lord, Admiral Sir Michael Le Fanu, the C-in-C Far East Station, and all their staff. During the second phase of the exercise there was recreational leave at the island of Tioman, and the manoeuvres concluded during the evening of 4 February, when *Fearless* returned to Singapore. Later that month, in company with *Andromeda, Fearless* made a five-day visit to Bangkok, where she secured alongside a berth in the New Port, some miles south of the city. On 27 February, following her return to Singapore, the men of 42 Commando, Royal Marines, were embarked and *Fearless* sailed for Hong Kong and a rendezvous with *Bulwark*, which had recently arrived in the Far East from Devonport. Exercises in the Hong Kong area followed, but on 21 March the assault ship returned to Singapore. In early April, after taking on board an embarked force of Gurkha Rifles, *Fearless* took part in 'Exercise Flying Fish' in the Tioman area of the South China Sea, together with *Bulwark* and *Triumph*. This time, however, instead of Wessex helicopters, she took on the more lightweight Scout and Sioux helicopters of the Commando Brigade Squadron, which made the flight deck crew's task easier. The main amphibious landing took place at Kuala Marang, with *Fearless, Bulwark* and *Triumph* anchoring off Pulau Kapas, from where the troops were ferried ashore. By 11 April, however, *Fearless* had returned to Singapore. Her time on the Far East Station was drawing to a close.

On Monday 13 April 1970, *Fearless* and her ship's company bade farewell to Singapore Naval Base as the assault ship left to make a nine-day non-stop voyage to Dubai, where she anchored during the early hours of 22 April. That evening, having refuelled, she continued her passage, arriving in Bahrain two days later. Before returning to the UK she was to carry out a joint exercise with the Army and RAF, and after a visit by General Sir Charles Harington, the exercise, code-named 'Entrold', began on 29 April. Operating with *Andromeda,* the landing ship *Sir Bedivere* and a squadron of RAF helicopters, *Fearless* landed and re-embarked a battalion of troops. Finally, however, after disembarking the air squadron and returning the troops to Bahrain, on Friday 8 May the assault ship began her long voyage home. On 20 May she called at Durban for five days, and seven days later she lay off Cape Town for an hour in order to collect a passenger. On Sunday 7 June she made her final 'foreign' visit of the commission when she secured alongside the breakwater at Funchal, Madeira. During her 48 hours alongside there were some unusual visitors in the form of students from the schools' cruise ship *Uganda,* who were invited on board to look over the ship. At 05.50 on Friday 12 June, four days after leaving Funchal, *Fearless* anchored in Plymouth Sound. A few hours later tenders began ferrying families out to the ship and at 11.15 she weighed anchor for the passage up the Hamoaze. At noon *Fearless* secured alongside No 6 wharf in Devonport Dockyard.

During her second commission *Fearless* had steamed 76,350 miles, she had recorded 2,400 helicopter landings, the LCMs had achieved 300 amphibious troop and vehicle landings and the LCVPs had made 180 troop landings. Altogether she had carried 7,500 troops and 1,300 vehicles with the largest embarked force being the 902 Gurkhas involved in 'Exercise Sea Horse'. It was the end of a successful commission and ahead lay a seven-month refit.

Fearless is secured alongside Tokyo's Hanumi Pier in September 1969 as, greeted by a military band, RFA *Stromness* prepares to manoeuvre alongside. *(Imperial War Museum, London, No HU 90947)*

Chapter Three

HMS *Fearless* - Third Commission 1970-1972

During the summer and autumn of 1970 *Fearless* lay in Devonport Dockyard's No 9 dry dock as she underwent her second major refit, and on 8 August her newly appointed commanding officer, Captain B. J. Straker OBE RN, visited the ship which, at that time, was in a state of organized chaos. He finally took up his appointment on 20 October 1970 and a few weeks later, on a grey November morning, he and the ship's company moved on board. On 22 January 1971 the Admiral Superintendent inspected the ship and three days later, at 10.50 on Monday 25 January, *Fearless* left the dockyard to begin her post-acceptance trials. Severe gales and heavy seas kept the assault ship at C buoy in Plymouth Sound that night, but next day she was able to put to sea and begin full-power trials in the Channel. During the three days in rough weather it became clear that because of the long refit many members of the ship's company had lost their sea legs, but after disembarking the LCMs off the Nab Tower, the ship returned to Plymouth Sound on the evening of 29 January for a short break before continuing machinery trials over the measured mile. The trials were concluded on Friday 5 February, when *Fearless* returned to Devonport Dockyard for rectification of machinery defects. Two days later steering gear was discovered to be damaged, and as it was apparent that it was deliberate, the police were called in to investigate, with the result that all shore leave was stopped for the day. In the event the incident was not serious enough to affect the ship's operational capability.

On Friday 12 February the Recommissioning Service was held on the tank deck, with the ship's chaplain conducting the religious service and the cake being cut by the guest of honour, Lady Hull. Twelve days later, on 24 February, *Fearless* sailed for an arduous four-week work-up at Portland. In addition to the usual naval programme the assault ship embarked troops and tanks from 24 Brigade, a hovercraft from Lee-on-Solent and Wessex helicopters of 846 Squadron as well as helicopters from 666 Army Air Corps Squadron, which provided plenty of training in her amphibious role. Following a successful inspection by the Flag Officer Sea Training, the work-up ended on Thursday 25 March and by noon the next day the assault ship had returned to Devonport for a hard-earned Easter leave.

On 26 April 1971 *Fearless* put to sea to carry out machinery trials and three days later she steamed up Southampton Water to 101 berth in Southampton Docks where, in the words of one member of the ship's company, 'we took on board hordes of pongos and their vehicles'. Despite the frantic activity on board, the ship's company was able to enjoy what was, for the Royal Navy, a more unusual run ashore. On 2 May the assault ship sailed north for the Mull of Kintyre where, in Carradale Bay in an exercise code-named 'Nelson's Touch', the first major amphibious landing of the commission took place. For two days logistical support was provided for the troops ashore, and whilst in Scottish waters 150 men of the 1st Royal Irish Rangers were embarked. On 7 May, escorted by the destroyer *Cavalier, Fearless* sailed for Denmark to carry out her second amphibious assault, 'Exercise Moon Lady', which was staged on the Danish coast below Copenhagen. Apart from the fact that the troops were landed about half a mile from the intended site, everything went well and the whole exercise was observed closely by East German intelligence services. The exercise also incorporated the assault ship's Operational Readiness Inspection, when Rear-Admiral J. D. Treacher, the Flag Officer Carriers and Amphibious Ships, scrutinized the ship's preparedness for amphibious duties. After five days of landings and re-embarkation, during which the naval landing parties were also put ashore, *Fearless* put into Copenhagen. Despite the high prices Tivoli Gardens and the plentiful lager were enjoyed by most, and after leaving the Danish capital the ship returned to Devonport to drop off the embarked force and to prepare for the first of several 'Meet the Navy' tours.

On 25 May, after leaving Plymouth Sound, *Fearless* steamed north via the Pentland Firth for Leith where an 'embarked force' of 200 Scottish schoolboys was taken on board for the eight-hour passage to Sunderland. The assault ship anchored there at 16.30 on 2 June and the event is described by a member of the ship's company thus: 'Here we landed them by LCM and picked up 200 little Geordies, who ran around happily until we reached Portsmouth asking questions in a dialect few could understand.' A week in Portsmouth was spent chipping and painting before another unusual 'embarked force' was taken on board in the form of the British Olympic Yachting Team, together with their yachts and cars. On 16 June *Fearless* left Portsmouth to set course for Kiel and 'Kieler Woche', which was doubling up as the venue for Olympic yachting events. The assault ship entered harbour two days later to secure alongside the Tirpitzmole in Kiel Naval Base, where she joined naval units from eight other countries. The week revolved around various international

Captain Straker takes the salute at the Recommissioning Service on 12 February 1971.
(Imperial War Museum, London, No HU 90952)

sporting events for which *Fearless* fielded teams representing the Royal Navy. The runs ashore in this picturesque German town, particularly the organized trips to Berlin and to local breweries, were enjoyed by all and on 26 June, with a lot of empty wallets and thick heads on board, *Fearless* left Kiel to make her return passage to Portsmouth, where she arrived two days later. That forenoon anyone taking a stroll along Eastney seafront must have been very surprised when two of the assault ship's LCVPs landed on the beach to disgorge a screaming horde of marines who were assisting in the making of a training film.

On 1 July, whilst alongside at Portsmouth, there was an emergency muster of all ships' divers from every unit in harbour when the submarine *Artemis* sank at her moorings alongside HMS *Dolphin*. Six of the nine men on board, together with three sea cadets, managed to escape from the submarine before she sank, but three were trapped in the forward end. Fortunately, they were rescued safely after ten hours on the seabed and *Fearless'* divers were able to return to the ship. On 5 July, with ship's company family members on board, *Fearless* left Portsmouth to make the short passage to Southampton where, once again, she secured alongside Union Castle Line's 101 berth to disembark the families and embark troops and vehicles for 'Exercise Drake's Drum', an amphibious landing exercise which took place in the Portland area. On 10 July, with the exercise over, *Fearless* returned to Southampton to disembark the troops and to spend nine days alongside 101 berth, next to Mayflower Park. During her stay a ship's company dance was held at the Royal Pier ballroom and during the weekend of 17/18 July the ship was opened to the public. During the forenoon of Monday 19 July, having embarked a group of 200 southern schoolboys for the second phase of her 'Meet the Navy' visits, *Fearless* left Southampton to make the six-hour crossing of the Channel to Cherbourg for a three-day visit to the French port. It was said that the French public was amazed to see the assault ship with such youthful crew members, complete with school uniforms. From Cherbourg *Fearless* made a 24-hour passage to Avonmouth, rendezvousing with the Iranian frigate *Saam* and carrying out a jackstay transfer. The Iranian vessel, which was carrying out its initial trials, had just been completed by Vosper Thorneycroft. After arriving alongside Avonmouth Docks on 23 July, the schoolboys were disembarked. As well as being able to take advantage of Bristol city's night life, liberty men also went along to the city docks to assist with the cleaning of Brunel's old steamship *Great Britain*, which had been returned to her original West Country port, having been rescued from Sparrow Cove in the Falkland Islands where she had been beached. After four days at Avonmouth 209 schoolboys from the West Country joined the ship for the overnight passage to Devonport where *Fearless* arrived alongside on 28 July.

During the next month in her home port *Fearless* took part in Navy Days, when she was opened to the public over three days, but on Wednesday 1 September it was time to start work once again and, having embarked Headquarters 3 Commando Brigade and with the frigate *Phoebe* for company, she sailed for Gibraltar and a Mediterranean deployment. During the passage south the hot sunny

33

Fearless arrives in Grand Harbour on 24 October 1971 to begin a ten-day maintenance period.
(Michael Cassar, Valletta, Malta)

weather was a portent of things to come, and within 48 hours the NAAFI kiosk had sold record quantities of suntan oil. On 7 September *Fearless* left Gibraltar to steam east for a series of manoeuvres which would culminate in the NATO exercise 'Deep Furrow', during which time she would have a permanent Soviet shadow in the form of an intelligence-gathering trawler or, during the main exercise, a Kashkin-class destroyer. As she steamed further into the Mediterranean and temperatures on board rose even higher, the engineers were kept busy repairing some temperamental air-conditioning plants, and during some nights mess deck temperatures rose to over 98°F. On 13 September the ship anchored off Dhekelia and the embarked force was landed in the LCMs and LCVPs for a three-day exercise ashore. Trouble with *Fearless'* main engines meant that the ship remained at anchor during the exercise, but with the stern gate lowered to provide an excellent lido platform, 'hands to bathe' was piped each afternoon. In the early hours of 17 September, with all the troops having re-embarked, the assault ship made a slow passage on one engine to Limassol for a five-day stopover which coincided with a local wine festival. Nursing some severe hangovers, but with her engines operating efficiently once again, *Fearless* returned to Dhekelia where there was another amphibious exercise with 41 Commando and Headquarters 3 Commando Brigade, which resulted in the ship's landing party, the 'blue berets', being surrounded by three members of the Parachute Regiment. On conclusion of this set of manoeuvres the assault ship weighed anchor on 1 October and set course for Brindisi where, three days later, she embarked an additional force consisting of the 8th Amphibious Brigade of the US Marine Corps for 'Exercise Deep Furrow'.

This exercise, executed around the Turkish area of Thrace, was NATO's biggest amphibious exercise since the end of the Second World War and after the naval phase, the amphibious operations on 12 October involved an assault landing at Saros Bay by embarked forces from both *Fearless* and *Bulwark,* with the destroyer *Norfolk* acting as escort. The men of 3 Commando Brigade and the US Marine Corps made a night helicopter landing to secure blocking positions some 25 kilometres behind the withdrawing 'enemy', which provided valuable training in cross-operations with British and US forces. On 13 October, with her troops ashore, *Fearless* put to sea and next day she received a visit from the First Sea Lord, Admiral Sir Michael Pollock. Four days later, after recovering her embarked force at Saros Bay, *Fearless* made a three-day visit to Istanbul for a short recuperation period. Unfortunately the assault ship was anchored a long way from the city centre, but for those who made the long trip ashore there was the reward of seeing the ancient mosques and fascinating bazaars of the region. After leaving Istanbul on 22 October *Fearless* set course for Malta, where she arrived two days later to undergo a ten-day maintenance period in Grand Harbour. During this time the embarked force left the ship for training at Ghajn Tuffeiha Camp, whilst the ship's company painted ship and cleaned the boilers. It was during this period that there was a change of Executive Officers, with Commander M. D. Joel RN being appointed to the ship. On Tuesday 2 November, having re-embarked Headquarters 3 Commando Brigade, the assault

A Westland Wasp helicopter coming in to land on *Fearless'* flight deck during 'Exercise Sun Pirate' which took place off Puerto Rico. There are already two Wessex and two smaller helicopters on the flight deck.
(Imperial War Museum, London, No HU 90950)

ship left Malta to set course for Cagliari, Sardinia, where she spent two days prior to her final exercise of the deployment, 'Sardinia 71'. The Royal Marines were joined by the San Marco Battalion of the Italian Marines for the amphibious assault of the Sardinian beaches on 6 November, following which *Fearless* anchored offshore to support the troops. On 9 November, with the weather too rough for the LCMs, the vehicles were recovered by helicopter. On the following day the troops themselves were re-embarked and, upon completion, the assault ship set course for Gibraltar and the first leg of her passage back to Devonport.

Lieutenant-Commander Doug Barlow, *Fearless'* Bosun, remembers an amusing incident which happened soon after the Commander arrived aboard: 'Upon his arrival from his MoD boat procurement job, the new Commander announced that he had made arrangements to change the 27 ft whaler with the latest motor whaler, a boat with no oars or sails, much to the disdain of the Boatswain who enjoyed his sailing in the old whaler. The time came when the excited Commander could try out his new 'toy' and the ship was stopped. The Commander had only invited his two 'ship's appearance' managers, myself and the Chief Bosun's Mate to accompany him and after being lowered to the water we slipped from the falls. As soon as we were clear of the ship the Commander, who clearly had no further use for oars and sails in the ship's boats, confidently demonstrated the engine start to us. The engine, however, had other ideas and it obstinately refused to start. Over and over the Commander tried and, as we drifted further and further away from *Fearless,* he became embarrassed, cross and very cross. Finally, someone on board *Fearless* decided we were getting nowhere, and the ship started to come astern to retrieve us. The much-vaunted engine trials ended with the three of us, the Commander, myself and Chief Bosun's Mate, paddling the new whaler with bottom boards until we reached the davits where, with a very red-faced Commander, and the duty watch stifling their laughter, we were hoisted back on board.'

On Friday 12 November *Fearless* arrived alongside Gibraltar's South Mole where, on Remembrance Sunday, there was a combined dockside parade of 650 sailors, Royal Marines and soldiers. The three-day stop at Gibraltar was an opportunity for buying last-minute Christmas presents, but by 15 November *Fearless* was at sea again and two days later, at just before midnight, she anchored in Plymouth Sound. Next forenoon she weighed anchor to steam up harbour and secure alongside No 7 wharf, where many families were waiting to welcome their loved ones home. Once alongside, Headquarters 3 Commando Brigade was disembarked and the ship's company began their seasonal leave. During her period in Devonport the assault ship was dry docked so that two new five-bladed propellers could be fitted and the underwater hull could be scraped and painted. Above the waterline the ship's side and superstructure were repainted, all in preparation for the FOCAS inspection which was due to take place early in the new year.

Fearless had been due to leave Devonport on Monday 3

January 1972 to sail north for Rosyth but, much to the delight of those who lived locally, problems with the main engines delayed sailing for three days. When she did leave harbour the assault ship sailed north to Rosyth to embark a company of Royal Marines from 45 Commando, together with their vehicles and equipment, to transport them to Elvegard, Norway, for 'Exercise Clockwork'. The exercise was intended to test both men and equipment in sub-zero temperatures, and *Fearless* steamed well inside the Arctic Circle to achieve the required weather conditions. During the passage from Rosyth some very severe weather was encountered, with wind speeds of up to 63 knots and huge waves. With the ship rolling as much as 35 degrees either way, normal day work on board was virtually impossible, and while the watchkeepers managed to maintain essential services, most mess decks were said to 'resemble mortuaries'. Doug Barlow the Bosun, remembers the passage well: 'Making my way to the bridge on that stormiest of nights was like moving through a ghost ship, not a person to be seen. My visit to the bridge was one of curiosity and upon arrival I found a very sick Officer of the Watch clinging to the binnacle. My offer to stand his watch was gratefully accepted with a promise he would do the same for me. I took over a never-to-be-forgotten middle watch. That mighty vessel was tossed around like a piece of driftwood with smashes and crashes filling the air. Calls from other parts of the ship came through the bridge telephones. The watch engineer rang from the engine room to compare roll indicators: "We registered 30 degrees that time, how about you?" These comparisons continued throughout the watch. An excited call came from the lower tank deck to the effect that a Centurion tank had come adrift and a major was underneath it, risking serious injury or even death, while attempting to re-secure it. Then came a report that the two after LCMs were shifting and colliding. This had never been heard of before and from then on, when securing for sea, the "chippies" placed wooden shores between them. It was my most exciting middle watch, and the officer whom I had relieved didn't return the favour.'

Never was the sight of land more welcome and to everyone's surprise, Andfjord was enjoying similar temperatures to those which had been experienced at Devonport, with not a flake of snow in sight. Once at anchor the marines of 45 Commando were disembarked and the ship's company got a run ashore at Harstad, but whilst at anchor there the LCVP *F6* had the misfortune to strike a rock and sink. Fortunately, the crew's cries for help were soon heard and, despite the hours of extended darkness, they were safely rescued, along with the waterlogged *F6*. Again Doug Barlow recalls the incident: 'The Royal Marines were carrying out a dawn sweep in the LCVPs and *F6* inadvertently sailed inside a navigation mark and perched herself on a pinnacle of rock. Although boats were able to approach and rescue the crew, *F6* was stuck fast and making lots of water. That afternoon I was dispatched to the scene with a salvage crew and initially I was going to do a tidal lift with an LCM lashed to each side of the stranded vessel. Unfortunately, however, the LCM's draught was too deep and despite the words of caution from "experts" in *Fearless* I ordered up two LCVPs to attempt the lift-off. Doubts were expressed whether this would work, especially without a strongback across all three boats. I was confident my plan would work, and positioning two LCVPs abreast of each other, on either side of *F6*, with their lifting bolts adjacent, I ordered my team to lash these bolts together with cordage and to wait in position with sharp knives at the ready. We then waited for what seemed to be an eternity in freezing conditions for the rising tide. Suddenly, without warning, all three LCVPs were floating, lashed together with barely a list on the supporting craft. We slowly returned to the ship and manoeuvred into the dock where *F6* was hoisted by crane onto the flight deck.'

On 18 January *Fearless* left Norway to steam back into the full fury of the Atlantic Ocean and North Sea, neither of which were any calmer since her last encounter. This time, however, it was a much shorter passage and on 21 January, three days after leaving Harstad, *Fearless* arrived in the River Tyne where she secured alongside, under the shadow of the Tyne Bridge. After several days of effort in cleaning and painting, as well as hectic runs ashore, Admiral Treacher's inspection took place which culminated in Divisions on the tank deck, followed by the presentation of the Fleet Seacat Aimers Trophy to a member of the ship's company. With the inspection over the ship's company could relax and concentrate on the runs ashore, where the people of Newcastle looked after them well. Without doubt the most popular visitors to the ship were the glamorous models who, despite the bitterly cold weather, demonstrated the Royal Marines Commando keep fit exercises for the local television station. The latter part of the Newcastle visit was taken up with the embarkation of 24 Brigade, Royal Marines, who were to form the embarked force during the next leg of the commission, a deployment to the Caribbean.

On 31 January *Fearless* left the Tyne and steamed south to Plymouth Sound where she embarked a flight of four Wessex helicopters from 845 Squadron, together with squadron personnel. However, with more severe weather conditions forecast it was decided to strike the helicopters into the LCMs and wedge them in the dock, and when she sailed a few hours later to begin a transatlantic crossing it was to sail into some appalling weather. For the first six days the assault ship was hammered by severe gales and heavy seas, the force of which actually distorted the forecastle breakwater. The final few days, however, saw hot sunshine and calmer seas and on 8 February the four

LCVPs *F5* and *F7* are lowered from the starboard davits during 'Exercise Sun Pirate'.
(Imperial War Museum, London, No HU 90938)

helicopters were lifted precariously by crane back onto the flight deck. Four days later *Fearless* arrived at the giant US Naval Base at Roosevelt Roads, Puerto Rico. The base itself covers an area of over 120 square miles, but apart from the PX it had very little to offer liberty men and most members of the ship's company preferred to travel the 30 miles to the capital, San Juan. On 13 February *Fearless* left Roosevelt Roads to make the short passage to nearby Isla de Vieques, which was the venue for 'Exercise Sun Pirate'. In company for the tri-service exercises were the LSLs *Sir Bedivere, Sir Tristram* and *Sir Galahad,* as well as the frigate *Phoebe,* all supported by the RFAs *Regent* and *Tidesurge*. With the beachheads having been secured, the LCMs spent many hours landing personnel and stores then, whilst *Fearless* left the area to play her part in the naval exercise, the ship's LCMs transported equipment to and from Roosevelt Roads. The exercise was overshadowed by a tragic accident when a Land Rover was badly damaged and three men lost their lives. Meanwhile, whilst the embarked force toiled with their exercise, the clear water, hot sun and golden beaches meant banyans on Beef Island (British Virgin Islands), and Vieques for *Fearless'* ship's company. On each occasion an LCM was loaded with recreational boats, a NAAFI beer team and Commander 'S', who took charge of the barbecue.

On conclusion of the exercise *Fearless* and *Sir Bedivere* paid a five-day visit to Bridgetown, Barbados, where, once again there were beautiful beaches and plenty of rum, which was actually cheaper than the accompanying Coke. Many members of the ship's company will have happy memories of the popular Coconut Creek Club and the local bars in Nelson Street, and Captain Straker even met up with a distant cousin, Emile Straker, a member of the chart-topping group 'The Merrymen'. On 29 February *Fearless* left Bridgetown and on departure one of the Wessex helicopters put on a flying display over the Coconut Creek Country Club, to be rewarded with a gallon jar of rum punch which, according to the flight crew, was broken before it could be returned to the ship. There then followed another ten-day passage across the Atlantic to Liverpool where, on the first night ashore, the proprietors of the Clubship Landfall (a converted LCT) laid on a special dance for the ship's company. Soon after her arrival the first of the ship's company Easter leave parties left the ship, but on 13 March, to a volley of sirens from other ships in harbour to mark Captain Straker's last voyage, *Fearless* left the River Mersey to steam south for Falmouth Bay, where the squadron personnel left the ship, and on to Portsmouth where she was to undergo a dockyard-assisted maintenance period.

On 22 March 1972, soon after her arrival in Portsmouth, there was a change of command for *Fearless* when Captain S. A. C. Cassels RN took over from Captain Straker. Three weeks later, with the maintenance period completed and having hoisted the flag of Rear-Admiral J. D. Treacher and embarked Headquarters 3 Commando Brigade, on a dull and wet 11 April the assault ship left Portsmouth Harbour to carry out post-refit engine trials in the Channel. With these completed and having rendezvoused with the frigate *Bacchante,* the two ships set course for Bordeaux and a five-day visit to the French port.

Four hundred and fifty men of the 2nd Battalion Scots Guards on *Fearless*' flight deck as they prepare for 'Operation Motorman', the opening up of 'no-go' areas in Londonderry.
(Imperial War Museum, London, No HU90944)

The purpose of the visit was to help celebrate the 25th anniversary of the twinning of the cities of Bordeaux and Bristol, the latter having 'adopted' *Fearless* as its ship. During her stay in harbour guests on board included the French Prime Minister, the civic officials of both Bordeaux and Bristol and, when opened to the public, some 10,000 local people. For the ship's company perhaps the most notable event was a special dance put on by the city and, apart from the fact that the bar ran dry after only an hour, it was a huge success. Fortunately, one of the assault ship's LCVPs was able to make an emergency trip up the Gironde River for more wine supplies. Fifty orphans from a nearby children's home enjoyed a slap-up party on board and the whole visit was deemed to be an outstanding success. On 17 April *Fearless* left harbour to make her way back into the Bay of Biscay and set course for Gibraltar from where, after a brief visit, she entered the Mediterranean and set course for Cyprus.

Six days after leaving Gibraltar *Fearless* anchored off Dhekelia where, together with the commando carrier *Albion* which had 848 Squadron and 42 Commando embarked, she took part in four days of landing and withdrawal rehearsals in readiness for the major NATO exercise code-named 'Dawn Patrol'. After the manoeuvres off Cyprus the ships steamed north to carry out more landing exercises on a beach close to the Greek fishing town of Kavalla. These were combined with a run ashore in the town itself where the assault ship's visit boosted sales of ouzo and trade in the local restaurants and cafes. 'Dawn Patrol' involved 100 ships from seven countries ranging over the whole of the Mediterranean Sea, with a variety of amphibious ships taking part, including *Albion*, *Fearless* and *USS Guadalcanal*. *Fearless* was joined by the frigates *Aurora* and *Juno,* the helicopter cruiser *Blake,* the RFAs *Lyness* and *Olmeda* and later, units of the French ASW Squadron. The main amphibious landing was staged at Kiparissia in western Greece, and on completion of the exercise the force made its way to Athens for a five-day visit. Despite the fact that Phaleron Bay was virtually jammed with ships of every nationality, the boat routines operated efficiently and with the city centre within easy reach everyone enjoyed the run ashore. Shortly before *Fearless* left Athens the new FOCAS, Rear-Admiral R. D. Lygo, made a brief visit to the ship and on 20 May she weighed anchor and set course for Malta where many were able to reacquaint themselves with the establishments of Strait Street. However, the stay was only short and after two days *Fearless* left Grand Harbour to set course for home. Apart from a mail pick-up, Gibraltar was bypassed and on 29 May *Fearless* arrived off Poole Harbour Buoy where one of the LCMs was landed*, before the assault ship set course for Devonport where she arrived next day for ship's company leave and a two-week maintenance period.

All too soon, it seemed, the leave period was over and on a very wet 13 June *Fearless,* with Headquarters 3 Commando Brigade embarked, left Devonport for 'Exercise Trial Strength' which was to be executed on the

---

* LCM *F3* was to take part in demonstrations for HRH the Duke of Edinburgh in his capacity as Captain General Royal Marines.

38

bleak and lonely beaches of the Orkney Islands. After collecting LCM *F3* from Poole the first stop was Rosyth where men and vehicles of the Royal Netherlands Marines were embarked, which brought the ship to 'overload conditions'. There was also a short visit to the ship by the Grand Duke of Luxembourg then, with the embarkation of troops completed, *Fearless* sailed for Scapa Flow. During the passage she underwent her Operational Readiness Inspection, and on 20 June she arrived in the famous wartime anchorage for the start of the exercises. Also taking part in 'Exercise Trial Strength' were the commando carrier *Albion,* the frigate *Salisbury,* the RFAs *Olna* and *Retainer* and two SRN6 hovercraft belonging to the Royal Corps of Transport which, in the absence of the LCMs, practised docking procedures. Although the weather was calm for the exercise it was overcast and damp, and the Dutch marines spent three uncomfortable nights ashore. The ship's company had some brief runs ashore in Kirkwall, then after bidding farewell to the Dutch marines, *Fearless* steamed south to Devonport, where she arrived on 27 June to disembark Headquarters 3 Commando Brigade and to embark the C-in-C Fleet, Admiral Sir Edward Ashmore and his staff for a short visit to Lisbon. The C-in-C was making the visit in his capacity as the NATO Commander Eastern Atlantic and was overseeing the opening of a new headquarters complex in the Portuguese capital. It was the first visit by a senior officer since 1966 and inevitably there were plenty of ceremonial duties to be performed. Indeed, on the forenoon of her arrival the Royal Marines Detachment, who provided the Captain's Guard, paraded seven times which, they claimed, was a record. Some members of the ship's company will remember the city's Texas Bar, and others will recall the well-organized coach tours to Sintra and the beach resort of Estoril. When the visit came to an end *Fearless* returned to Devonport before continuing her 'Meet the Navy' tour which took her, complete with an 'embarked force' of schoolboys, up the Bristol Channel to squeeze through Swansea Harbour's narrow entrance for a five-day visit to the city. During her stay she played host to a Dental Association conference, as well as hordes of schoolchildren and, during two afternoons, to local residents.

After leaving Swansea *Fearless* headed north to take part in Rosyth's Navy Days, and during the passage she rendezvoused with her sister *Intrepid* and stayed with her long enough for an inter-ship sports day which was held on *Intrepid's* flight deck, with 50 competitors being transferred from *Fearless* by jackstay. Navy Days at Rosyth was washed out by heavy rain, which limited the numbers of visitors to the ship, and on leaving the Scottish naval base *Fearless* steamed north to Cape Wrath for an annual naval gunnery exercise 'Wrathex'. The exercise was cut short, however, on receipt of instructions to steam immediately to Gareloch on the Clyde and speculation as to the ship's future

itinerary ran riot, with any broadcast over the ship's tannoy which was prefixed by 'Captain speaking' being guaranteed to silence even the noisiest member of any mess. On arrival in the Gareloch the 2nd Battalion Scots Guards was embarked, supplementing Headquarters 3 Commando Brigade who were already on board, and it soon became clear that the troops were bound for Northern Ireland, for a special operation in the troubled Province.

In 1972 Northern Ireland had seen a sharp increase in civil strife, which was of great concern to the British Government as a result of which, in March that year, direct rule from Westminster was imposed. In both Belfast and Londonderry Republican leaders had established what had become known as 'no-go' areas by erecting street barriers, behind which gunmen had kept out the forces of law and order and this had led to a state of virtual anarchy in parts of Londonderry. The Government, in order to re-establish a police presence, had decided to use overwhelming force to open up the areas once again and *Fearless* was to play a vital role in the operation which was code-named 'Motorman'. As well as men of the Scots Guards the assault ship also embarked four armoured bulldozers belonging to the Royal Engineers, which had been brought from their base in Germany, and during the late evening of Sunday 30 July *Fearless* anchored in Lough Foyle, about 25 miles from the city of Londonderry. Under the cover of darkness, and escorted by the minesweeper *Gavinton,* the LCMs set off from the anchorage down the lough to a beach on the outskirts of the city. As it was not known whether the operation would be opposed in any way, weapons and ammunition had been issued and all the LCM crews were equipped with steel helmets. Fortunately the journey was uneventful, and at just before midnight the troops and bulldozers were landed. By 07.00, in a dawn action which involved 12,000 troops, all the barriers had been removed and police and army patrols were once again operating throughout Londonderry. By 09.00 the bulldozers were back on board the assault ship. *Fearless* had completed another successful operation and many messages of appreciation were received on board. After leaving Lough Foyle that same day, the assault ship arrived in Devonport on Tuesday 1 August when summer leave began and the armoured bulldozers began their journey back to Germany.

During the period spent at Devonport *Fearless* was dry docked in order that her stern glands could be repacked and she also took part in Plymouth Navy Days, when some 27,000 people visited the ship. On board rumours were circulating to the effect that the commission, which had been due to end in October, was to be extended. As a result of industrial action in the dockyard her scheduled refit could not begin on time and, because of mechanical defects on board the commando ship *Bulwark, Fearless* was ordered to take her place in the Mediterranean. With the leave and maintenance period over and having embarked

In line abreast during 'Exercise Corsica 72' in the Mediterranean are *Fearless*, *Intrepid*, *Bulwark* and *Ark Royal*.

(*Ron Slater*)

Headquarters 3 Commando Brigade, and members of the US Navy's Seal Team 2 (the equivalent of the Special Boat Service) *Fearless* left Devonport in early September and set course for Holland. Once safely alongside the new Europoort at the mouth of Rotterdam's New Waterway, *Fearless* embarked a company of Dutch marines and sailed for Rosyth where other units were also at anchor. On September 11, when she left Rosyth, she joined a force which included *Ark Royal* (flag FOCAS), *Blake, Fife, Juno* and the RFAs *Olwen* and *Retainer,* for the NATO exercise code-named 'Strong Express'. It was to be the organization's largest exercise since its formation in 1951 and it involved some 64,000 personnel, 300 ships and 700 aircraft. *Fearless'* role was to land her embarked force on the Lofoten Peninsular in order to reinforce NATO's northern flank. On 15 September, the Dutch marines were subjected to a rather wet landing on a beach in the exercise area near Harstad which, coupled with their Orkney experience must have left them with some soggy memories of *Fearless*. During the exercise the assault ship played host to a steady stream of VIPs, including two junior government ministers, the C-in-C Fleet, Admiral Sir Edward Ashmore, the Secretary of State for Defence, Lord Carrington, and the Commandant-General Royal Marines, Lt-General B. I. S. Gourlay. On completion of the landings the LCMs were detached for a period to team up with 45 Commando, in a night attack on a Norwegian 'enemy'. While in the area shore leave was limited to a few 'expeds' for the hardier members of the ship's company, then on completion of the exercise the assault ship returned the Dutch marines to Europoort before steaming to Rosyth for post-exercise conferences. On 4 October she sailed south to Portsmouth for a one-week break.

As *Fearless* had been due to begin a long refit her stores had been allowed to run down, and during her seven days alongside at Portsmouth the ship was quickly replenished in order to prevent any deficiencies which might arise. On 12 October after embarking four Wessex helicopters of 848 Squadron, she left home waters bound for the Mediterranean. Her main task during this period, whilst standing in for *Bulwark*, was to act as a troop carrier for 41 Commando who were scheduled to exercise in Cyprus during the last week of the month. After a brief stop in Gibraltar *Fearless* steamed east to Malta where, on her arrival, she embarked the commandos and their equipment and made the three-day passage to Dhekelia for the amphibious landing. Once the troops were ashore *Fearless* was not required to take any further part in the exercise and, on 25 October, flying the flag of Rear-Admiral Templeton-Cotill, the Flag Officer, Malta, she steamed north to the Greek port of Volos. The passage was made by way of the Scarpanto Strait, round the picturesque island of Stampalia and through the Sartorin Passage, arriving at Volos during the forenoon of 27 October. Although the town was a popular holiday resort during the summer months, by early autumn it was very quiet and although some managed to acquaint themselves with the local ouzo, there was little else to entice liberty men ashore. As an alternative a series of banyans and 'expeds' were organized and the LCMs were kept busy dropping the parties off at various beaches and picking them up 24 hours later. Although the weather was fine for most of the visit, one 'exped' party was forced to spend a night out in the open in torrential rain. On leaving Volos *Fearless* returned to Dhekelia to re-embark 41 Commando and deliver them back to Malta, where *Fearless* met her sister ship *Intrepid;* her ship's company was busy preparing the ship for Admiral's inspection - which gave them an excuse to decline all *Fearless'* sports challenges.

During her two-week stay in Grand Harbour 50 wives and girlfriends flew out to the island for a very pleasant reunion and, in anticipation of the end of the commission, all the Chinese cooks and stewards flew back to their homes in Hong Kong. On 18 November *Fearless* left Malta to rendezvous with *Intrepid* and to carry out trials which involved the dropping of depth charges from helicopters. Following these *Fearless* returned to Marsaxlokk Bay where, once again, 41 Commando was embarked. The assault ship's final amphibious exercise of the commission was code-named 'Exercise Corsica' and with *Intrepid* and *Bulwark,* which had finally made it out from the UK, landings were made on the beaches of Corsica which were defended by the Green Scorpion Battalion of the French Foreign Legion, who proved a formidable 'enemy'. On conclusion a sports day was organized at Calvi, and after leaving Corsica, *Fearless,* flying the flag of FOCAS, and *Intrepid* made a five-day visit to Toulon. There the local beauty queen, assisted by two glamorous helpers, added the rum to the Christmas pudding being prepared on board *Fearless* and a band of nubile drum majorettes showed off their marching routines on the flight deck. Finally, with FOCAS having returned to the UK by air, *Fearless* and *Intrepid* also left for the passage home, making a short stop at Gibraltar where many took the opportunity to buy last-minute Christmas presents. Soon after weighing anchor, however, *Intrepid* was forced to return to Gibraltar with a damaged hull, leaving *Fearless* to continue the passage alone. After a bumpy crossing of the Bay of Biscay, *Fearless* arrived in Plymouth Sound on 10 December 1972 and was soon safely alongside in Devonport Dockyard.

Shortly after her arrival the ship received a visit from her sponsor, Lady Hull, accompanied by Field Marshal Sir Richard Hull which, for Captain Cassels, rounded off a successful commission during which *Fearless* had steamed some 65,000 miles. Ahead, however, lay a very different role for the assault ship.

41

Chapter Four

HMS *Fearless* - Dartmouth Training 1973-1978

During the first six months of 1973 *Fearless* was under refit in dry dock at Devonport and, being far from habitable, her much reduced ship's company was accommodated ashore in HMS *Drake*. Each day the ship became a hive of activity with a cacophony of noise from 'windy hammers', pneumatic drills, pumps and the continual lifting and shifting of stores. At the same time there was the seemingly never-ending scraping, chipping and painting, to say nothing of the scrubbing and washing, and all the main passageways were clogged with flexible pipes and hoses of every description. Gradually, however, as the summer approached and the completion date drew nearer, the ship took on a semblance of order and the ship's company was able to move back on board. On 18 June 1973 there was a change of command when Captain J. B. Rumble RN took over, and on 6 November Flag Officer Plymouth carried out an inspection of the ship. Next day *Fearless* put to sea to undergo her post-refit trials and work-up, but two days later she was back in Devonport for five days of repairs to the main condenser's circulating pump. The work-up continued, but was once again punctuated by condenser troubles, but in mid-November, with Headquarters 3 Commando Brigade back on board, she took part in her first major amphibious exercise for 12 months. Taking place in the Lulworth Cove area of Dorset the exercise also involved *Bulwark*, *Intrepid* and the LSL *Sir Galahad*, and between them they landed War Maintenance Reserves in order to set up a Brigade Maintenance Area and a Forward Air Base on Salisbury Plain. The work-up ended on 7 December when *Fearless* returned to Devonport, and three days later she assumed the role of Dartmouth Training Ship. In this role she would make three main training cruises each year. By tradition she would follow the sun to the Caribbean and West Indies in the spring, relocating to Scandinavia and the Baltic in the summer and to the Mediterranean in the autumn. She would cater for midshipmen-under-training, who were generally in their sixth month in the Royal Navy when they joined *Fearless* for their first sea experience. From the moment they stepped on board they were caught up in, and often caught out by, a training schedule which occupied their energy entirely until they disembarked some nine weeks later. The programme for each cruise was carefully planned by the navigating officer, to give a balance between coastal navigation, sea training, visits for adventurous training and banyans, and 'showing the flag'

visits to major ports and cities. Their days were spent in one of three ways: working part of ship alongside members of the ship's company, with the Buffer imparting words of wisdom from his experience, under instruction in the 'schoolrooms' on the tank deck or on duties which ranged from departmental messenger to midshipman of the watch. It was said that living and working with the ship's company not only broadened the young officers' vocabulary, which it certainly did, but it also created a mutual understanding and respect between them.

In early January 1974, after embarking a flight of 848 Squadron's Wessex helicopters at Portland, and with 110 midshipmen embarked, *Fearless* left for her first nine-week training cruise in the Caribbean area. After a rough transatlantic crossing sunny weather was encountered at last and among the places visited was Port of Spain (Trinidad), on 30 January. During the five-day visit members of the touring MCC cricket team and the West Indies side met a team of officers and men from *Fearless* for a friendly match. Both teams autographed a cricket bat which was raffled on board, with the proceeds going to the children's ward of RNH Stonehouse. On 9 February, at Antigua, Captain Rumble handed over to the English Harbour Authority three capstans, built by the engineering department of HMS *Vernon*, replicas of those which had once stood in Nelson's Dockyard. These were subsequently put into place by enthusiasts who were restoring and maintaining this delightful harbour. During the deployment *Fearless*, together with 13 other units which included *Bulwark*, *Blake*, *Devonshire* and *Kent*, took part in a series of exercises code-named 'Caribtrain', which culminated in a fleet gathering off Virgin Gorda to bid farewell to the First Sea Lord, Admiral Sir Michael Pollock. During the day there was banyan leave, and during the balmy tropical evenings *Bulwark* played host ship for a number of sporting activities, including 'horse races'. On 21 February *Fearless* arrived at Miami where, with the temperatures in the high 80s, the Royal Marines Band attended the opening ceremony of the Miami International Boat Show where they played to a packed auditorium. Among the visitors to the ship were the film star Douglas Fairbanks Jnr and Danni Messinger, who had just been awarded the title Miss Florida. On the official side there were receptions and cocktail parties for civic dignitaries as well as the traditional children's party. and whilst in the Caribbean the Royal Marines Detachment provided a

Two excellent views of *Fearless* as...

training team to work with the Guyana Defence Force, which meant they missed most of the runs ashore and rejoined the ship in mid-February. Finally, the cruise drew to a close with a visit to Nassau before *Fearless* made the return crossing of the Atlantic Ocean, arriving in Devonport on 12 March.

After Easter leave and maintenance, late April saw *Fearless* in the Mediterranean and in company with the newly designated commando carrier *Hermes* for 'Exercise Dawn Patrol 74', a medium-scale NATO southern region naval and amphibious exercise. As it was the first occasion that *Fearless* and *Hermes* had operated together in the amphibious role, they carried out a brief work-up period off Cyprus code-named 'Double Bass', during which 41 Commando from *Hermes* and Headquarters 3 Commando Brigade from *Fearless* were landed in the Dhekelia area for manoeuvres ashore. These landings were used to test the Command and Control procedures between the ships, Brigade Headquarters and the naval staffs. From Cyprus the UK elements sailed for Kalamata Bay in southern Greece for the pre-'Dawn Patrol' conference, where all the participating commanding officers met for the first time and final orders were given. From the conference area the Task Force sailed some 40 miles north to the Kiparissia area for a run-through of the landing. Headquarters 3 Commando Brigade, commanded by Brigadier R. J. Ephraums RM, and a signal squadron were embarked in *Fearless* while 41 Commando was in *Hermes*, with LSL *Sir Lancelot* being used for advance force operations. Italy and Greece were also represented in their own amphibious ships. Commanding the Task Force was Vice-Admiral Murphy USN, with the Flag Officer Carriers and Amphibious Ships (FOCAS), Rear-Admiral A. D. Cassidi, flying his flag in *Hermes*; the Commodore Amphibious

...she leaves Plymouth Sound in October 1973. *(Maritime Books, Liskeard and Ron Slater)*

Fearless is opened to visitors during her visit to Venice in June 1974. *(Imperial War Museum, London, No HU 90946)*

Warfare, Commodore D. Smith, flew his pennant in *Fearless*. Of the 60 ships participating in the exercise the Royal Navy was represented by *Fearless, Hermes,* the guided missile destroyer *Hampshire,* the frigates *Achilles, Lowestoft* and *Sirius,* the submarine *Opportune,* and the RFAs *Regent* and *Tideflow.*

The scenario for the amphibious phase of 'Dawn Patrol' involved an imaginary island, Butrekia, represented by the Cape Teulada training area in southern Sardinia, which had been overrun by an 'enemy' made up of a company of US Airborne Infantry and four platoons of Italian tanks and mechanized infantry. The landing by Advance Force Operations involved British, US, Turkish and Italian commando teams who were put ashore before the main landings. This involved a night assault by helicopter and landing craft in order to achieve maximum surprise and it went ahead in ideal conditions, with flat, calm seas and a bright, full moon. By dawn the initial objectives had been secured and by evening on the first day the force was safely established ashore. Thereafter the exercise continued with a slow advance through the training area and a full programme of live firing on the Teulada Range. Air strikes were made by Greek, Turkish and Italian aircraft, as well as RAF Buccaneers from Malta. Altogether the exercise was a great success and during her Mediterranean deployment *Fearless* visited Naples on 13 May, Venice on 23 May and Izmir on 1 June. From the Turkish port she steamed to Malta where, in Grand Harbour, she underwent a 13-day maintenance period. On the way home there were visits to Taranto and Villefranche, with banyan leave being given at Sardinia's La Maddalena, before she returned home.

Once back in home waters, and operating in the Portland area, on 18 July 1974 *Fearless* received a royal visit from Princess Margaret and her two children, Viscount Linley and Lady Sarah Armstrong-Jones. The royal party had arrived at HMS *Osprey* by helicopter to spend the day watching the Navy at work, which began with visits to married quarters at Westcliffe. At 14.00 Viscount Linley arrived by fast patrol boat alongside *Fearless,* which had just completed a major NBCD exercise, to be transferred to LCM *F7* and treated to a landing demonstration on the beach, where his mother and sister were waiting for him. The 'landing force' was drawn from the Royal Marines Detachments from HM Ships *Diomede, Gurkha* and *Tartar* together with the Blue Beret Platoon (a landing party made up of members of the ship's company) from *Fearless.* For the finale the Wessex helicopters of 845 Squadron put on a flying display which coincided with a simulated naval bombardment. After leaving the beach the royal party returned to *Fearless* for a tour and for tea, before being flown ashore by helicopter while the assault ship departed for a rendezvous with an RFA to carry out a fuel replenishment.

In September 1974 *Fearless* paid a weekend visit to Antwerp and the French port of Le Havre to join in celebrations on the 30th anniversary of their liberation.

Fearless in the River Thames at Greenwich in the summer of 1975 when a Hawker Siddley Harrier landed on the flight deck and took off again, demonstrating its amazing versatility. *(Fleet Air Arm Museum, Yeovilton)*

After taking *Fearless* into Le Havre Harbour, past the luxury liner *France,* Captain Rumble had to move the assault ship further out to sea when mutinous members of the liner's crew 'took over' the ship and blockaded the harbour in a vain attempt to prevent the vessel from being taken out of service.* The visits to Antwerp and Le Havre were followed by the NATO exercise code-named 'Northern Merger' which ran for the last two weeks of September off the Jutland area of Denmark. Operating with *Hermes, Fearless* started the exercise with a rehearsal landing at the Barry Budden training area near Dundee, which proved to be a useful prelude to the main landing. This was followed by a six-day 'opposed' transit in deteriorating weather conditions, after which the main landing took place at the Oksbol training area on the Jutland Peninsular. Poor weather hampered operations and this was aggravated by shallow coastal waters and a very real mine threat, a leftover from the Second World War. In the event both *Fearless* and *Hermes* had to operate further offshore than had been planned, which slowed down the build-up ashore. The land phase of the exercise lasted for three days and was controlled by the Danish Army, who provided a formidable 'enemy'. Meanwhile, at sea more than 150 ships were exercised in anti-submarine warfare, minelaying and countermeasures, control of merchant shipping and anti-aircraft warfare. After the exercise the participating forces gathered in Copenhagen for the wash-up and to sample the lager. In October the ship took part in exercises off the Dorset coast and received visits from a number of senior officers.

On 9 January 1975, after a maintenance period at Devonport and with a complement of Dartmouth midshipmen on board, *Fearless* left for an Atlantic crossing to the Caribbean. During this period life on board was hectic with mini-amphibious exercises involving marines and sailors from the USA, France and Colombia. On 24 January the ship arrived in Bridgetown, Barbados, for a five-day stopover and was visited by the former motor racing ace Stirling Moss. Leaving Barbados *Fearless* spent five days in the French Grenadines from where she exercised with the new helicopter carrier FNS *Jeanne d' Arc.* During their Caribbean encounter near Martinique there was an exchange of midshipmen, using both helicopters and light jackstay. Captain Rumble presented a badge and a framed photograph to his French counterpart with, for good measure, a bottle of Scotch Whisky. The reply came back in the form of a 'broadside' consisting of a case of champagne. The two ships were in company for about four hours before going their separate ways. In Venezuela *Fearless* put into La Guira, the port for Caracas, where a lot of sport was played followed, inevitably, by most generous hospitality. After arriving at Cartagena on 24 February, 150 Spanish-speaking Colombian marines were embarked for an amphibious exercise carried out largely by using sign language and a great deal of patience on both sides. In March, with *Hermes* and *Ark Royal,* she took part in 'Exercise Westlant 75' off Roosevelt Roads and the island of Vieques. Also taking part were Dutch and US Navy

* After rusting at Le Havre for five years *France* was given a new lease of life as the cruise ship *Norway.*

Fearless steams past Drake Island in Plymouth Sound during her post-refit trials in July 1976. *(Imperial War Museum, London, HU 90940)*

units, together with HM Ships *Hampshire* and *Tartar*. During the manoeuvres the LCMs were detached to the island of Tortola to assist local people in clearing wrecks from the seabed, dumping unwanted vehicles at sea and moving items of heavy plant around the islands. Meanwhile, back at Vieques the LCVPs streamed ashore with the Royal Marines Detachments from *Hampshire* and *Tartar* and the Blue Beret Platoon. The object of their exercise was to practise giving assistance to local people in the event of a major natural disaster. There was also a contribution from the Band of the Royal Regiment of Fusiliers who were on board for the cruise, with the most embarrassing episode coming during the exercise when one member of the band lost his clothes ashore, and caused some consternation when he returned to *Fearless* resplendent in just his beret, vest and life jacket. After stopping at Roosevelt Roads to pick up one of *Ark Royal's* broken Buccaneers from *Hermes* and carrying out a final amphibious exercise, this time with 47 Light Regiment, Royal Artillery, *Fearless* made her passage home via Bermuda. The crossing was uneventful and as the ship steamed into the Atlantic swell, the opportunity was taken to stage a traditional 'Sods Opera'. At Devonport families were embarked, and as the assault ship steamed up harbour the sight of a front-line Buccaneer aircraft on the flight deck evoked a few puzzled looks from those on shore.

During *Fearless'* period alongside, Easter leave was taken, and as the ship underwent an assisted maintenance period, a Government Defence Review was published in which it was stated that plans to build two more amphibious ships had been abandoned, and although *Fearless* and *Intrepid* would remain in service, only one of the two would be operational at any one time. For *Fearless*, however, the commission would continue as scheduled and early May saw 85 midshipmen-under-training from ten different countries on board, among them Prince Alai Tukuaho, the son of the King and Queen of Tonga. Also embarked were 24 Air Portable Brigade who were bound for an amphibious exercise code-named 'Tidy Flow', and they were disembarked off the Dorset coast. There was a fleeting glimpse of *Intrepid* as *Fearless* left Portland for Stockholm where she arrived in mid-May for a week-long visit. On arrival in harbour the C-in-C Fleet, Admiral Sir Terence Lewin, was embarked, together with his Royal Marines Band, which meant a constant round of honour guards for the ship's Detachment. Shortly after *Fearless* arrived the C-in-C was officially welcomed to the city by Cecilia, a local beauty who had been crowned 'Queen of Lake Malaren' and who acted as the official host for visitors to Stockholm. The hospitality in the city was tremendous, which was fortunate because an independent run ashore in the city could be a ruinously expensive undertaking. Among the round of social activities was a ship's dance to which the Swedish girls turned out in large numbers and which one of the marines described as having, '...left most of us breathless.' The visit ended, as it had begun, in warm sunshine, and *Fearless* steamed south for Germany and the River Trave which was close to what was then the East German border. The German visit took the assault ship to Neustadt and Lübeck where, once again, the men were shown wonderful hospitality. From Germany *Fearless* went on to Stavanger for sailing and 'exped' training, and then Kristiansand in Norway, before completing her Scandinavian cruise. Before returning to Devonport *Fearless*

Heavy weather in the North Sea during September 1976. The Wessex helicopters of 845 Squadron and the Scout helicopters had to be well lashed down.
(Fleet Air Arm Museum, Yeovilton)

Sea spray cascades over one of 845 Squadron's Wessex helicopters during her passage between Texel and Esbjerg. This was one of the drawbacks of not being fitted with an aircraft hangar, and it was a serious problem for the maintenance crews.
(Fleet Air Arm Museum, Yeovilton)

undertook an important visit to the River Thames, anchoring off Greenwich for a NATO seminar at the Royal Naval College. During the visit the world's press, Members of Parliament and Defence representatives from 16 other navies, including the Argentinian Navy, were invited to witness the amazing versatility of the Hawker Siddley Harrier vertical take-off and landing aircraft which the Government had recently announced was to be developed for service with the Royal Navy. The College provided a magnificent backdrop for this engineering design feat as the Harrier, flown by test pilot John Farley, roared overhead, came in low over *Fearless* and, in a cloud of spray, hovered above the assault ship and landed gently on the flight deck. A short time later, the Harrier roared vertically up into the air in an impressive take-off which amply demonstrated to the spectators its versatility and manoeuvrability. Visitors to the ship included the King and Queen of Tonga, accompanied by Princess Pilolevu, who as well as being principal guests at a Naval College dinner, had the opportunity of meeting up with their son.

On leaving Greenwich *Fearless* made a mini-cruise to Casablanca and Madeira, which were final ports of call before she returned to Plymouth for summer leave and, with her Dartmouth Training role having been taken over by *Intrepid,* to decommission for a long refit. Since taking on the role in January 1974 she had steamed some 44,000 miles and had visited 38 ports in the Caribbean and around Europe. Her ship's company had been involved in a busy programme of visits, international liaison duties and much hard work, having taken part in numerous amphibious exercises.

During the winter of 1975 and the spring of 1976 *Fearless* lay at Devonport and any visitor to the ship could be forgiven for thinking that her interior compartments had been dismantled, with the bits and pieces never to be put together again. On 13 August 1975, soon after arriving back in Devonport, there had been a change of command when Captain L. A. Bird MVO RN took over from Captain Rumble. It must have been particularly poignant for Captain Bird to take command, for he had stood by the ship whilst she was under construction at Harland & Wolff's Belfast shipyard. It was also decided that in the future the Royal Marines Detachment would be known as the Assault Squadron, which reflected the duties they carried out in the assault ship. On 25 November 1975, the tenth anniversary of the first commissioning, a 'birthday' cake specially made for the occasion was cut by the captain. By the early summer of 1976 a semblance of order had been restored to the ship and she had once again taken on the Role of Dartmouth Training Ship from *Intrepid,* which was about to go into Reserve. On Friday 2 July, at the end of her long refit, a short ceremony of rededication was held on board. Divisions were fallen in on the jetty while families and official guests arrived, with music being provided by the Band of the 3rd Battalion, the Royal Regiment of Fusiliers, who had served with *Fearless* on previous commissions. Among the guests were Field Marshal Sir Richard Hull and Lady Hull, and the honour guard was provided by the 4th Assault Squadron, Royal Marines. After the ceremony the rededication cake was cut by the commanding officer's wife and the youngest rating from *Fearless,* JMEM Mellor. Later the guests and ship's company took lunch in the various mess decks. During Navy Days at Plymouth that summer *Fearless* proved to be a major attraction, with over 22,000 people visiting her in the space of the three days.

In early September, following her post-refit trials and work-up, and with summer leave having been taken, *Fearless* engaged in her first major amphibious exercise. 'Exercise Teamwork 76' was one of a series of national and NATO exercises designed to coordinate all the NATO manoeuvres which fell within the organization's Allied Command Europe. The scenario for 'Teamwork 76' depicted a series of political events which began with uncontrolled inflation in Europe and culminated in an attempt by the Warsaw Pact to persuade Scandinavian countries to leave NATO. Threatening speeches and provocative troop movements made against Denmark resulted in a request by her for military assistance. The maritime part of the exercise was designed to demonstrate and refine NATO's striking fleet, its capability to deploy forces rapidly to Northern Europe and to project sea power ashore to reinforce its northern flank. In all it involved some 80,000 personnel, 250 ships, 24 submarines and over 900 aircraft. Starting at Portland *Fearless* embarked Headquarters 3 Commando Brigade and elements of 42 Commando, together with Wessex and Scout helicopters of 845 Naval Air Squadron, while the remainder of 42 Commando, Dutch Marines, 79 Commando Light Battery RA and elements of 59 Independent Squadron RE were embarked in the LSLs *Sir Bedivere, Sir Geraint, Sir Percivale* and *Sir Tristram.* After steaming through Force 8 gales, and carrying out a rehearsal landing on the island of Texel, the force sailed for Esbjerg. During the passage they steamed into more appalling weather with 40-knot winds and heavy seas and, with the ship rolling heavily, all the helicopters and vehicles, particularly the tanks, had to be well stowed and lashed down. Being a 'deterrent landing' rather than an amphibious assault it meant that *Fearless* and the LSLs would have the use of the host nation's port which in this case was Esbjerg. However, a crippled Russian cargo ship prevented *Fearless* from going alongside, and the severe weather meant that in the initial stages of the exercise she was unable to use her LCMs. Last-minute changes saw Headquarters 3 Commando Brigade being disembarked by helicopter. Fortunately, a break in the severe weather enabled the LCMs to operate through the port of Esbjerg, from where the troops were moved in Danish Army transport to the 'frontier', where they linked up with the 2nd Jutland Brigade to prepare defensive positions. Two days later, having re-embarked the troops, *Fearless* steamed back into gale force winds and via the Pentland Firth to Scapa Flow, where a large NATO fleet was already at anchor.

The second phase of the exercise, which also involved the US Navy's command ship *Mount Whitney,* the giant aircraft carrier *John F. Kennedy* and the helicopter carrier *Guadalcanal,* began on 14 September at Scapa Flow and despite forecasts of a rough passage, *Fearless* made a smooth, but 'opposed' crossing of the Norwegian Sea to Trondheim Fjord. The scenario for this part of the exercise was developed from the situation in Denmark to one of open hostilities between NATO and the Warsaw Pact, with the latter having occupied parts of Norway where, around Namsos, they had surrounded two Norwegian battalions; it

"Nostos Vassos Athene"

7th Nov. '76

The drama of the fire on board MV *Nostos Vassos Athene* in November 1976 is captured in this series of photographs.
(Brian M. Ahern)

The fire-fighting team from Fearless *who successfully extinguished the dangerous fire in* Nostos Vassos Athene.
(Brian M. Ahern)

was in this area that the amphibious landing would be made. On 20 September, off Namsos *Fearless* and the remainder of the amphibious force made a combined and coordinated sea and helicopter assault on either side of the Namsen Fjord in order to link up with the Norwegian Army and militia units. As expected the exercise attracted a large number of distinguished visitors, including King Olav of Norway, senior NATO commanders, numerous ambassadors and politicians. Once again, despite gloomy predications from the meteorologists, the weather remained fine for the re-embarkation in Namsen Fjord, and so ended one of *Fearless'* biggest amphibious exercises.

On 4 October 1976, after a short break at Devonport, *Fearless* resumed her Dartmouth Training role, and with an 'embarked force' of 90 midshipmen and the Wessex helicopters of 846 Squadron's B Flight, she sailed for the Mediterranean. After a short stop at Gibraltar the assault ship steamed east to the Italian port of Civitavecchia, the seaport for Rome, to embark elements of 41 Commando. From here some members of the ship's company travelled to the Vatican for an audience with the Pope, but for the majority there were more secular activities to be enjoyed in the bars of Civitavecchia itself. From Italy *Fearless* set course for a ten-day stay at Malta where, with 41 Commando, she took part in 'Exercise Wild Thyme' off the island. The exercise was an opportunity to practise the landing and recovery of the commandos, together with their vehicles and equipment, in the military training areas of Malta. The highlight came when, as an exercise in disaster relief, 90 'refugees' played by wives and relatives of the men, were evacuated from Kalafrana at the southern end of Marsaxlokk Bay. During the operation the helicopters of 845 Squadron accomplished the 1,000th deck landing, which was cause for a small celebration. On board for the landings, recovery and the 'civilian evacuation' was FOCAS, Rear-Admiral J. H. F. Eberle, who joined the ship to carry out the annual sea inspection and he stayed with her for the next two visits - to Venice and Toulon.

Fearless' arrival in Venice on 29 October coincided with torrential rain, which meant the unique city was somewhat wetter than usual and for a few days LCVPs were seen making their way along the Grand Canal in company with the gondolas. After Venice the assault ship returned to Grand Harbour, this time to pick up a film crew who were to shoot a sequence of scenes for the James Bond film, 'The Spy Who Loved Me', which starred Roger Moore and Barbara Bach. Unfortunately poor weather prevented filming for most of the time they were aboard, but 7 November was a sunny and calm Sunday forenoon and filming appeared to be going well. However, just as *Fearless* was about to steam over the horizon into camera shot an SOS call was received from a nearby ship which was on fire about four miles away, and five miles off Malta. Leaving the film cameramen stranded in an LCM *Fearless* immediately turned away to go to the aid of the 6,550-ton cargo ship *Nostos Vassos Athene*. Mick Ahern who was a

CMEM on board *Fearless* remembers the incident well: 'It was a lovely sunny Sunday forenoon off Valletta. I had just drawn the keys to the Fleet Chiefs' bar and I was idly passing a few minutes watching the helicopter crew prepare to fly off and film some aerial shots for the James Bond film "The Spy Who Loved Me", before opening up and enjoying a pint of beer. Suddenly, without any warning, I was abruptly called away to be told that a Greek merchantman was on fire close by and was listing heavily. Some 20 minutes later myself and the First Lieutenant, Lt-Cdr Peter Luce, were being flown in one of the Wessex helicopters towards the burning ship. When we arrived at the scene we could see thick black smoke pouring from its funnel, and from the after superstructure. One of *Fearless*' LCMs was already lying off the ship and we were lowered into it. After being taken alongside we climbed aboard in order to assess the situation and ascertain exactly what fire-fighting equipment would be needed. On board the ship it was clear that the crew had abandoned her and we found ourselves standing on a canvas which covered the deck cargo. I asked one of the Royal Marines in the LCM what cargo the ship was carrying, and I remember his reply as if it were yesterday, "Ten tons of aerosol lighter fuel". On hearing that we moved smartly away from the canvas and onto the forecastle in order to continue our planning. It soon became apparent to us that the seat of the fire was in the engine room and that we would need to enter the compartment in order to extinguish it. Meanwhile, unknown to us, Captain Bird had manoeuvred *Fearless* to a position alongside the freighter's starboard side, which was no mean feat given the thick black smoke, but it meant we had the use of the ship's fire-fighting facilities. I organized a small fire-fighting party and we slowly made our way through the dark, smoke-filled passageways to the ship's engine room where, as it was a diesel fuel fire, we were able to fight it with foam equipment. Gradually we managed to get the blaze under control, while on board *Fearless* other fire parties were enthusiastically playing a number of high-power water hoses onto the ship, and as the amount of water on board increased, so did the merchantman's list. Eventually it became so steep that it began to cause us some concern. Fortunately, we were able to stop the upper deck fire hoses and by the early afternoon we had extinguished the engine room fire. This was not the end of the problem, however, for we then found that the fire had spread into the after hold where, at the bottom, some of the cargo had ignited. We decided that the only way to tackle this blaze was to cut our way through the engine room bulkhead into the after hold, which took some time to complete. We eventually got into it and were soon able to put that fire out, pump all the water out of the ship's holds and bilges, and sail her into the safety of Grand Harbour. The fire party, which was made up of young men from all departments of the ship, including the Assault Squadron, were magnificent and, considering their youth, they were a credit to both *Fearless* and to the Service. As for my pint of beer, it was the following Wednesday before I was able to enjoy it, and some time later I saw the James Bond film at the cinema.'

Mick has modestly understated his own and Lt-Cdr Luce's part in the incident, for both men were in constant danger, not only from the fire, which was spreading rapidly out from the engine room and through the superstructure, but also from the potentially lethal deck cargo of lighter fuel and acid. Both were constantly soaked with water and foam and had to contend with thick acrid smoke, the heat and the deafening noise. In spite of these appalling conditions both men maintained an exemplary standard of calm and displayed great presence of mind in fighting the fire. Mick Ahern led and directed the fire-fighting teams which boarded *Nostos Vassos Athene,* but on board where they were confronted with an unfamiliar and smoke-filled ship, which lacked power and light and was burning fiercely, Mick's unwavering confidence in success enabled them to extinguish the main blaze within two hours. Once the fire had been extinguished Mick continued to lead his team in the vital tasks of cooling down and pumping out the ship, tasks made all the more difficult by the dangerous conditions in the engine room which was, hot, dark and partially flooded. Both Lt-Cdr Luce and CMEM Ahern were, quite deservedly, awarded The Queen's Commendation for Brave Conduct. In the event seven other bravery awards went to the officers and men who successfully dealt with the dangerous situation, and saved the cargo ship.* Meanwhile, with *Fearless* having left the merchant ship, the film crew were able to complete their shoots and before leaving they sent the following message of thanks: 'From James Bond film unit to *L10* HMS *Fearless*. Many thanks for a good shoot. A highly eventful week when many were stirred but none were shaken. Signed 007.'

Before returning home to Devonport there were two more visits for *Fearless,* the first being to Toulon on 10 November, where the Royal Marines provided two ceremonial guards. The first occasion was for the Armistice Day Parade in the city, where they joined units from the French armed forces, and where the local crowd applauded enthusiastically as they marched off. One marine recalled, '…it was difficult restraining some of the squadron from going back for an encore.' The other ceremony took place on Remembrance Sunday at the British cemetery in Marseilles where, once again, they were well received by both the local people and the British community. The final run ashore of the deployment was Gibraltar, where the

---

* The Queen's Commendation for Brave Conduct went to Lt-Cdr P. Luce RN and CMEM Ahern. C-in-C's Commendations went to Cdr T. W. J. Hale RN, Lt G. Armstrong, CMEM Elder, MECH1 Reed, FCOEA Stephens, LMEM Lee and LMEM Yeates.

'Rock Race' was held in which the midshipmen-under-training beat the Royal Marines into second place. Meanwhile, on the lower vehicle deck, a BBC Radio Two team led by the presenter Dave Allen, recorded a session for the 'Dave Allen Country Club' programme. On 21 November, having left Gibraltar, *Fearless* set course for home, but not for a rest. During two days in Plymouth Sound the midshipmen were disembarked and elements of the Commando Logistics Regiment were embarked for 'Exercise High Tide'. Set in Holland, it was a week-long exercise with the embarked force being landed at Den Helder for training, at the end of which *Fearless* returned to Devonport for a five and a half week maintenance period, and for Christmas and New Year leave.

On 11 January 1977, with the leave period having passed all too quickly, *Fearless* embarked 80 midshipmen, along with the Fife and Drum Band of the Guards' Training Depot, Purbright, and 30 Guardsmen who had just completed their training and who were now to get some practice in chipping and painting. She then steamed out of Plymouth Sound, past 'Charlie Buoy' and into the Channel bound for the sunshine of the Caribbean. After a bumpy crossing of the Atlantic, when all many wanted was a quiet bunk and a handy pusser's bucket, on 22 January Trinidad hove into sight and suddenly the queues for the dining hall were back to their usual length. Port of Spain, with its sandy beaches and steel calypso bands, came as a brief but welcome respite and for five days everyone was able to relax. One important visitor to the ship during this period was President Ellis Clarke who toured the ship after first inspecting a Royal Marines Honour Guard. When *Fearless* left Trinidad she spent 14 unbroken days at sea, the longest continuous period for some time, during which she took part in 'Exercise Caribex 77', a medium-scale NATO exercise which also included units from the USA, Canada, Brazil and the Netherlands. *Fearless'* role was to transport Dutch marines from the island of Curacao to Vieques, which meant a three-day passage at 'overload' conditions with most of the embarked force sleeping on the lower vehicle deck and at one stage, after detaching *Tartar,* the assault ship closed to within 50 miles of Belize. One member of the ship's company described conditions on board as being reminiscent of the 'Black Hole of Calcutta'. The assault ship's role in the exercise was minimal, but her own Royal Marines Assault Squadron did manage to get ashore for some training.

Having completed her part in 'Caribex' *Fearless* reverted to her Dartmouth Training role and, most importantly for the ship's company after a long period at sea, she was able to make some welcome visits to foreign ports. The first stop was Cartagena, Colombia, where the Corps of Drums of the Guards Depot Beat Retreat in the old walled city. After leaving Cartagena on 14 February *Fearless* steamed to Kingston, Jamaica, and on to Port au Prince, Haiti, where the vibrant sounds and colours of a Haitian carnival are amongst the most vivid memories of those on board the assault ship. The ship's company actually took a full part in the festivities by entering a model of the ship in a procession of floats which signalled the start of the exciting and noisy three-day carnival. During the passage from Cartagena a team of shipwrights had built the float, the base of which was a four-ton lorry belonging to the 4th Assault Squadron. Although the fifes and drums of the Guards had difficulty competing with the enormous amplified stereo systems which were fitted to the local floats, they were still very popular with the local people and they played non-stop for four hours. Undoubtedly the best run ashore for most members of the ship's company came on 26 February when *Fearless* put into Charleston, where many made new friends in this east coast port of the USA. The return passage to Devonport was made by way of Bermuda's Ireland Island naval base and on 16 March, *Fearless* arrived in Plymouth Sound to be greeted by 850 relatives and friends who were brought by LCM out to the ship where they were given lunch on board while making the passage up harbour. On 6 April the C-in-C Fleet, Admiral Sir Henry Leach, hoisted his flag in *Fearless* and ten days later the assault ship was at C buoy in Plymouth Sound, embarking troops for her next exercises which took place on the coast of Dorset.

On 30 April *Fearless* embarked another 120 midshipmen who, according to one member of the ship's company, 'looked identical to the last lot', and then sailed for her summer deployment to northern Europe. After steaming by way of the Irish Sea, Scapa Flow and the Pentland Firth the first call, on 5 May, was Copenhagen where, despite the high cost of living, for six days most of those on board enjoyed the attractions of the Tivoli Gardens, or visits to the Tuborg and Carlsberg breweries. Other organized tours included the Cherry Heering and the Royal Copenhagen Porcelain factories, while back at the quayside over 2,000 people toured the ship. On 17 May, with the Junior Band of the Household Division embarked, *Fearless* made a six-day visit to Bordeaux, which coincided with an International Trade Fair in the city. The exhibition, which was housed in an enormous hall, included a British trade mission and on 'British Day' the band shared the musical programme with French military bands. On the two days when the ship was opened to the public a total of 3,600 took the opportunity to look round. The Queen's Silver Jubilee holiday weekend was spent at Scapa Flow, and this was followed by a six-day visit to Kristiansand in Norway and to Kiel where *Fearless* arrived on 15 June, in time for the start of 'Kieler Woche', the annual festival of sailing regattas, during which warships of many nations gather at the German base. *Fearless* was the first foreign warship to arrive and she received a warm welcome from the local people who laid on many social

Fearless looks immaculate anchored at Spithead for the Queen's Silver Jubilee Fleet Review in June 1977. *(Mike Lennon)*

A stern view of *Fearless* at Spithead for the Silver Jubilee Fleet Review. Two LCMs are entering the dock and floodlighting fittings can be seen on the port side. (Mike Lennon)

events for the ship's company.

Inevitably the highlight of *Fearless'* summer programme was the Queen's Silver Jubilee Fleet Review at Spithead, for which the ship's company put in a lot of hard work, tackling more than the usual quota of chipping, painting and polishing. The assault ship took her place between *Ark Royal* and *Blake* for what was to be the first Review at Spithead since 1953. Over the three days spent at anchor some last-minute paint and polish was applied and, without doubt, *Fearless* was in pristine condition for the event. During her short period at Spithead the Royal Marines Honour Guard was paraded for a record number of times, and the ship's company rehearsed 'Man and Cheer Ship' more times than had ever been done before. On Monday 27 June, the day before the Review, Admiral of the Fleet Lord Mountbatten paid a visit to *Fearless,* the main purpose of which was to meet the midshipmen. That day also saw a full Review rehearsal with RFA *Engadine* acting as HMY *Britannia*. Afterwards the fly-past by rotary and fixed-wing aircraft of the Fleet Air Arm was rehearsed which, in the event, was the only time that the full fly-past was seen. On the big day poor weather marred the occasion, but at 11.19, as *Britannia* passed the Spit Refuge Buoy, the fleet fired a 21-gun salute and the royal yacht took up her position at the head of the Review Lines. At 14.30 *Britannia,* preceded by the Trinity House vessel *Patricia,* entered the lines followed by HMS *Birmingham* with members of the Admiralty Board, then *Engadine* and the LSLs *Sir Geraint* and *Sir Tristram*. As the royal yacht approached *Fearless* the Alert was sounded and the ship's company came smartly to attention, the Guard and Band did their bit, whilst the rest of the men on the flight and weather decks gave the traditional three cheers. *Britannia* then anchored for the eagerly awaited fly-past, but because of the overcast weather conditions it was limited to 90 helicopters. Next day came the steam past off the southern side of the Isle of Wight when, led by *Ark Royal,* 61 units of the Royal Navy acknowledged the retirement of Admiral of the Fleet Sir Edward Ashmore. At the end of the ceremony *Fearless* left her position of third in line behind *Ark Royal* and *Hermes,* to prepare for 'Exercise Forest Venture', with 41 Commando's Salerno Company in Loch Alsh and off the west coast of Scotland, after which the ship returned to Devonport for a six-week dockyard assisted maintenance period, which included a spell in dry dock, and a well-earned summer leave.

On 24 August 1977, whilst *Fearless* was at Devonport, there was a change of command when Captain W. R. S. Thomas OBE RN took over from Captain Bird. In the last week of August *Fearless* nosed her way out of dry dock to secure against the sea wall and Captain Thomas took the opportunity to address the ship's company. He praised the ship's proud reputation for punctuality in sailing, but clearly this was tempting fate for next afternoon there were problems in the engine room and her departure was delayed. After a considerable hold-up, on 1 September the assault ship finally left harbour and after undergoing sea trials and experiencing a run ashore at Portland, she set course for the Mediterranean on 15 September in her Dartmouth Training role. This time, as well as carrying

Following the Review and steam-past *Fearless* sailed west to prepare for 'Exercise Forest Venture'. Here she is seen off the Isle of Wight. *(Mike Lennon)*

midshipmen, she also had on board MEA apprentices from HMS *Caledonia* who, when not working in the engine and boiler rooms, were to be found in all parts of the ship. Together with the midshipmen they crewed the ship's motor boats, and took full advantage of their first foreign runs ashore. Also embarked for the deployment was 41 Commando's Salerno Company. Five days after leaving home waters and in warmer weather off Gibraltar, a live Seacat missile shoot was carried out before the ship spent a night alongside. After leaving Gibraltar *Fearless* steamed east to Malta, where she spent five days and some of the 'first timers' became acquainted with the dubious delights of 'The Gut'. For the more energetic, however, there was also a full sports programme.

After leaving Malta, and whilst on passage to Venice, Salerno Company was transferred to USS *Guadalcanal* for 'Exercise Display Determination'. On the last day of September *Fearless* arrived in Venice and secured some 200 yards from St Mark's Square, where she presented an imposing sight, particularly at night when she was floodlit. During the five days alongside the ship was visited by Princess Margaret, who was in Venice to open a fashion show, the proceeds of which would go towards saving the city from the encroaching water levels. From Venice it was back to Malta, picking up Salerno Company from *Guadalcanal* en route, with the next visit on the agenda being Navarino Bay, Greece. Here, on 19 and 20 October,

Fearless took part in celebrations to mark the anniversary of the Battle of Navarino in 1827, when 12 British, seven French and nine Russian warships defeated a combined Turkish-Egyptian fleet in the last major fight under sail. This was followed by a longer stop of five days at Piraeus, the port for Athens, where some Royal Marines were detached for a three-day stay with the Greek Parachute Regiment. On their return to *Fearless* they were heard to say, 'If anyone thinks the food is bad in our Corps, they should visit the Greek Paras'. After leaving Piraeus course was set for Cagliari which, for most, is not noted as one of the best runs ashore but, nevertheless, the waterfront bars saw a good increase in trade. After leaving Cagliari on the last day of October, *Fearless* was involved in a four-day amphibious exercise on the Sardinian coast, during which the ship's Amphibious Beach Unit was landed onto a very picturesque beach backed by attractive sand dunes, which the marines quickly rearranged. LCM and LCVP vectoring and beaching drills were practised along with other evolutions, while simulated air strikes were laid on from a distant *Ark Royal*. On 4 November *Fearless* rendezvoused with the carrier and the assault ship streamed a splash target astern which the *Ark's* Buccaneers then subjected to a very spectacular and impressive bombing and rocket strike.

Following the exercise there was another visit to Malta and on 9 November, during the return passage to Devonport, *Fearless* called at Villefranche for five days, where she was joined by FOCAS, Rear-Admiral W. D. M. Staveley, who inspected Divisions and presented a number of awards to the ship's company. At a ceremony ashore to mark Armistice Day an impressive British presence was provided by the Royal Marines of the 4th Assault Squadron who, in company with the Royal Marines Band and members of the ship's company, marched through the picturesque town. The final stop was Gibraltar, and on her return to Plymouth Sound the midshipmen and apprentices were disembarked before *Fearless* returned to her original role and, with 41 Commando, took part in 'Exercise High Tide' at Den Helder in Holland. Following this there came some much-needed Christmas leave at Devonport.

On 17 January 1978, *Fearless* made her now-traditional westbound crossing of the Atlantic for the Caribbean and the West Indies with midshipmen and MEA apprentices embarked, arriving in Antigua 12 days later. During the deployment she also called at Tortola, Barbados and, on 23 February, Roosevelt Roads. This visit was marred, however, by the death of LSA Sandy, who was killed in a road traffic accident ashore. After five days in Miami *Fearless* returned home by way of Bermuda, arriving in Portsmouth in late March for maintenance and for Easter leave. The assault ship's spring and summer cruise saw her in the Mediterranean in May and on 16 June she was back in home waters for a four-day visit to Sunderland This was followed on 24 June by six days at Kiel for 'Kieler Woche', returning to Devonport in July. On 30 August, after summer leave and Plymouth Navy Days, *Fearless* began the final phase of her commission with a three-week exercise code-named 'Northern Wedding', which involved some 200 ships. Her role began with landings of Dutch marines in their home country, before she moved up the North Sea to rendezvous with *Hermes*, three LSLs and an amphibious Task Force of nine US ships. The whole force then steamed to Scapa Flow for two days of practice landings with 40 Commando. Once they had re-embarked the force made an 'opposed' passage through stormy seas to Arendel in Norway where *Fearless* landed her troops before returning to Devonport for a long weekend prior to her autumn deployment in the Mediterranean.

At the end of September, *Fearless* left Devonport bound, once again, for warmer climes. She was back in her Dartmouth Training role with midshipmen and apprentices embarked, as well as the Band of the Royal Greenjackets. A long westerly swell stayed with the ship all the way to Gibraltar where mail was dropped and collected, before she headed south for Gran Canaria and the port of Las Palmas. By the time she reached the island on 4 October the sun was shining and everyone enjoyed this more unusual run ashore, with its long crescent beach of fine golden sand. From Las Palmas the ship steamed into the Mediterranean and on 16 October she arrived in Malta for seven days of maintenance. After leaving Grand Harbour the assault ship steamed south to Alexandria where she spent seven days, before moving on to Istanbul and Toulon, before returning home by way of Gibraltar. The end of the commission also marked a change of allegiance for *Fearless* as she moved her base port from Devonport to Portsmouth. After handing over her operational role to her sister *Intrepid*, *Fearless* steamed into Portsmouth Harbour with her paying-off pennant flying on 30 November 1978 to pay off and to undergo a period in Reserve prior to a long refit. It would be three years before she was operational once again.

Chapter Five

HMS *Fearless* - War In The South Atlantic 1979-1982

For 20 months *Fearless* lay at Portsmouth in a state known as 'Preservation by Operation', perhaps better known as Reserve, but on 4 July 1980 she was towed to South Shields for a refit on the River Tyne. During the 14-month overhaul the few members of her ship's company became familiar with 'Rupert's' nightclub and its half-price 'wets', whilst on board *Fearless* herself looked distinctly inelegant under a massive 'shed' structure which covered the flight deck and stern area. Under the cover of this temporary protection from the weather much of her old equipment was modernized, with new specialist radio and satellite terminals being fitted. In addition to this her machinery was overhauled but, outwardly, the work left her appearance and profile largely unchanged. During the spring of 1981, as *Fearless* neared the end of her refit, a Government Defence Review spelt the end for both assault ships as it was announced that *Fearless* would pay off for the last time in 1984. For her sister *Intrepid* the end was to come even sooner, with her withdrawal from service scheduled for 1982. Although the announcement would not affect *Fearless*' forthcoming commission, it was a blow to the Navy which was only just recovering from swingeing cuts in the 1960s. They were all part of a process which had been carried out steadily by all governments since the end of the Second World War, and they paralleled the shedding of Britain's worldwide colonial commitments. The Conservative Government of Margaret Thatcher was, however, soon to find out that this was almost a 'cut too many'. On 4 May, soon after the announcement of the assault ship's coming demise, her new commanding officer, Captain E. S. J. Larken RN, joined *Fearless* and soon afterwards the ship's company was brought up to strength. On 27 September 1981 a rededication ceremony was held on board, with the guest of honour being Lady Hull, who had launched the ship almost 18 years earlier. Next day *Fearless* sailed for her post-refit trials and on 20 October, after final adjustments to her main propulsion machinery, she waved goodbye to the River Tyne as she steamed south for her home base of Portsmouth.

On 3 November 1981 *Fearless* sailed for Portland for Flag Officer, Sea Training's sea checks and for her work-up. The first week of these saw the ship alongside with the ship's company being tested for fire-fighting, damage control and other skills, including 'aid to civil power' and 'natural disaster' relief. This was followed by two weeks of amphibious exercises, when the Assault Squadron was put through its paces. Units of the Blues & Royals, together with four Chieftain Tanks and nine Scorpions, exercised

During the forenoon of Tuesday 6 April 1982, a cold and windswept day, with her ship's company and embarked force manning the decks, *Fearless* left Portsmouth for the South Atlantic.
(*Mike Lennon*)

the newly designated LCUs (Landing Craft Utility - formerly known as LCMs) in the movement of armour, spending a night aboard before they were put ashore at Arish Mell beach. *Fearless* then sailed for Plymouth where she embarked part of Headquarters 3 Commando Brigade to continue her work-up. The next few days saw her landing and re-embarking troops and a great variety of vehicles which tested the LCUs, various helicopters and members of the ship's Assault Squadron. During this period, whilst *Fearless* was anchored at Spithead, the Secretary of State for Defence, John Nott, visited the ship and he appeared impressed with the ship's capabilities, which may well have influenced his decision as to the future careers of both *Fearless* and *Intrepid*. Following her successful work-up *Fearless* was operational once again in a remarkably short space of time, and she returned to Portsmouth Dockyard to secure 'back-to-back' with her sister *Intrepid*, from whom she would take over as the Navy's operational assault ship. Whilst stores and equipment were transferred from *Intrepid* to *Fearless* Christmas leave got under way, and when the ship's company returned to the ship it was to find they had been joined by an 'embarked force' of 150 midshipmen and 75 engineering apprentices, all eager to start their two months' seagoing training. *Fearless* was back in her Dartmouth Training role.

On 7 January 1982 *Fearless* sailed from Portsmouth bound for Bermuda and the warmer waters of the Caribbean. At no stage during her crossing could the weather be described as calm, but five days out of the Solent a totally unexpected Atlantic storm blew up with 70-knot hurricane force winds and huge seas battering the ship. For over 12 hours *Fearless* weathered 'Hurricane Trevor' during which, surprisingly, little serious damage was suffered, although two Wessex helicopters which were lashed down on the flight deck were badly corroded by the sea salt and spray, and neither was flown during the deployment. Weather reports were immediately sent out from the ship, and six hours later they were received back in *Fearless* in the form of Meteorological Office storm warnings to Atlantic shipping. Eventually, however, after picking up the Flag Officer Third Flotilla (FOF3), Vice-Admiral John Cox, off Bermuda, the assault ship set course in more typically warm, calm, sunny Caribbean weather, for San Juan, Puerto Rico. *Fearless* was joined for the deployment by the frigate *Achilles* and three RFAs, and over the period spent in the Caribbean, using helicopters from the RFAs, both midshipmen and apprentices were transferred daily to and from other ships. The second port of call on 27 January was Port of Spain, Trinidad, where most of the men were able to enjoy Maracas beach during the eight-day maintenance period. After leaving Trinidad, on 5 February *Fearless* visited Curacao where she joined up with *Achilles*, which had visited Barbados and Antigua, and both ships' companies were able to sample the delights of the Dutch colonial island. Whilst at Curacao the C-in-C Fleet, Admiral Sir John Fieldhouse, joined the ship for several days. On 11 February the LCVP *F6*, with the C-in-C aboard, was lost off Arashi Beach, which left Admiral Fieldhouse wading ashore in four feet of water. After leaving Curacao with *Achilles,* a two-day low-key amphibious exercise code-named 'Aruba' was carried out en route. Those landed included 35 Dutch marines, the midshipmen and the apprentices, together with the Royal Marines Band of FOF3, who marched from the landing craft into chest-deep water playing 'A Life "in" the Ocean Wave'. From Aruba and its magnificent sandy beaches, lavish hotels and plush nightclubs, *Fearless* sailed east to the island of Bequia in the Grenadines, where a ship's banyan was laid on. The assault ship anchored half a mile offshore where most off-duty personnel packed into LCUs and headed for the beaches to set up barbecues and a cold beer stall. The last port of call in the West Indies was Kingstown, St Vincent, which was only a few miles steaming from Bequia. Here many overdid the consumption of the local brew, 'Sunset Rum', resulting in more than a few sore heads on board. The Caribbean cruise came to an end on 22 February 1982, when *Fearless* left St Vincent to make her voyage home.

As *Fearless* steamed across the Atlantic Ocean diplomatic problems had arisen between Britain and Argentina over negotiations in respect of the Falkland Islands. Although the basic problem went back many years, the current difficulties had started following General Leopoldo Galtieri's succession as President of Argentina. By late January 1982 the Argentine Government was showing a new belligerence in its dealings with Britain and they delivered a communication to the British Ambassador in Buenos Aires stating that British recognition of, 'Argentine sovereignty over the Malvinas (Falkland Islands), South Georgia and the South Sandwich Islands' remained an essential requirement for the settlement of the dispute. In early March, however, as *Fearless* arrived in Plymouth Sound to disembark her men under training and to reassume her amphibious role, few took any interest in what was still a diplomatic problem. Having completed her rapid role-change *Fearless* sailed for 'Exercise Alloy Express', north of the Arctic Circle. On 8 March, at Trondheim, she picked up a large embarked force of engineers and gunners for landing in Gratengen Fjord where, despite the bitterly cold weather, the sea remained calm. The ship's company's first run ashore since St Vincent was Harstad which, with temperatures of minus five and heavy snow, was quite a contrast to the 30°C of the Caribbean. For two days *Fearless* 'hid' from air reconnaissance in the fjords, where a 'snowman-building contest' provided some lighter moments. In mid-March, however, when *Fearless* returned to Portsmouth to undergo a period of dockyard assisted

Followed by her four LCUs, *Fearless* steams past The Hard on her way out of Portsmouth Harbour. The Gosport Ferry can also be seen astern, as can the masts of HMS *Victory* and Semaphore Tower. *(Derek Fox collection)*

maintenance, the political dispute over the sovereignty of the Falkland Islands, South Georgia and the South Sandwich Islands had taken a more ominous turn.

In March 1982 political negotiations were overshadowed by events on the island of South Georgia and by the actions of a hitherto unknown scrap metal dealer. Constantino Davidoff was a scrap merchant from Buenos Aires who, in 1978, had approached Christian Salveson, the Edinburgh-based company which managed Crown leases for the disused whaling stations on South Georgia. In the following year he signed a contract giving him an option to purchase equipment from the stations, and in 1980 he exercised the option. Between 1979 and late 1981 Davidoff was in occasional contact with the British Embassy in Buenos Aires, but on 16 December he left Buenos Aires in the Argentine naval ice-breaker, *Almirante Irizar,* to inspect the scrap on South Georgia. However, the British Embassy in the Argentine capital was not notified until after he had left and only two days before he arrived at Leith on 20 December. On 31 December 1981 the Governor of the Falkland Islands reported to the Foreign and Commonwealth Office in London the unauthorized presence of *Almirante Irizar* in Stromness Bay, South Georgia. The Governor recommended that proceedings be instituted against Davidoff and a strong diplomatic protest be made to the Argentine Government. However, the Government in London did not wish to provoke the Argentines and it was agreed that if Davidoff reported to the British Antarctic Survey at Grytviken and requested entry permits for himself and the naval vessel, then they would be granted. On 9 February 1982 the British Ambassador in Buenos Aires lodged a formal complaint with the Argentine Government at the breach of sovereignty, but this was rejected by the Foreign Ministry in Buenos Aires. It was apparent that the Argentines were testing British reactions to their aggression and, unfortunately, the signals they were receiving appeared to confirm their suspicions that the British Government took no interest in its South Atlantic possessions. Two weeks later, on 28 February, Davidoff visited the British Embassy in Buenos Aires where he apologized for the problems caused by his visit to South Georgia and announced that he wished to make another visit to the island. He appeared anxious not to cause any more international incidents and asked for instructions on how to proceed. On 11 March 1982, before he received any reply or instructions, he left for South Georgia in the Argentine naval support vessel *Bahia Buen Sucesco* and arrived there eight days later. That same day the British Antarctic Survey members noted a sizeable Argentine naval presence ashore, heard shots being fired and saw an Argentine flag raised. Clearly Davidoff's visit was another front to challenge British authority and in London it was agreed that HMS *Endurance* (which had also been earmarked for disposal by the Government) should sail for South Georgia with a detachment of marines to evict the Argentinians.

On Monday 22 March *Bahia Buen Sucesco* left Leith and on the same day the Governor of the Falkland Islands telegraphed London to say that Davidoff's party was deliberately flouting British regulations and that more illegal landings were likely, probably on the Falkland Islands themselves. Over the next two days diplomatic relations between London and Buenos Aires deteriorated rapidly. By 25 March it became apparent that Argentine warships were being sent to South Georgia to prevent *Endurance* from evicting the Argentinians there and that another Argentine supply ship was at Leith unloading stores, with three landing craft and a military helicopter operating from the vessel. In London it was feared that any attempt to resolve the situation effectively would result in a full-scale military offensive by Argentina and further diplomatic efforts were made to persuade the Argentines to remove the men. On Saturday 27 March it was clear that there was intense naval activity at the Argentine bases in Mar del Plata and Puerto Belgrano, with the embarkation of marines and the sailing of several ships. At midday on 29 March information was received in London that five Argentine warships, including a submarine, were sailing to South Georgia and that another four warships, including the aircraft carrier *Veinticinco de Mayo,* were also at sea. It was immediately recognized by the Ministry of Defence that the presence of Argentine ships some 800 miles north of the Falkland Islands, as well as warships close to South Georgia, was a dangerous situation and it was decided to dispatch three nuclear-powered submarines to the South Atlantic. Consideration was also given to forming a larger naval force in case it were to be required but, as far as a deterrent force was concerned, it was too late.

By the evening of Wednesday 31 March, reliable intelligence reports indicated that the Argentinian armed forces were set to invade both the Falkland Islands and South Georgia, and there followed some frantic, last-minute, diplomatic efforts to head off the invasion. The Argentine plans had been laid in December 1981 by the country's Military Junta, and no diplomatic manoeuvrings would deflect it from its aggression. At 23.00 local time on Thursday 1 April 1982, Argentine marines of the Amphibious Commando Company landed from the destroyer *Santissima Trinidad,* which was anchored a mile off the coast of East Falkland, to attack the Royal Marines Barracks at Moody Brook. In the event the camp was empty, with the small resident garrison having moved to the capital, Stanley, in order to defend Government House. Next morning, at 06.30, the main Argentine force landed just north of Stanley and by the end of the day a huge invasion force had overwhelmed the small 80-man garrison of Royal Marines which, as luck would have it, was at double its normal strength. In Britain there was an

As *Fearless* steams into the Solent her four LCUs follow like ducklings. *(Official, courtesy Maritime Books, Liskeard)*

During the passage south, as well as intensive training, there was still time for some relaxation. Here the Crossing the Line ceremony has drawn a good crowd of spectators and even a Sea King helicopter has provided a viewing platform.
(Royal Marines Museum, Eastney, No 7/20/18 - 304)

unprecedented national sense of shock and outrage, and it was quickly decided to send a large Naval Task Force to the South Atlantic to retake the islands and to restore the legitimate British sovereignty. Although it was a simple task for the politicians to announce the dispatch of the force, actually assembling the huge armada of warships, troop transports and supply vessels, to sail 8,000 miles south posed huge logistical problems for the First Sea Lord, Admiral Sir Henry Leach, and the C-in-C Fleet, Admiral Sir John Fieldhouse. They immediately set about organizing both units and personnel, but the irony of the situation was obvious to all. The politicians who were desperately looking to the service chiefs to rescue them from the seemingly impossible situation in which they found themselves, were the same people who only a few months earlier had insisted on swingeing cuts in the Defence budget, which would have seen the disposal of the aircraft carriers *Invincible* and *Hermes,* as well as the assault ships *Fearless* and *Intrepid.*

Meanwhile, on 2 April in Portsmouth Dockyard, *Fearless* was just a week into her assisted maintenance period and this had been long enough for the dockyard to have opened up all her main propulsion machinery for repair and maintenance. In addition the aft main boiler was defective with casing cracks and brickwork defects, problems which, under normal circumstances, would take several weeks to repair. With the work well under way many members of the ship's company were on leave, but that day the ship was brought to immediate notice for steam and the dockyard's Fleet Maintenance Group and the

ship's company worked round the clock to get the assault ship ready for sea. All those away from the ship and on leave were recalled, storing got under way and the boiler casing and brickwork was repaired and replaced. By late Monday 5 April the sick boiler had been flashed up, and by the following day *Fearless* was ready to sail. On board she had Headquarters 3 Commando Brigade, two troops of the Blues & Royals and approximately a quarter of 846 Squadron's personnel. In addition the flight deck was packed with stores and chacons, but with enough room to land on and stow three of 846 Squadron's Sea King helicopters, and three Scout helicopters belonging to 3 Commando Brigade Air Squadron. At 10.00 on Tuesday 6 April 1982, a cold, wet and windswept day, *Fearless* slipped from Fountain Lake Jetty and, with her four LCUs following astern like a brood of ducklings, she made her way down Portsmouth Harbour. What was not generally known was the fact that the assault ship was actually steaming with only one main boiler on line, as the new brickwork on the after one was slowly drying out. As she moved towards the Solent her siren boomed out and people began to gather on the harbour walks and on the Round Tower at Old Portsmouth. Many were wives, sweethearts and mothers, and as she nosed out past Fort Blockhouse there were both cheers and tears for the departing assault ship. There was, however, from her bellicose appearance, no doubting her purpose for her flight and weather decks were lined with men from the ship's company and aft there were ranks of Royal Marines in battle fatigues, with the guns and equipment for the force of 600 men on board. At

Fearless, with the troopship *Canberra* and other units of the amphibious force, at anchor off Ascension Island.
(Author's collection)

her masthead she flew the pennant of Commodore Michael Clapp, who commanded the Amphibious Task Group, and on her arrival at Spithead *Fearless* paused to take on her LCUs before steaming out into the Channel. That evening Commodore Clapp arrived on board by Sea King helicopter and, with the assault ship steaming into heavy rain and rising seas, the deck landing was, 'certainly outside flying limits for Sea Kings on LPDs'. The assault ship then set course for Ascension Island where the amphibious group would rendezvous for final training and preparations before sailing for the Falkland Islands.

As *Fearless* steamed south there was a great deal of hard work to be undertaken, particularly by the engineering department who had to get the second main boiler on line. The electricians faced the task of bringing the ship's damage control systems to a high standard, while in the communications department there was more signal traffic in the space of a few days than was usually handled over the period of a full commission. In the medical section there were enormous quantities of stores to be sorted and prepared for use, including individual morphine doses, and the paperwork included some unfamiliar forms, such as death certificates. The Air Department had to get used to integrating with the squadron personnel and taking every opportunity to carry out flight deck training, particularly as *Fearless* and 846 Squadron had little experience of operating together. It was also the first time that Sea King helicopters had operated from the assault ship's flight deck. Conditions on board were, according to one member of the ship's company, 'on overload', with camp beds appearing in all sorts of unlikely places, and one junior rates mess deck being occupied by senior Army officers. On 11 April *Fearless* was ordered to proceed to Ascension Island independently, although there was still time for relaxation and, on 15 April, a full-scale Crossing the Line ceremony was held on the flight deck, with Heads of Departments finding themselves in the makeshift ducking pool. On 16 April the Commander of the Carrier Battle Group, Rear-Admiral John (Sandy) Woodward, visited *Fearless* by helicopter from *Hermes* for the first of many high-level conferences on board the assault ship. Next day *Fearless* arrived off Pyramid Point, on the north-west side of Ascension Island, where she would spend the next three weeks.

Ascension Island is characterized by extinct volcanoes and huge rocks of lava which surround Green Mountain, so named because it is capped by the only vegetation on what is a hot and arid island. Whilst at anchor, however, there was an opportunity for training and the ship's engineers were able to carry out a great deal of repair work and finishing of jobs which had been abandoned when the maintenance period at Portsmouth was suddenly curtailed. The troops and Assault Squadron were kept very busy and much valuable experience in operating the LCUs and LCVPs was gained. 846 Squadron underwent a 'reshuffle' which, until the arrival of *Intrepid*, resulted in *Fearless* becoming the main operational headquarters and maintenance base for seven of the squadron's Sea Kings. For the squadron as a whole it was a busy period as they transported stores, troops and ammunition around the amphibious section of the Task Force. By 20 April, as well

On 19 May 1982, in the Southern Ocean, 600 men of 40 Commando were transferred from *Canberra* to *Fearless* by LCU. It was a tricky operation, but it was completed successfully. Here two LCUs, which have been hastily given some camouflage paint, carry men from the troopship to the assault ships.

(Royal Marines Museum, Eastney, No 7/20/18 - 822)

With 600 extra men on board *Fearless* was in 'mega-overload' and even the Junior Rates' Dining Hall was converted to sleeping accommodation.

(Royal Marines Museum, Eastney, No 7/20/18 - 655)

Under 'mega-overload' conditions even the LCUs became dormitories. This photograph shows the tank deck packed with men and equipment.

(Royal Marines Museum, Eastney, No 7/20/18 - 661)

65

as *Fearless,* the ships of the amphibious section at Ascension included the LSLs *Sir Galahad, Sir Geraint, Sir Lancelot, Sir Percivale* and *Sir Tristram,* together with the troop transport *Canberra,* which arrived that day. In the early hours of 26 April some loud and unidentified sonar transmissions were heard on *Fearless'* hull and this was quickly followed by 'Hands to Action Stations. Ship's divers muster at the diving store'. Meanwhile, *Canberra* was immediately ordered to sea and the assault ship's divers prepared to search the hull thoroughly, looking for limpet mines or any sign of explosive devices, for the probability of attack from Argentine mini-submarines could not be discounted. Surrounded by hundreds of brilliantly coloured tropical fish the diving team made the 500ft search in about 30 minutes, after which, fortunately, they were able to give the 'All Clear'.

On Wednesday 5 May *Intrepid,* together with *Atlantic Conveyor* and two oil tankers, arrived off Ascension Island, and as various political initiatives failed to find any solution and remove Argentine forces from the islands, it became increasingly clear that a military invasion would be the only way to evict them. On 6 May the troopship *Canberra,* which was carrying 40 and 42 Commandos and the 3rd Battalion Parachute Regiment, left Ascension Island bound for the Falkland Islands. Next day *Fearless,* having re-embarked her troops and having readjusted the huge quantity of stores she was carrying, left her anchorage and set course for the Total Exclusion Zone (TEZ) which had been declared around the Falkland Islands. On Monday 10 May, 1,000 miles north-west of Tristan da Cunha, with *Intrepid* having caught up, the two assault ships rendezvoused with *Ardent, Argonaut, Canberra, Atlantic Conveyor, Norland, Europic Ferry* and *RFA Stromness.* This was now the all-important troop convoy and security for its voyage south was vital. During the afternoon of 11 May there was a submarine 'Red Alert' which lasted for an hour, during which time all vessels steamed at 16 knots while carrying out zigzag manoeuvres. In the event there was no threat to the convoy. Next day the island of South Georgia was retaken and by 15 May the convoy was some 810 miles east-north-east of Port Stanley. By now, with the convoy well into the 'Roaring Forties', the barometric pressure was falling and by the evening they were steaming into Force 9 gales, with winds and spray so bad that bridge wing lookouts had to be brought in under cover. Plans for the assault were well under way, and that forenoon commanding officers of all ships held an 'amphibious assault conference' in *Fearless.*

On 13 May, with the amphibious force some 900 miles from Port Stanley, 60 officers assembled in the wardroom of *Fearless* to hear the Brigade Commander, Brigadier J. H. A. Thompson, give orders for the amphibious landing on East Falkland Island. The mission was to land in the Port San Carlos area and establish a beachhead from which to launch offensive operations. It was to be a silent night landing in three phases, the first being a simultaneous beach assault by 40 Commando and 2 Para to secure San Carlos and Sussex Mountain respectively. In Phase Two, 45 Commando and 3 Para were concurrently to secure Ajax Bay complex and Port San Carlos Settlement, and Phase Three was a helicopter move of artillery and air defence to cover the beachhead, while the SBS and SAS were to take an enemy position on Fanning Head and carry out diversionary operations near Goose Green. At 14.45 on Sunday 16 May, 650 miles east-north-east of Port Stanley, there was a further rendezvous when the frigates *Antrim* and *Plymouth,* together with the LSLs *Sir Galahad, Sir Geraint, Sir Lancelot, Sir Percivale* and *Sir Tristram,* along with MV *Fort Toronto,* joined forces. The convoy now consisted of 19 ships, and as they approached the Total Exclusion Zone tension mounted. On Tuesday 18 May, on a glassy sea with a cold winter chill and a clear sky, when they were some 200 miles east-north-east of Port Stanley and on the edge of the TEZ, the convoy rendezvoused with the aircraft carriers *Hermes* and *Invincible* and their escorts, and as one member of the ship's company recalled, 'It was a magnificent sight to behold, ships of all shapes and sizes from horizon to horizon.' The whole force was now on a war footing and during the night, with all ships darkened and without even navigation lights, the bridge watchkeepers and all lookouts were very much on their toes as, in the inky darkness, 22 ships manoeuvred together. Next day, during the middle watch, an order came from the C-in-C Fleet at Northwood, who had decided against keeping three major assault units in one ship (*Canberra*), to transfer 1,200 men to *Fearless* and *Intrepid.* However, weather conditions and the state of the sea seemed to rule out a boat transfer and the helicopters, which would be essential for the final assault and beyond, had logged too many flying and engine hours to be used. At one stage the feasibility of carrying out the operation by jackstay transfer was considered, but as this would have taken about 15 hours to complete and there was a high chance of men being injured or killed, it was discounted. In the event, and to everyone's relief, the heavy seas abated somewhat and at 09.30, with the troopship *Canberra* close to *Fearless'* port quarter, the cross-decking of 600 men of 40 Commando by LCU began. Bobbing about in a sea-state 4, the assault ship's LCUs circled *Canberra* while, one at a time, they came alongside the liner's E deck gun port doors. The commandos, with all their combat gear, bergans and rifles, queued along the liner's Promenade Deck, down the stairs and passageways on D and E decks and through to the gun port doors. After handing down their equipment they had to gauge the moment when the LCU would bob to the lip of the hatchway. In the five-foot swell any split-second miscalculation could have been fatal, and it nearly was. Secured high above by lines passed to *Canberra's*

A magnificent aerial photograph of *Fearless* at sea. *(FotoFlite, Ashford, Kent)*

Fearless at Spithead, with Isle of Wight ferries and the Haslar coastline in the background. *(FotoFlite, Ashford, Kent)*

67

Fearless with her LCVPs and LCUs in formation alongside. *(Derek Fox collection)*

On 18 March 2002, a blustery day in the Solent, *Fearless* entered Portsmouth Harbour to pay off for the last time.
(Derek Fox collection)

Fearless in the South Atlantic operating Sea Kings of 846 Squadron.
(Fleet Air Arm Museum, Yeovilton)

Promenade Deck the LCUs were slamming regularly against the liner's side and half an hour after the start of the operation one marine lost his footing and fell into the icy waters of the South Atlantic - between the LCU and *Canberra*. With only seconds to spare before the LCU would be banged against *Canberra's* side, crushing the man, he managed to recover instantly from the shock and swim to the stern of the LCU, where he was hauled to safety. By 11.00, however, the operation was completed, and with 600 extra men of 40 Commando on board *Fearless,* the vessel, according to one member of the ship's company, was in 'mega-overload'. Life for everyone became difficult, with even the Junior Rates Dining Hall having been converted to sleeping accommodation for the extra troops.

On Thursday 20 May, which was D-day minus one, the convoy was less than 100 miles north-east of Port Stanley and early in the morning all ships took station on *Sir Lancelot*. All round the assault convoy the destroyers and frigates of the screen, *Antrim, Brilliant, Broadsword, Yarmouth, Ardent, Plymouth* and *Argonaut,* were providing protection, whilst ahead of the force anti-submarine helicopters were on patrol 'dunking' their sonars. Also in company, and providing air cover, was the aircraft carrier *Invincible*. By 20.00 the troop convoy had changed formation into three waves, with *Fearless* and *Intrepid* in line ahead leading the way in Wave One. Forty minutes later, with everyone at Action Stations, the escorting warships commenced a barrage to soften up Argentine positions on Fanning Head and elsewhere in the area. At 20.58 on Friday 21 May *Fearless* and *Intrepid* passed Jersey Point and three hours later, at just before midnight on a cold and starlit night *Fearless* anchored in Falkland Sound,

off Chancho Point. Complete surprise had been achieved, but owing to a problem with the ballast pumps there was a delay before the first LCUs carrying units of 40 Commando were able to slip silently out into the inky darkness to the landing area at San Carlos Settlement. At the same time 3 Para were landed at Fanning Head to deal with enemy troops and within hours troops were streaming ashore to consolidate the bridgehead. By 07.30 Phase One of the operation was complete, and on Fanning Head the SBS were engaged in a fierce fight with a company of Argentinians, with explosions and tracer lighting up the sky. Meanwhile, as daylight dawned over Falkland Sound, a tranquil scene greeted the ships' companies, with geese flying in formation in the clear blue sky and seabirds bobbing on the water, but anti-aircraft gunners and Seacat operators awaited the inevitable air attacks. At this stage *Fearless'* defensive armament consisted of four quadruple Seacat surface-to-air missile systems and two 40/60 Bofors AA guns, but they would soon be supplemented by a variety of additional weapons, including captured 20mm Oerlikons, 35mm anti-aircraft guns, light machine-guns and even self-loading rifles. At 08.50 local time the first enemy Pucara aircraft made a reconnaissance mission over the area and 40 minutes later two low-flying Mirage jets swept in to launch a bombing raid. For the first time since the end of the Second World War the Royal Navy came under sustained air attack, and by 10.00 *Fearless* had moved to an anchorage in San Carlos Water.

It was not long before all the ships in Falkland Sound and San Carlos Water were being subjected to regular air attacks and as each wave of enemy aircraft flew over, most at just over masthead height, *Fearless* vibrated to the noise

D-Day in San Carlos Water and an Argentinian Mirage fighter swoops low over *Fearless* as it attacks the shipping at anchor.
(PO Pete Holdgate, courtesy Maritime Books, Liskeard)

Fearless docked down in San Carlos Water. (*Royal Marines Museum, Eastney, No 7/20/18 - 703*)

A Harrier refuelling on *Fearless'* flight deck during operations to retake the Falkland Islands. (*Royal Marines Museum, Eastney, No 7/20/18 - 349*)

A weather-beaten *Fearless* on the morning of 14 July 1982, on her return from the South Atlantic, as she docks down in the Solent to offload the LCUs prior to her triumphant entry into Portsmouth Harbour.
(Mike Lennon)

of Bofors guns firing and the Seacat missiles soon claimed their first kill, when a Mirage fighter was brought down. Early on the first day there was a portent of things to come when *Antrim* was hit by cannon fire, which caused one casualty and left an unexploded bomb lodged in the ship. Later in the day *Ardent* was seriously damaged, and later sank, and *Argonaut* was hit by enemy bombs. A team from *Fearless* assisted the frigate's ship's company in keeping their ship seaworthy and also carried out both First Aid and fire-fighting duties, as well as helping to restore electrical power and repair machinery. During the first six days of the land campaign *Fearless* remained at anchor and, in fact, she and *Intrepid* became the longest serving inhabitants of what became known as 'bomb alley'. During this period she suffered four casualties on board, with one man being wounded in the leg and being evacuated from the ship. Three other seamen were wounded by shrapnel, treated and retained on board. On 22 May, with anti-aircraft missile batteries being set up ashore, there was a respite from the air raids, but the next day saw the resumption of repeated attacks on the ships at anchor. This time *Antelope* was hit and later that day the bomb exploded, sinking the frigate. Her ship's company was rescued by LCUs and LCVPs from *Fearless* and the men were accommodated for the night in the assault ship before being transferred to *Canberra*. On 24 May there were further air attacks in which the LSLs *Sir Galahad* and *Sir Lancelot* were damaged by unexploded bombs. Next day, Argentine Independence Day, saw continuous air attacks and there was little respite for the anti-aircraft crews as wave after wave of low-flying aircraft came in over the anchorages to bomb and strafe the ships. For some days the air battle had hung in the balance, but the withering hail of fire put up by the ships eventually began to bring results. One Argentine pilot actually ejected from his damaged Skyhawk and landed in the sea just astern of *Fearless*. He was picked up by one of the LCUs and brought on board as a prisoner of war and treated in the sickbay for a dislocated left knee, which he had incurred on leaving his aircraft. He was later transferred ashore for further surgery. That day five Argentine jets were 'splashed' over the anchorages and the combat air patrols accounted for another five, but at sea it was an unhappy day when *Coventry* was sunk with the loss of 20 men and *Atlantic Conveyor* went down with the loss of 12 men, two Chinook and eight Wessex helicopters, and large quantities of equipment.

On 26 May there were fewer air attacks and for *Fearless* it was a relatively quiet day. Ashore orders were given for the breakout from the San Carlos bridgehead, with 2 Para attacking Darwin on 28 May. On 27 May *Fearless'* gunners had claimed two Mirage fighters shot down and next day the assault ship put to sea and steamed to an area outside the TEZ in order to refuel. Whilst at sea she embarked the Commander Land Forces Falkland Islands, Major-General Jeremy Moore, and other senior officers before rendezvousing with *Hermes* and the carrier group for a senior officers' conference. On conclusion of the meeting *Fearless* returned to San Carlos Water, where she anchored before dawn on 31 May. While at anchor she experienced trouble with her turbo-alternator cooling systems when krill, which are abundant in the waters of the Falkland Islands, jammed open two of the cooling water inlets. The ship's divers, who had been busy searching the underwater hull of an RFA, were asked to blank off one of the inlets.

been acting suspiciously and, with the permission of the Red Cross, they searched the vessel.

During her period at anchor carrying out support operations *Fearless*' ship's company performed some invaluable tasks, from providing fire-fighting and damage control parties to running a captured Argentine oil rig supply vessel, which had been operated by the Argentine Navy. The helicopters of 846 Squadron flew simultaneously from *Fearless* and *Intrepid,* transporting troops forward, resupplying them and moving their gun batteries in behind the front line. This latter duty also involved the constant supplying of ammunition and on a number of occasions the helicopters came under fire. They were also engaged in search and rescue operations on ships which had been damaged or sunk. The main galley staff also worked flat out with never less than 1,000 people to feed on a daily basis and on most days they were also required to feed at short notice varying numbers of troops who would arrive on board needing substantial hot meals. Meanwhile the stores accountants and writers had to contend with the problem of an 8,000-mile supply line and as well as their normal duties they were also employed in operational or first aid roles throughout the fighting. The 4th Assault Squadron were kept extremely busy, working an average of 18 hours each day as the LCUs and LCVPs carried out all manner of duties which included, on one occasion, rescuing an oil-covered penguin.

On 6 June *Fearless* made a night passage to a point off Elephant Island close to Choiseul Sound where half a battalion of Welsh Guards was disembarked and taken ashore in two LCUs. Two days later, at Bluff Cove, the LSLs *Sir Galahad* and *Sir Tristram* were bombed by enemy aircraft and both were set on fire, killing 63 and wounding 83. A few hours later LCU *F4,* from *Fearless,* which was on passage from Port Darwin to Fitzroy, bringing up vital communication Land Rovers, was attacked by enemy aircraft and sunk in Choiseul Sound, with the loss of six members of her crew, four Royal Marines and two seamen.

Another view of *Fearless* as she offloads her LCUs before,...

However, continuing air raids meant that they had to work after dark and, with the help of a clearance diving team, they worked at a depth of 30 feet in bitterly cold waters for four days, during which time they had little sleep. Once they had completed this task they had only a brief respite before they were called upon to remove one of the sunken *Antelope's* hawsers from around a screw. On 31 May, *Fearless*' Principal Medical Officer joined a boarding party on the Argentine hospital ship *Bahia Paraiso* which had

73

...her mission to the South Atlantic over, she makes her entry into harbour. *(Both Mike Lennon)*

Three days after the tragedy at Bluff Cove a team from *Fearless* was dispatched to Fitzroy in order to survey the hulk of *Sir Tristram*. As they made their way through smoky passageways they found the forward compartments were untouched, but the after section had been reduced to mangled rubble and molten aluminium. They found that the generators were still intact and it did not take them long to restore electrical power and to provide hot water. As a result of their efforts the LSL was able to provide much-needed shelter to troops who would otherwise have had to live in tents. On 12 June the final battles around Stanley began, with 3 Commando Brigade, in a night attack, capturing high ground to the north of the town and, two days later, 5 Infantry Brigade took the high features to the south. That day, at 20.59 local time, General Moore accepted the Argentine surrender and, once again, the Union Flag flew over Government House.

On Tuesday 15 June, Major-General Mario Menendez, the commander of the Argentine forces, and four of his senior officers, were temporarily accommodated in *Fearless*, with the General occupying the Landing Force Commander's cabin. Next day it was decided to move the assault ship closer to Stanley and at 21.00 she left San Carlos Water for an overnight passage to Port William, the capital's outer harbour. For four days the ship's company was able to assist with the clean-up operations in and around Stanley and on 17 June, with General Galtieri having been deposed, it was clear that the campaign was definitely over. Finally, on 25 June, some ten days after the surrender, with Headquarters 3 Commando Brigade embarked, *Fearless* left the Falkland Islands and set course for Ascension Island and home. Happily the passage north was faster than the outward bound voyage, and on 3 July there was a short break at Ascension. Ten days later *Fearless* arrived in Plymouth Sound where her embarked force and 846 Squadron were landed, and HRH the Duke of Edinburgh visited the ship and spent over an hour on board. Next day, to a tumultuous reception, *Fearless* and her sister *Intrepid* arrived at Portsmouth. Without any doubt she had played a vital role in the retaking of the Falkland Islands and one of her first visitors in Portsmouth was the Secretary of State for Defence. *Fearless* had been away from her base port for exactly 99 days and, sadly, six members of her ship's company had not returned.

Chapter Six

HMS *Fearless* - Return To Training 1982-1985

On her return from the South Atlantic in July 1982 *Fearless* was able to complete her dockyard assisted maintenance period at Portsmouth, and the ship's company could finish their leave which had been so rudely interrupted earlier in the year. By September, however, the ship was ready for sea once again and before she set course for the Mediterranean in her Dartmouth Training role she took part in a major NATO exercise in the Baltic. 'Exercise Northern Wedding' saw her landing US Marines in Denmark, and operating US Navy Sea Stallion, Sea Knight and Cobra helicopters, with one of the latter being accommodated overnight on the flight deck. The exercise was followed on 16 September by a five-day visit to Newcastle upon Tyne to renew the friendship which had been built up during her 14-month refit at South Shields. Civic receptions were held in Newcastle and South Shields as Tyneside opened its arms to *Fearless* and her company. At the city's Odeon cinema members of the ship's company watched a special showing of the film 'Who Dares Wins' and met two of its stars - Ingrid Pitt and Lewis Collins. During the two days that the assault ship was open to the public, 5,000 people toured her and a further 2,000 were turned away as there was no more time for them to get aboard. With the visit over *Fearless* returned to Portsmouth to take on her 'embarked force' of midshipmen and apprentices, before setting course for warmer Mediterranean climes.

As always the first port of call when bound for the Mediterranean was Gibraltar and on 4 October 1982, when leaving the port, as well as two Wessex helicopters of 845 Squadron, she had on board two passengers. The assault ship's visit had coincided with a change of Gibraltar's Governors, and General Sir William G. F. Jackson, the outgoing Governor, together with Lady Jackson, took passage in *Fearless* to Naples, her next port of call. After a glittering and moving ceremony in which Sir William bade farewell to friends and colleagues, he handed over the keys to the fortress and embarked in the assault ship. After boarding, Sir William inspected a Royal Marines honour guard and the Staff Band of the Royal Engineers then, accompanied by the frigate *Rhyl* and a host of small boats, *Fearless* sailed from Gibraltar to the crash of a 17-gun salute. With the Flag Officer Gibraltar, Rear-Admiral D. J. Mackenzie, on board, the frigate *Rhyl* steamed past *Fearless* when they were off Europa Point as a final salute to the outgoing Governor. During the passage to Naples General and Lady Jackson took part in many of the assault ship's activities, including a flight in one of the Wessex helicopters, a band concert and the general drills which the midshipmen and apprentices under training regularly undertook. After ten days at Naples, *Fearless* visited Split, Istanbul and Venice. The autumn cruise to the Mediterranean ended with a two-day visit to the French port of Brest and after leaving on 25 November, she returned to Portsmouth for Christmas leave and maintenance.

In early January 1983, when *Fearless* left Portsmouth for her Dartmouth Training Squadron spring term deployment in company with the frigate *Londonderry*, her role in 'Operation Corporate' (the Falklands Campaign) was well and truly behind her. Although her primary role was still that of an assault ship, the major part of each year's sea time was spent in her secondary role of training ship, giving officers and engineering apprentices under training their first experience of life at sea in a Royal Navy warship. For this spring cruise, as well as men under training, she also had embarked two Wessex helicopters and personnel of 845 Squadron. There was a brief stop in the Azores where *Fearless* and *Londonderry* refuelled from *British Elk*, an oil tanker which had been taken up from trade by the MoD, and the helicopters carried out an extensive training programme which included the last firings of 2-inch rockets from Royal Navy aircraft. During the second leg of the westbound transatlantic crossing the assault ship supplied *Londonderry* with fuel, a close-quarter manoeuvre which had only rarely been practised before. As she steamed closer to the Caribbean a signal was received from the Government of Tortola in the British Virgin Islands requesting the help of the assault ship. When *Fearless* arrived off the island her ship's company was kept busy using a helicopter to lift a three-ton crane from a sunken pontoon in Paraquita Bay. The team of men from *Fearless*, led by Commander John McGregor, included ship's divers, explosive experts and a willing party of volunteers from the engine room department, and between them they managed to shift the crane and clear the entrance to the bay, which was used as a hurricane shelter for yachts. As well as helping the harbour authority, other working parties adjusted the post office clock and rehung Tortola's church bells.

After leaving Tortola *Fearless* rejoined *Londonderry*, which had called at nearby Virgin Gorda, and the two ships exercised with the US Navy. One of the manoeuvres

Whilst exercising in Norwegian waters in late 1982, white camouflage nets were hung over the side to confuse aircraft.

(Royal Marines Museum, Eastney, No 14/2/10 - 153)

included streaming splash targets for aircraft from the brand new USS *Carl Vinson,* and for two hours wave after wave of Corsairs and Intruders swept past the assault ship's stern as they 'attacked' the elusive targets. The next stop, on 20 January, was San Juan, which had always been a regular port for Dartmouth Training units, and here there was an opportunity for the midshipmen to join up with Puerto Rico's National Guard for an exercise in nearby mountains. The two ships then moved on to Pensacola where, on 29 January, *Fearless* underwent an eight-day maintenance period, and a competition was held to see who could get the furthest away from the ship. The four LCVPs, under the guise of a navigation exercise, did exceptionally well, with their Royal Marine crews transiting the Intra-Coastal Waterway between Pensacola, Florida and New Orleans, and attracting a great deal of local attention in the process. Once back at sea *Fearless* took part in more exercises with US forces, with two Navy CH53 helicopters staying overnight and then taking Captain Larken on a reconnaissance flight over the Mississippi Delta. On 11 February *Fearless* and *Londonderry* were joined by the West Indies guardship, HMS *Zulu,* and together the three units steamed into the Mississippi River for the passage up to New Orleans for the highlight of the deployment - the Mardi Gras. That weekend *Fearless* was joined by the Flag Officer Third Flotilla, Rear-Admiral Derek Refell, and all three ships' companies were able to soak up the incredible atmosphere and wild sights of the festival, where FOF3's Royal Marines Band, as well as the Admiral himself, took part in the final parade. From New Orleans the ships steamed south for a Flag visit to Freeport, Grand Bahama, during which the local Defence Force Commander visited the assault ship to meet the Bahamian midshipmen who were on board. A well-known millionaire provided free buses and cars for the ship's company, and there were 70 complimentary tickets on offer for a Dave Brubeck Quartet concert. The visit provided *Fearless'* ship's company with their final opportunity to enjoy the Caribbean sun and warm sea, before returning to home waters where the ship would undergo a temporary role change.

On 4 March 1983, on her arrival in Plymouth Sound, *Fearless* disembarked her men under training and in just four hours she reverted to her role as an amphibious assault ship. There was also a change of command, with Captain R Trussell RN taking over from Captain Larken. After making the quick change to her amphibious role *Fearless* steamed north for the rigours of the Norwegian Sea and the appropriately named 'Exercise Cold Winter'. During this exercise she embarked elements of Headquarters 3 Commando Brigade, together with their transport and four of their Lynx helicopters, with all of them being landed at Tovik in Norway. During the deployment there was a visit to Andalsnes, and on completion of the exercise *Fearless* disembarked her passengers and returned to Portsmouth for an assisted maintenance period. The assault ship's summer cruise, as was traditional for the Training Squadron, took her north to Scandinavia and the Baltic, and after picking up an RAF volunteer band at Faslane, on 11 May she made a six-day visit to Malmo where there was an opportunity for football fans to watch some European Cup Winners matches. This was followed by visits to Aarhus and the city of Helsinki and whilst in the Baltic the ship's four LCUs carried out a successful 'Navex' in perfect weather, sailing 400 miles without refuelling and suffering no mechanical failures. The LCUs left *Fearless* in Kiel Bay, as the assault ship was about to begin a visit to the German naval base, from where they split into two pairs and circumnavigated the Danish island of Fyn in opposite

76

directions. One pair visited Odense and the other called at Aeroskobing. On the fourth day of their voyage all four LCUs were reunited at Kiel's Tirpitzmole, where the rest of the ship's company was enjoying Kiel Week. The deployment ended with a three-day visit to Hamburg before she returned to Portsmouth.

With summer leave over, on 5 September *Fearless* left Portsmouth for a mini-amphibious work-up off Portland, during which she was visited by the Secretary of State for Defence, Michael Heseltine. Following this, with units of 45 Commando embarked, the assault ship and the LSLs *Sir Geraint* and *Sir Percivale*, and HMAV *Ardennes*, left for the passage to Danish waters. On 9 September, as they steamed north, a major naval exercise code-named 'Botany Bay' was held with various aircraft, fast patrol boats and submarines of the West German and Danish Navies 'attacking' the troop convoy. As they steamed through the Kattegat a mine clearance operation was carried out, and on 16 September the main amphibious exercise, 'Ample Express', began. This involved a rehearsal landing on the coast of Zealand, and a final transit round Bornholm for a landing at Fakse Ladeplads, where two Anglo-Danish military groups were deployed. *Fearless* then undertook a three-day visit to Copenhagen before the commandos re-embarked for the return trip to Rosyth.

After disembarking her troops, *Fearless* again completed a fast role-change, embarking midshipmen and apprentices for a Mediterranean deployment, but on 29 September, whilst in the Channel south of Portland and en route from Rosyth to Casablanca, the assault ship was in collision with the German oil tanker *Gerhardt*. Fortunately neither ship was seriously damaged, but *Fearless,* with damage to her stem, had to make an unscheduled stop at Portland for repairs and most of those on board were able to manage an unexpected, mid-deployment, home leave. However, it also meant the cancellation of the proposed visit to Morocco. On her way to the Mediterranean *Fearless* spent six days off the Azores in company with the oil tanker *British Tamar*, which usually refuelled Royal Navy units off the Atlantic Islands as they made the voyage between Britain and the Falkland Islands. The tanker was able to assist with the training of midshipmen when, each day, six young officers would transfer by helicopter for extra instruction in bridgemanship, coastal navigation and officer of the watch duties. Guided by the staff of the Officers Training Department and the RFA liaison officer, the students manoeuvred the tanker in various formations as if she were a frigate. Exchange visits between ships' officers were also arranged and it proved to be an interesting six days for the tanker's crew as they exercised various methods of refuelling at sea. On 17 October, after leaving Palermo, the Mediterranean deployment took *Fearless* to Cyprus as well as to Naples where, on 31 October, she began a nine-day self-maintenance period. The first transit of the Strait of Messina was accompanied by violent and vivid electrical storms, which even seemed to keep Mount Etna quiet, and the Royal Marines Detachment landed at the Akrotiri Sovereign Base Area of Cyprus for two days of military training. In mid-November, however, the regular *Fearless* training role, by which many set their annual calendar, (a winter training cruise to the Caribbean, a Scandinavian exercise, Easter leave, a Baltic cruise, summer leave, followed by a Mediterranean cruise and Christmas leave), was suddenly disrupted when Captain Trussell announced to the ship's company that, 'We are required to proceed to Portsmouth and store for war in the best possible time.' Speculation on board was rife as rumours circulated round the ship about which war *Fearless* was to become involved in.

Within 36 hours of her arrival in Portsmouth on 18 November *Fearless* was converted from a place of instruction to an assault ship, with the Portakabins being removed from the tank deck, down the apron to the end of the dock before being lifted off by crane. Thanks to the magnificent efforts of the Dartmouth midshipmen in destoring and restoring the ship, most ship's company members were able to get home for a brief period at least. Finally, with the tank deck resembling a huge naval store, *Fearless* left Portsmouth late the next evening after some tearful farewells, bound once again for the Mediterranean, and the troubled country of Lebanon*. On 27 November, the assault ship, with part of 846 Squadron embarked, relieved HM Ships *Brazen* and *Glamorgan* off Beirut, where British troops had formed part of an international peacekeeping force since December 1982. Here she would provide logistical support and recreational facilities for men of the Queen's Dragoon Guards in Lebanon. The four Sea Kings of 846 Squadron linked the ship with the troops ashore, and naval parties were flown into Beirut to improve protection and habitability in an old tobacco factory which was serving as the British Headquarters in this dangerous city. Hercules aircraft from RAF Akrotiri in Cyprus delivered mail and stores to the troops, but when Beirut airport was closed the airlift was undertaken by RAF Chinook helicopters, which used the flight deck on *Fearless* as a refuelling pad. In company with the assault ship were the frigate *Achilles* and RFA *Brambleleaf,* and during the deployment *Fearless* hosted a combined services entertainment group which gave a concert on the tank deck in front of an appreciative audience of about 450 sailors and troops. Two of the assault ship's LCUs were used to transport stores from RAF Akrotiri to the port of Jounieh, north of Beirut, and as recounted by one of their crew members: 'We were escorted by HMS *Achilles* who insisted on treating us like ducklings. The skill and stamina of the two coxswains was ably demonstrated on the return journey when, because of inclement weather, we had to

---

* Lebanon as a country was created by France in September 1920, as part of its League of Nations Mandate under the Treaty of Sévres, when Britain and France between them virtually carved up the Levant countries which had formed part of the Ottoman Empire. Prior to this the area had formed part of Syria.

On 2 September and looking immaculate, *Fearless* leaves the Solent for 'Exercise Botany Bay'. *(Mike Lennon)*

Fearless in Scandinavian waters for 'Exercise Teamwork 84'.
(Royal Marines Museum, Eastney, No 2/18/25A - 302)

take shelter in the lee, between six and 30 feet off the frigate's starboard quarter. It certainly added a new dimension to station keeping.'

While *Fearless* enjoyed a 'stand down' period anchored off Cyprus, some limited leave was granted with the use of sports facilities ashore. Whilst off the island four Chelsea Pensioners, with a combined age of 297, who were guests of British Army units, braved a choppy boat trip out to the assault ship to be entertained on board for the day. Christmas and New Year were celebrated with the improvisation for which the Royal Navy is renowned, and the hard work of the cooks in preparing a slap-up Christmas dinner was much appreciated, as was the additional beer issue. The traditional Christmas Day 'rounds' were conducted by 'Captain' Des, usually known as Steward Cuthbert, the ship's youngest member. He was joined by 'Santa' in the form of CPO Stwd Saddler, who was also the subject of a 'Guess the Weight of Santa' competition. However, as 10 January 1984 approached, anxious eyes scoured the horizon for RFA *Reliant*, which was taking *Fearless*' place on station. To everyone's relief the handover was on schedule, and with revolutions being rung on for the passage home, *Fearless* set course for the west. There was a short stop at Gibraltar, where some shore leave was granted, and on 20 January 1984 the assault ship returned to Portsmouth, where she was greeted by families and friends. For the ship's company there was an additional three days' leave as recompense for the disruption caused by the unscheduled deployment to the Eastern Mediterranean.

With leave and her maintenance period having passed by far too quickly, in March 1984 *Fearless* sailed north for Scandinavia and 'Exercise Teamwork 84' with both midshipmen and apprentices, as well as an embarked force on board. During the amphibious phase the assault ship's LCUs and LCVPs moved more than 8,000 vehicles, and at one stage ferried some 800 of them in 12 hours. The exercise also involved carrying Royal Marines to and from Scandinavia, working closely with the DFDS ferry *Winston Churchill* which provided welcome comfort for some of the marines in the Commando Logistics Regiment. Having landed and re-embarked her troops in the Tromso area, *Fearless* returned to Plymouth Sound in severe gales to disembark the Royal Marines at Mountbatten Slip, and to take on a 'force' of teenage sons of ship's company members who took passage from Plymouth to Portsmouth. This proved to be a tiring adventure, but was an outstanding success for the boys. Upon her arrival in Portsmouth Dockyard the assault ship was taken in hand for an assisted maintenance period, which meant more leave for the ship's company. It was late May when *Fearless* sailed again to carry out a mini-work-up at Portland and Arish Mell, where the Assault Squadron were put through their paces, after which, in her training role, the assault ship set course for Newcastle upon Tyne and Copenhagen where she arrived on 2 June. During the visit the 4th Assault Squadron were invited to attend the 700th anniversary celebrations of the Swedish town of Jonkoping, situated in the centre of southern Sweden, at the foot of Lake Vattern. In order to get to the town the four LCUs, led by Captain Rob Need RM, sailed from Copenhagen to Gothenburg to begin a transit of the Gota Canal. The first leg of the canal transit took the LCUs to Lake Vanern, where they anchored for the night and next day they continued the journey to their first port of call, Sjotorp. The crews received a friendly welcome here, then the next leg to Karlsborg took them through 27 locks and some very narrow sections of waterway where, at several points, there were only six inches to spare. At Karlsborg they took a short break before setting out for Donsand, where they were joined by the British Ambassador to Sweden, who was an ex-Royal Marine, for the final approach to Jonkoping, where over 1,000 people had gathered to give them a great welcome. Three days and nights of official and informal celebrations followed, which taxed everyone's stamina, and the departure from the town was spectacular as they sailed at midnight to navigate Lake Vattern, bound for Motala. The next stop on the Gota Canal was Linkoping, where the crews were put up for the night in a Swedish Army barracks, and as the craft headed for the Baltic they were greeted enthusiastically at each lock. The last stop was Soderkoping at the eastern end of the canal before they locked out into the Baltic where, on 12 June, they rejoined *Fearless* for a visit to Stockholm. At the Swedish capital the assault ship mounted a trade exhibition devoted to British Leyland and Jaguar cars, which attracted a great deal of local interest. From Sweden *Fearless* moved on for her final visit of the schedule to Kristiansand in Norway, where the city was in the middle of its annual summer carnival. The last days of the deployment were spent on exercise off Cape Wrath, and after landing the midshipmen at Dartmouth *Fearless* sailed for a Families Day off Portsmouth, when more than 1,000 relatives and friends were embarked. Following this the assault ship steamed up harbour to secure alongside Middle Slip Jetty.

With her summer leave and maintenance over, *Fearless* left Portsmouth for Devonport where, with the ship at anchor in Plymouth Sound, her sponsor Lady Hull came to visit. Next day on Monday 3 September, Headquarters 3 Commando Brigade was embarked after which *Fearless* sailed for Copenhagen and 'Exercise Bold Gannet'. During the exercise, which was carried out under the scrutiny of NATO chiefs, Commodore Amphibious Warfare, Commodore Peter Dingemans, hoisted his broad pennant in the assault ship. It was the Navy's job to transport the Royal Marines, together with Dutch marines, from the UK to the Baltic. Augmented by forces from Denmark, Germany and the USA, the exercise was designed to test the deployment of the UK Mobile Force, as well as the UK and Netherlands Amphibious Force. In company with *Fearless* was the destroyer *Newcastle,* which would provide anti-aircraft support, and also included in the troop convoy were the LSLs *Sir Bedivere, Sir Geraint* and *Sir Percivale,* with the RFAs *Olmeda* and *Resource* in support. Backing up the force were the Army's logistic vessels HMAVs *Arakan* and *St George,* together with five chartered merchant ships which carried both British and Dutch forces. Also involved were the helicopters of 845 and 846 Squadrons and 17 landing craft from the German amphibious group. It was the biggest movement of troops from the UK to Europe since the end of the Second World War.

During the sea passage, which included a naval exercise in the form of an opposed transit of the North Sea, code-named 'Exercise Lionheart', *Fearless* and *Newcastle* steamed through the Strait of Dover and the Skagerrak into the Kattegat. They then sailed through the Store and Femer Baelts and round to Copenhagen where the final exercise details were agreed and where the troops landed for cross-training with the Danish Army. During her four days in the Danish capital, from 8 to 12 September, *Fearless'* ship's company was able to enjoy what had become a familiar run ashore and the MoD's sales organization arranged a military equipment sales exhibition. Having re-embarked her troops *Fearless* left Copenhagen for the Baltic Sea where she represented part of an 'Orange' amphibious invasion force approaching south-west Zealand. On 13 September the assault ship exercised with the merchant vessels which had been taken up from trade, and she received a visit from the Chief of the Defence Staff, Air Marshal Sir Donald Hall, who was able to see at first hand the problems of trying to adapt merchant ships to such a highly specialized role. On 15 September, in strong winds and a heavy swell, the main amphibious landing took place on the coast of Zealand, but with fuel contamination having temporarily grounded the Sea Kings and Wessex helicopters, the LCUs bore the brunt of the work, which continued until nightfall. The exercise lasted for two weeks, after which *Fearless* returned her embarked force to Plymouth Sound where she carried out another quick role-change and embarked 70 midshipmen and 100 engineering apprentices for her annual autumn training cruise to the Mediterranean.

After calling at Gibraltar *Fearless* made a five-day visit to the Spanish port city of Barcelona, where she occupied a prime city-centre berth and attracted over 3,000 local people when she was opened to the public. From Barcelona the assault ship went on to Piraeus, for Athens, where, once again, the MoD's sales organization had arranged an important military exhibition, with all manner of products and pyrotechnics on display on the tank deck. Whilst the exhibition attracted senior military figures, the ship's company enjoyed time off in the Greek capital, some boosting trade in the local bars, others preferring to visit sights such as the Acropolis and Delphi. One visitor to the ship was the overseas manager of a large British bank, who had done his National Service as a writer in the Navy, and he 'dined out' six members of the S & S department as well as providing a chauffeur-driven car for a party visiting Delphi. During the deployment *Fearless* visited Istanbul, and on her return to Portsmouth she underwent an assisted maintenance period before preparing for her final duties before handing over to her sister *Intrepid.*

On 11 December 1985, at Portsmouth, Captain P. G. J. Murison RN took command of *Fearless,* and in early January 1986, with her 'embarked force' of midshipmen

On 7 January 1985, *Fearless,* with an 'embarked force' of midshipmen and apprentices, left home waters for her spring training deployment to the Caribbean.
(Mike Lennon)

and apprentices on board, *Fearless* left home waters for her spring training cruise to the Caribbean. During the deployment she called at Tortola, where a team of 132, which included the 4th Assault Squadron and apprentices, carried out a number of tasks on behalf of the local people, including the disposal of a 60-foot sunken motor vessel, a bulldozer and derelict cars. The operation lasted for four days, and among other tasks completed was the laying of a road by the Royal Marines. The removal of MV *Maudelle* at Hodges Creek was the most difficult job, but it provided the ship's divers and demolition teams with some valuable experience. The apprentices refurbished and repainted the Fort Charlotte Children's Centre at Roadtown, and to mark the centre's reopening the apprentices financed and organized a party for the children. The end of the 'Military Aid' programme was marked by two days of recreation, with an official cocktail party on board. Other visits during the deployment included Martinique and Barbados, and later the ship spent eight days in Mayport, Florida, before returning to Portsmouth for leave to be given.

Fearless' final deployment took place in April and May 1985 when, in her training role and with 220 trainee midshipmen and apprentices embarked, she sailed for northern waters. Also on board was a detachment from 845 Squadron and the band of the King's Own Scottish Borderers. Along with *Invincible, Glamorgan, Newcastle, Cleopatra, Jupiter* and *Yarmouth,* she took part in 'Exercise Cold Winter' which, with thick pack ice in the Baltic approaches, lived up to its name. There was a visit to Oslo, and during the exercise, which involved forces from the UK, Netherlands and Norway, there was an 'attack' on Norway's west coast and the navigation of picturesque fjords for a helicopter-borne assault. In May, whilst most of the British units paid an official visit to Hamburg, *Fearless* put into Oslo where, flying the flag of FOF3, Rear-Admiral R. G. A. Fitch, she took part in the 40th anniversary celebrations of the country's liberation from German occupation. During the four-day visit an honour guard, formed by the midshipmen under training, paraded in a wreath-laying ceremony at the British cemetery. There were visits to the ship by the Prime Minister of Norway, and the President of the Norwegian Parliament, who called on Admiral Fitch.

In early June 1986 *Fearless* undertook her final duties of the commission when, with *Invincible, Glamorgan, Phoebe* and *Nottingham,* she took part in Staff College Sea Days in the Channel. Hundreds of VIPs, Members of Parliament and foreign dignitaries were given an insight into operations undertaken by the Royal Navy. As far as *Fearless* was concerned, however, the most important guests were embarked for the final day, when 1,350 relatives and friends of the ship's company joined the ship, including Admiral Fitch, his wife and son. *Fearless* sailed from Spithead in company with the other units, led by Flag Officer First Flotilla in *Invincible,* to carry out a light jackstay transfer with *Phoebe,* witness a fly-past by *Invincible's* aircraft and, as the highlight of the day, perform a period of close-quarters manoeuvring with *Intrepid,* which had just completed her amphibious work-up. After *Intrepid* had formally taken over as the operational amphibious and training ship, *Fearless* steamed into Portsmouth Harbour flying her paying-off pennant.

On 19 July 1986, within a few weeks of her arrival at Portsmouth, the commission ended and *Fearless'* ship's company had been reduced from 650 officers and men to just 50, and the process of dehumidification had begun, as the ship was prepared for the Reserve Fleet. She would remain at 30 days' notice for steam until the late summer of 1988, when she was due to begin a refit which would prepare her for operational service once again.

Chapter Seven

HMS *Fearless* - A Royal Review 1988-1995

Fearless remained at Portsmouth until the summer of 1988 when she was shifted under tow to Devonport Dockyard to undergo a major two-year refit which would cost some £50 million. Inevitably in a vessel of her age, a large amount of extra work was found to be necessary. A complete overhaul of the ship's main propulsion machinery took place, as well as hull maintenance and the updating of the main galley. The aviation fuel capacity was increased considerably to cope with the thirstier Sea King helicopters, and also the EH101 (Merlin), when it finally came into service. Although it was not easy to spot the difference, the assault ship's mast was shortened by 12 feet and new communications aerials were added to what remained. *Fearless* retained two of the Navy's last operational GWS-20 Seacat missile systems, but to give her more 'punch' these were supplemented by two Vulcan Phalanx air defence guns, capable of firing 3,000 rounds per minute. She was also fitted with two BMarc, close-range guns capable of firing 600 rounds per minute and two general-purpose machine-guns to supplement her firepower. To augment her defensive protection Seagnat chaff launchers were fitted. The operations room was fitted with the latest Plessey command system, and enhanced military communications systems and a computerized message handling system were installed, all improvements which were essential to *Fearless*' capability during amphibious operations when she would act as a joint naval and military headquarters. Finally, the flight deck was strengthened so that two Sea King helicopters were able to use it at any one time. Overall she could operate four of these large helicopters, although the lack of a hangar meant that as

before a permanent ship's flight would rarely be carried.

In November 1989 the ship was moved out of dry dock and on 6 February 1990, with the ship still in refit, *Fearless*' new commanding officer, Captain S. R. Meyer RN, joined and a few weeks later her ship's company was brought almost to full strength. Early September 1990 saw some hectic days on board as the ship was prepared for the Flag Officer's 'Ready for Sea' Rounds, but these passed off without any problems and less than two weeks later, on Saturday 15 September 1990, having been out of action for four years, *Fearless* left Devonport Dockyard. To everyone's amazement she steamed unassisted through the morning haze down the Hamoaze, past the Royal William Yard and into Plymouth Sound. She was followed closely by the brown and black camouflaged LCUs and LCVPs of the 4th Assault Squadron, and in Cawsand Bay the assault ship docked down to embark her landing craft. For the remainder of September, October and into November, *Fearless* carried out a busy period of trials, tests, training and defect rectification. On 9 November 1990, *Fearless* was recommissioned at Devonport, with the ceremony taking place on a rather crowded tank deck, which had been cleaned up and fitted out to seat 1,000 people. Along with

Raiding craft leave *Fearless* during exercises off the British Virgin Islands in the summer of 1991.
(Royal Marines Museum, Eastney, No 14/2/10 - 148)

Dressed overall and anchored at Spithead, Fearless looks immaculate for the D-Day Anniversary Fleet Review.
(Mike Lennon)

families and friends of the ship's company, the principal guests at the ceremony were Vice-Admiral Sir Alan Grose, the Flag Officer Plymouth, and the Lord Mayor of Portsmouth. The 20-man Royal Marines Guard would have done a 'King's Squad' proud, and the commissioning cake was cut by Mrs Erica Meyer, ably assisted by 17-year-old JS Martin, the youngest member of the ship's company. With the pomp and ceremony over *Fearless* sailed for a short shakedown cruise, during which, for the last time, she met her sister *Intrepid* at sea. The event was combined with a Families Day - and the meeting of the two 'grand old ladies of the fleet', which were now the longest serving operational units, saw them steaming side by side for over an hour. After completing her initial post-refit trials, *Fearless* presented herself to Flag Officer Sea Training and his staff for a two-week 'Operation Granby' contingency training session.

In August 1990 the Iraqi Army of Saddam Hussein had invaded and occupied the oil-rich Emirate of Kuwait. Iraq had never accepted the validity of the borders of this tiny Emirate since the two days in late August 1921, when Britain's representative in Baghdad had arbitrarily decided where the modern borders of Iraq (made up of the Ottoman provinces of Basra, Baghdad and the Kurdish-dominated Mosul), Saudi Arabia and Kuwait would be established. Most Iraqis regarded Kuwait as part of their Basra province, which British colonialists had taken from them and, according to one senior British diplomat in the Middle East at the time, 'We protected our strategic interests rather successfully, but in doing so we created a situation where people felt they had been wronged.' Whatever the historical background, however, the fact remained that Kuwait's South Rumaila oilfields were the world's third largest oil producer and if Saddam Hussein thought that the Western powers would allow this act of aggression to succeed, then he had badly misjudged them. In response to appeals from the Kuwaitis for international assistance, a coalition of Western powers, led by the USA and including Britain, began a massive military build-up in neighbouring Saudi Arabia with the aim of retaking Kuwait. The British contribution to the build-up was code-named 'Operation Granby' and in the autumn of 1990 it was not known whether *Fearless* would be required to take part. For the ship's company, however, the rigours of Portland were rewarded by a five-day visit to Rotterdam which, after a busy three-month period, was followed by Christmas leave. In the new year of 1991 it became clear that the assault ship would not, in the immediate future, be going to the sunny climes of the troubled Middle East and that she was bound for Portland and a more comprehensive dose of sea training which, as always, taxed all departments to their limits.

During the work-up *Fearless* steamed north towards the Arctic Circle to take part in a combined winter exercise with Norwegian and Dutch forces. The assault ship carried men of 40 Commando, who worked alongside Army units from the two European countries, as she completed a number of amphibious landings along the frozen fjords of northern Norway. During this period *Fearless* found herself in a 'tight spot' while steaming under the Tjeisund Suspension Bridge near Narvik, as she cleared it with only a few inches to spare. There was a run ashore in Narvik which, tongue in cheek, some described as, 'almost as exciting as Portland'. After a successful visit to the historical city of Trondheim, *Fearless* joined the Type 42 destroyer *York* and the frigate *Amazon,* as the flagship of Commodore

Peter Grindal, Commodore Amphibious Warfare, for 'Exercise Adger 91'. This involved all participating units, including Dutch marines and Norwegian naval units, in a combined land, amphibious, maritime and air operation. An amphibious assault in the Skagerrak with combat and maritime operations completed the exercise and, although dense fog kept the aircraft away, unseasonal mild weather in its turn kept the usual snow and ice at bay. After leaving northern waters *Fearless* returned to Portsmouth, and in May she made a coastal cruise which included a call at her newly adopted town of Scarborough. Courtesy of an amateur radio society the visit received worldwide publicity and over 1,000 well-wishers, from as far afield as Malaysia, Australia and the USA, contacted the ship. On 15 May, after leaving Scarborough and making a two-day cruise round the coast, *Fearless* arrived in Plymouth Sound to prepare for a deployment to the Caribbean. After embarking Royal Marines Commandos, Lynx helicopters from 651 Squadron AAC, which were normally based in Germany, and a Sea King from 826 Squadron at Culdrose, all of which took a great deal of coordination, the assault ship slipped her moorings and set course for the British Virgin Islands.

After an 11-day transatlantic crossing *Fearless* arrived off Beef Island where, at first light, the Royal Marines carried out a full-scale assault of the island's Long Bay Beach. It was said that one marine explained to a bewildered looking local policeman, 'It's okay mate, we're just invading.' However, when it was realized that the policeman had not been warned of the 'invasion', hurried explanations were given. Once ashore the 4th Assault Squadron set up an operations base in record time, and in phase two of the assault barbecue equipment was landed for the Royal Marines' banyan. The first 'civilized' port of call was Aruba, where the marines undertook a full programme of exercises in conjunction with the Aruban militia. From Aruba *Fearless* steamed to Curacao which, in turn, was followed by a four-day visit to Montego Bay. During her visit to the island of Dominica the authorities ashore requested that the Royal Navy assist them in finding a final resting place for the 150-ton coaster, and ex-Dunkirk veteran, *Ile de Serk* which had been driven ashore in 1988 during a severe storm. A salvage team led by Lt-Cdr Graham Binningsley, working with the public works department and even prisoners from the local jail, laboured round the clock to dig the vessel free from a position beside the island's main highway, in the centre of the town of Rousseau. Once free, *Fearless,* keeping as close to the shore as possible, while contending with the wind and currents, dragged the coaster towards the sea using a 600-ft towing hawser. Once afloat a huge roar went up from the enormous crowd which had gathered on shore, and this was echoed by the ship's company lining the assault ship's weather decks. The four LCUs then towed *Ile de Serk* four miles out to deep water where a demolition team led by Sub-Lt Radbourne placed

In the summer of 1994, during her deployment as Caribbean guardship, the 'yellow bird' funnel badges of the old West Indies Squadron replaced *Fearless'* Combined Operations badges. *(Commodore A.J.S. Taylor)*

charges round the coaster's hull and set the fuses. To ensure that the coaster sank quickly, a team of Royal Marines from the 4th Assault Squadron set up two Gustav anti-tank weapons on *Fearless'* forecastle and, as the demolition charges exploded, they fired four rounds into the stricken vessel which sank, bow first, within a minute. The final port of call in the Caribbean was Antigua where the embarked force rejoined the ship for the passage home to the UK, having split up for two different exercises, 'Steel Band' in Jamaica and 'Trade Winds' in Dominica.

By the autumn of 1991, in common with other major Royal Navy units, *Fearless'* accommodation had been modified to adapt the ship for a mixed male and female ship's company and during the remainder of her naval service she would carry a complement of female personnel, both officers and ratings. With her summer leave and maintenance period over, and prior to a Mediterranean deployment with the Dartmouth Training Squadron, *Fearless* was engaged in her amphibious landing support role. During a week-long exercise off the west coast of Scotland which began on 13 September 1992, she operated as flagship of the Commodore Amphibious Warfare, with elements of 45 Commando, the Army's Blues & Royals and the Royal Corps of Transport, conducting loading and offloading, cross-decking and beach assaults. Other ships involved included the LSLs *Sir Galahad* and *Sir Tristram*, the destroyer *Manchester* and MCMVs of the Mine Countermeasures Squadron, as well as helicopters of 845 Squadron. On 24 September, on conclusion of the exercise, *Fearless* returned to Portsmouth to disembark her Royal Marines and Army units and replace them with an 'embarked force' of young officers under training from the Royal Naval College at Dartmouth. The first port of call on this Mediterranean deployment, during which she was in company with the frigate *Minerva*, was Gibraltar, where the Assault Squadron asserted its dominance in sporting events, including the Rock Race. The next stop was an uneventful visit to Naples where many visited Pompeii, and where others found their entertainment at various Neapolitan bars and clubs. The highlight of the Mediterranean deployment was a visit to the Soviet Union's Black Sea port of Sevastopol, which was scheduled for 6 October 1991, less than eight weeks before the break-up of the Soviet Union. *Fearless* was flying the flag of Rear-Admiral Bruce Richardson, Flag Officer First Flotilla, and during the passage to the Black Sea time was spent cleaning and painting the ship, sprucing up uniforms and learning enough Russian to ensure street survival. With *Minerva* visiting the Bulgarian port of Varna, *Fearless* secured alongside at Sevastopol, the Crimea's principal city, which having been closed to foreigners, had not seen a British warship in its harbour for over 40 years, a period which had encompassed the darkest days of the Cold War, as well as the changes which had resulted from the effects of 'Perestroika' and 'Glasnost'. The assault ship's visit was part of a programme of building stronger ties between the Soviet Navy as it still was and the Royal Navy. However, it came at a time when the Soviet Union was clearly in its death throes, and there lay ahead the very real prospect of the Soviet Empire fragmenting, which would leave its armed forces facing a very uncertain future. In the Crimea in particular there were Ukrainian Nationalists who wished to set up their own Navy and take over the Soviet Black Sea Fleet. None of these domestic tensions, however, interfered with the warmth and openness of the welcome given to *Fearless* and her ship's company.

The Deputy Commander of the Black Sea Fleet, Rear-Admiral Stanislav Alexeyev, threw all his considerable energies into getting the most out of the goodwill visit, arranging for hundreds of Soviet sailors and young naval officers to visit the assault ship. He astonished his British visitors by giving them an impromptu tour of the submarine base at Balaclava, a fjord-like harbour filled with submarines, which had never been visited by Western military parties before. The Kara-class cruiser *Azov* was the host ship for the visit and here too Royal Navy officers were virtually given the run of the ship, to examine in detail her weapons, electronics and layout and, more importantly, to sample the vodka in her wardroom. The friendly atmosphere was not just confined to military circles, and when *Fearless* was opened to visitors, the crowds were so enormous that Soviet sailors had to be brought in to hold them back. Over 60 local families took members of the ship's company, male and female, into their homes, an extremely generous gesture given the hardships and shortages which they had to endure, with meagre food availability and even water supplies rationed to three hours a day. To most members of the ship's company the glimpses of life in Sevastopol that the visit afforded were a revelation, and although the town was generally clean and tidy, the shops were small with little in the way of foodstuffs for sale. Often there were just pickled vegetables and tinned fish on sale, with few signs of fresh produce. One member of the ship's company recalled that whilst looking round the shops, the only items he found on sale in a toy shop were plastic buckets. However, he and his 13 shipmates were able to enjoy a two-course meal in a restaurant, complete with wine, vodka and champagne, for a total of four pounds. Every day local people came on to the jetty to barter, with soap and chocolate being much in demand, and everywhere ashore members of the ship's company were literally mobbed by both adults and children, all eager for their autographs. One member of the ship's company summed up the experience thus: 'Sevastopol proved to be the experience of a lifetime. We were astounded at the controlled poverty of society, the high cost of living and the total lack of consumer goods in the shops. However, we soon found the majority of Russians to be friendly and exceptionally generous with what little they had.' Two members of the 4th Assault Squadron spent an evening as guests of the Black Sea Naval Infantry Brigade Officers' Mess, where they partook in what turned out to be a vodka tasting extravaganza. Other organized activities included guided tours of Crimean battlefields, including the infamous 'Valley of Death', where the Charge of the Light Brigade took place, and Balaclava itself. On the sports pitches the ship's teams, when faced with national athletics and Olympic veterans, struggled gallantly, but when the time came to leave one officer summed up the feelings of most members of the ship's company: 'The visit was made by the genuine hospitality of the people, added to the fact that we were witnessing such a change as political events were almost overtaking us.'

After leaving Sevastopol *Fearless* steamed across the

A Royal Marines Sioux helicopter lands on the flight deck. In the dock two neatly stowed Landing Craft Air Cushions (LCACs) can be seen.
(Official, courtesy Maritime Books, Liskeard)

Black Sea to the port city of Constanta in Romania which, after the Crimean visit, was something of an anti-climax after which everyone was quite happy to return to the warmer climes of the Mediterranean. Whilst *Fearless* was off the coast of Greece the LCUs carried out a 'Navex' through the Ionian Islands, and no sooner had they re-embarked than it seemed the ship would be required to assist with the evacuation of British nationals in and around Dubrovnik. The city had come under siege from the Serb-dominated Yugoslav Army, and on board *Fearless* there was some hasty contingency planning. In the event, however, the assault ship, which was once again in company with *Minerva,* was not required and she continued her passage to Venice. The remainder of the deployment was busy, but relatively uneventful, and there were two short goodwill visits. The first was to Palermo, where a small contingent left the ship to cycle back to the UK, and the second was to the naval base at the Spanish city of Cadiz. On 6 December, having experienced a diverse range of European cultures, *Fearless* arrived back in Portsmouth. Her arrival coincided with the announcement that plans were under way to replace both *Fearless* and *Intrepid,* with a government minister stating: 'Amphibious forces, by virtue of their inherent flexibility, are likely to be of increasing utility in peace, crisis and conflict.' It would be over ten years before these plans came to fruition and with *Intrepid* laid up at Portsmouth, and considered unlikely ever to go to sea under her own steam again, *Fearless* was now the Navy's sole amphibious assault ship. She also had the distinction of being the last operational steam-powered surface vessel. On 18 December 1991 there was another change of command, with Captain S. Moore RN taking over from Captain Meyer.

In February 1992, after leave and maintenance, *Fearless* embarked Y Company, 42 Commando and steamed north to Rosyth en route for amphibious exercises in the fjords of Norway. In early May, once again carrying Y Company and Sea Kings of 846 Squadron, *Fearless* returned to the warmer weather of the Mediterranean where she took part in an amphibious demonstration at Limassol for the newly appointed Flag Officer Surface Flotilla, where there was also an opportunity for some shore leave. The next port of call was Rhodes where most members of the ship's company were able to scatter all over the island during the five-day official visit in search of the best beaches, the ultimate suntan and the opportunity to meet some of the female holidaymakers out on package tours from Britain. On 3 June *Fearless* left Rhodes for a six-day passage to Toulon, during which damage control exercises and other evolutions were undertaken. The tenth anniversary of the end of the Falklands Campaign was commemorated with a memorial service on the flight deck, and on 9 June the assault ship arrived in the French naval base of Toulon for pre-exercise briefings. 'Exercise Farfedet' was to be an exercise in landing an amphibious force into a country which was experiencing severe internal disorder, and which was bordered by a hostile state poised to invade. In order to make the whole thing more realistic most of the various phases of the operation were to be 'hot planned' as events took place. Refugee evacuation and hostage release exercises would be carried out, as well as the winning of 'hearts and minds' of local people. These were to be the main tasks for the landing force which, in addition to the ship's embarked force, would include two companies of French commandos and the Italian San Marco Group. The amphibious task group consisted of four amphibious ships, including *Fearless* and FS *Orage,* and they were supported by two carrier groups. On leaving Toulon *Fearless* set course for Sardinia, joining up with the carriers en route, before carrying out rehearsal landings on the Italian island. On leaving Sardinia *Fearless* steamed to the Perpignan area of southern France where the main landings took place, with the role of the Royal Marines being to hold vital routes in order that French forces could evacuate refugees. Royal Marines' patrols into local villages were often persuaded into local cafes for 'refreshments' and, judging by the gifts of wine, the winning of local 'hearts and minds' was a success.

The exercise was followed by a week's rest and recuperation in Toulon, and a working visit to Gibraltar to support 'Exercise Purple Monarch', a Joint Force Headquarters command and control exercise. This was combined with the Top of the Rock race which, despite strong competition from two ship's company teams and a team of US Navy SEALS, was won by the 4th Assault Squadron. On returning to the UK *Fearless* was immediately involved in an amphibious demonstration off the south coast, for the benefit of the Secretary of State for Defence, Malcolm Rifkind. This important event was viewed as a great success and no doubt helped to ensure the need for replacement amphibious assault ships. *Fearless'* summer deployment ended with a visit to Scarborough, the ship's affiliated town, and on that enjoyable high note, she returned to Portsmouth after a busy six months to undergo an extended refit which would keep her out of service for almost nine months.

It was the spring of 1993 before *Fearless* was operational once again, and post-refit trials were followed by two amphibious work-up exercises. Both involved elements of 42 Commando, 3 Commando Brigade Air Squadron and 79 Battery, 29 Commando RA. The first was a landing at Browndown Beach and the second, 'Dragon Exchange', a Non-Combatant Evacuation Exercise, took place in early May at Lulworth. For the Royal Marines involved there was a sleepless night setting up a camp to process 'refugees', and the subsequent evacuation and surprise attack by local insurgents was thoroughly quashed. After re-embarking all units *Fearless,* together with the LSLs *Sir Bedivere* and *Sir Tristram,* set course for the Mediterranean and Cyprus. As

An excellent aerial view of *Fearless* with a fuel bowser and a Sea King helicopter on deck. *(Derek Fox collection)*

she steamed south the weather became warmer and all the embarked units were able to carry out valuable training exercises, before everyone relaxed during a three-day stop at Gibraltar. With the visit over, *Fearless* and the RFAs steamed east to Cyprus where the assault ship anchored off Akrotiri in order to land 42 Commando, who were to carry out a week of training exercises in the Akamas area in the north-west of the island, and further south in the Episkopi and Troodos areas. While the embarked force was ashore *Fearless* made a five-day visit to the Israeli port of Haifa, which was hosted by the Israeli Navy who arranged visits to Jerusalem, Bethlehem, Nazareth, the Dead Sea and the nearby ancient site of Masada. Although Haifa was an unusual port of call for the Royal Navy, it had once, during the late nineteenth and early twentieth centuries, and during the British Mandate of Palestine, been a regular port of call for many units. On leaving Haifa *Fearless* returned to Akrotiri to pick up her embarked force before sailing west once again for her passage home. This was marked by an eight-day visit to Lisbon in mid-June, where the embarked force carried out a 36-hour exercise with Portuguese marines and the ship's company enjoyed the attractions of the city. Some members of the ship's company took the opportunity to fly their wives out for the visit, before the assault ship steamed back down the River Tagus to join a Portuguese group for amphibious exercises prior to her return to her home base.

On 30 July 1993, whilst at Portsmouth undergoing a period of assisted maintenance, there was a change of command when Captain A.J.S. Taylor RN joined the ship, and on 1 September she sailed for a shakedown cruise in the Channel which ended in Plymouth Sound three days later. After taking on an embarked force the ship carried out her amphibious work-up in the form of 'Exercise Green Wader' at Browndown Beach in the Solent, following which there was a weekend break at Portsmouth before work began in earnest. *Fearless'* Operational Sea Training began at Portland on Monday 13 September, and it lasted for four arduous weeks. The period included a major disaster relief exercise, involving both a Disaster Exercise, when *Fearless,* with three Sea King helicopters, eight landing craft, two JCBs and the threatened use of the

BARV, completely overwhelmed Flag Officer Sea Training and his staff, and an Evacuation Operation. Every effort was put into making the latter as realistic as possible during the evacuation of the population of the 'Caribbean tourist island of Nosirp', with parts played by 200 Royal Marines, 24 Wrens and 40 teenagers from local schools, who were on 'holiday'. As well as fighting fires, tending the injured and extricating people from ruined buildings, the ship's company, together with landing craft and Sea King crews, also assisted in evacuating the 'tourists', alias sixth form students and their teachers. The work-up was followed by a three-week maintenance period which got under way on 16 October at Portsmouth for, with *Fearless* now the Navy's oldest operational fighting unit, and the last of the operational steam-powered surface ships, her steam turbines, the brickwork of her main boilers and her auxiliary machinery all required a great deal of overhauling. On 8 November, when *Fearless* put to sea again, she carried out amphibious drills in the Solent and seven days later she sailed for Flushing to embark Dutch marines for amphibious exercises off Texel, which included a weekend visit to Rotterdam. By the end of November, however, she had returned to Portsmouth for leave and maintenance.

On 1 February 1994 *Fearless* left Portsmouth for exercises in the Channel, before putting into Plymouth Sound for a long weekend in order to load an embarked force and their equipment. On Monday 7 February the assault ship left the Sound and, in company with the LSLs *Sir Bedivere*, *Sir Galahad* and *Sir Tristram*, she set course for the west coast of Scotland and 'Exercise Tartan Surprise', which saw the landing and continued support of a Commando Logistics force. The LCUs and LCVPs provided a major part of the support, supplying beach units with all manner of stores and equipment. The exercise was followed by amphibious operations in the Cromarty Firth after which, on 18 February, there was a long weekend break at Rosyth which meant a run ashore for the ship's company, while the senior officers attended briefings for the next series of exercises, JMC 941. On 21 February *Fearless* left the Firth of Forth, and headed into some stormy weather to join an impressive array of warships, including *Broadsword*, *Cardiff*, *Avenger* and units of the First Mine Countermeasures Squadron to begin the Joint Maritime Course series of manoeuvres. The amphibious operations took them north to Scapa Flow, Loch Erribol, Loch Ewe and Stornaway Bay to deal with surface, air and submarine attacks during a large-scale amphibious landing against 'enemy' forces all under the watchful eye of an army of camera-wielding members of the national press. With the troops ashore support operations continued day and night in adverse weather conditions, with both the ship's company and the landing craft crews working long hours. Finally, however, on 8 March 'Endex' was called and *Fearless* returned to Plymouth, for the amphibious offload.

On 11 March the assault ship arrived alongside at Portsmouth for leave and maintenance.

It was 25 April when *Fearless* left Portsmouth again and set course for Plymouth Sound to carry out her amphibious embarkation before sailing for the Arctic Circle and exercises in northern Norway in company with *Sir Galahad*, FGS *Glucksburg* and RFA *Orangeleaf*. This was followed by a passage south and exercises with Spanish units en route to Palma, Majorca, where she arrived on 4 May. Gathered in Palma Harbour was a large NATO fleet, while USS *Saratoga* almost filled Palma Bay, all of which meant a run ashore in a very crowded town. The manoeuvres, codenamed 'Dynamic Impact', were major multi-national NATO exercises involving some 93 warships from ten countries, which were designed to test the organization's ability to protect sea lines of communication in the Mediterranean as well as carrying out a major amphibious landing. The aircraft carrier *Ark Royal* led the Royal Navy's contingent which along with *Fearless* included *Edinburgh*, *Coventry* and *Avenger*, as well as the LSLs *Sir Galahad* and *Sir Tristram*, all supported by the RFAs *Fort Austin* and *Orangeleaf*. The part played by *Fearless* in 'Dynamic Impact' was divided into three phases, the first of which was a cross-training package and the second a demanding refugee evacuation exercise. On completion of the first two phases came the main amphibious assault at Cape Teulada, Sardinia, where the embarked force undertook raids, night helicopter and LCU landings and tank and infantry ambushes. On 18 May, with the exercise completed, *Fearless* began her return passage, via Gibraltar and Plymouth Sound, to Portsmouth where, after disembarking her landing craft, she arrived alongside on 27 May.

The highlight of 1994 for *Fearless* and her ship's company came in June when, on both sides of the Channel, the 50th anniversary of the D-Day landings was celebrated, beginning with a Spithead Fleet Review. It was the biggest naval event in home waters since the Queen's 1977 Jubilee celebrations, with some 60 ships making up the D-Day armada. The 16 Royal Navy units committed to the event included *Fearless*, the aircraft carrier *Illustrious* and the destroyer *Edinburgh*, as well as frigates and minesweepers. Among the 24 foreign warships taking part, by far the largest was the mighty 102,000-ton aircraft carrier USS *George Washington*, which dwarfed the other vessels from France, Canada, the Netherlands, Belgium, Norway, Greece and Poland. Among the merchant vessels present were the passenger liners *Canberra* and *QE2*, both veterans of the Falklands Campaign, which had been detailed to take D-Day veterans from Portsmouth to Normandy, as would *Fearless*. Preparations on board *Fearless* began on 3 June when the ship was moved to the Oil Fuel Jetty on the Gosport side of Portsmouth Harbour, and next afternoon she took on an 'embarked force' of veterans from the 'LST and Landing Craft Association',

On 13 March 1995, having completed her amphibious offload at Browndown, Lee-on-Solent, *Fearless* returns to Portsmouth Dockyard.
(Mike Lennon)

journalists and other invited guests. At 14.30 on what was a cloudy and wet day *Fearless* slipped her moorings and steamed out of harbour to take her place with *Illustrious* in the Spithead Review anchorage. By next day the weather had improved, rendering the famous stretch of water an impressive sight. Under a sharp blue sky the sea was churned to a glistening white by foaming wave crests as the wake of many dozens of small boats streaked among the anchored giants. At shortly after midday, preceded by the Trinity House vessel *Patricia* and followed by her escort frigate HMS *Active*, the royal yacht *Britannia*, immaculately dressed overall, nosed out of Portsmouth Harbour. As she steamed out to the Review area she was followed by a swarm of pleasure boats and yachts, and on shore every vantage point was crowded with thousands of spectators. On *Britannia's* after deck there was gathered a galaxy of monarchy, presidents and prime ministers lined up to review the fleet: the Queen and the Duke of Edinburgh, the Princess Royal and Princess Margaret, the President of the United States, Bill Clinton and his wife Hillary, King Harald of Norway, Prince Bernhardt of the Netherlands and the Prime Minister John Major. Other heads of state included President Havel of the Czech Republic, President Kovac of Slovakia and President Walesa of Poland. As the royal flotilla left harbour, a Swordfish biplane headed a fly-past of 120 aircraft, including one of the last serviceable Lancaster bombers, four Spitfires and a Dakota. They were followed by the scream of modern jet engines as Jaguars, Tornadoes and Harriers ripped the Solent sky apart. When *Britannia* approached the double line of ships for review, the aircraft carrier *Illustrious* fired a 42-gun salute, with the whole of the Solent, from Portsmouth to the Isle of Wight, seemingly covered with a seething mass of small ships. As the royal yacht steamed past *Fearless* she was saluted by both the ship's company and the embarked veterans who were manning the decks, and after passing down the Review lines *Britannia* set course across the Channel for Normandy. Simultaneously, the 14 National Flags of the participating nations were embarked from Southsea by LCVP to *Fearless* for the Channel crossing.

At the end of the Review the assembled fleet began to disperse and *Fearless* weighed anchor and set course for Normandy where she was due to take part in the ceremonies off the French coast. At 22.00 she anchored off Arromanches which had been code-named 'Gold Beach' 50 years earlier, in the company of *Edinburgh* (Flag Officer Surface Flotilla, Rear-Admiral M. Boyce) and *Avenger*, USS *Dallas* and *Doyle*, the Belgian frigate *Westdiep*, the French destroyer *Duguay-Trouin*, the Dutch frigate *Abraham van der Hulst*, the Norwegian frigate *Bergen*, the Greek frigate *Adrias* and the Polish landing ship *Krakow*. Meanwhile, on board *Fearless*, among the media complement was the BBC's chief television news reporter Kate Adie who, according to one correspondent, became the focus of attention in the wardroom.

Monday 6 June brought overcast skies, but good visibility, and at dawn *Fearless* and *Edinburgh* weighed anchor to move closer inshore in order to land the National Standards. Commodore Taylor remembers that: 'To the very second, on the beaches of Normandy, the D-Day veterans joined 4 Assault Squadron for a re-enactment. One old boy was given the privilege of putting an LCU on the very beach he had previously seen 50 years before.' As the ramps of the landing craft were lowered on the French beaches, a 21-gun salute from *Edinburgh* shattered the early morning peace, just as the massive naval barrage had done some 50 years earlier. Following the ceremonies *Fearless* set course for Plymouth Sound where, next day, she embarked E Company of the Commando Logistics Regiment, four Gazelle helicopters, and 539 Assault Squadron with two of their Landing Craft Air Cushions (LCACs). These were essentially hovercraft, each of which could carry 16 fully equipped marines in relative comfort over a long distance, and with a choice of landing places. Made of aluminium and powered by diesel engines they had the handling characteristics of a fast boat. However, unlike a boat, they could traverse mud, marsh, ice, snow and flooded areas, easily gaining access to terrain such as tidal mud flats. The hovercraft had a range of 300 miles, which was three times that of a rigid raider, and a top speed of 33 knots.

Fearless was bound for the Caribbean and a ten-week deployment as the West Indies Guardship, which was the first time this duty had been undertaken by an assault ship. During the Atlantic crossing via the Azores amphibious drills were carried out and the helicopters practised day and night landings which came in useful when the squadron was required to carry out a 50-mile casualty evacuation to the Azores, which was combined with a mail run. As *Fearless* was carrying out guardship duties, Captain Taylor decided to replace the Combined Operations funnel badges with the 'yellow bird' of the old West Indies Squadron. This was accomplished by one of the engineering officers who undertook some 'instructive and entertaining abseiling' down the outboard side of the funnels. The first amphibious exercises were carried out off Georgetown, Guyana, where, because of the undredged approaches, *Fearless* had to remain some 20 miles offshore. The Royal Marines of the embarked force were split into two detachments, with one being landed for some gruelling training in the steaming jungles during what was Guyana's wet season. The ship, meanwhile, left the area for Trinidad and on 25 June, whilst at anchor in Staubles Bay, she embarked men of the Trinidad & Tobago Defence Force and a Royal Marines Band. With the embarkation complete *Fearless* steamed to Curacao in company with RFA *Oakleaf,* for amphibious exercises with the Dutch forces, including HNLMS *Willem van der Zaan*. There was time for a long weekend at Willemstad, which was followed by more Anglo-Dutch exercises and manoeuvres, this time in the vicinity of the islands of Grenadine and Tobago. On 10 July the ship was again off Guyana for five days, during which time the ship's company carried out one of the most ambitious aid projects ever undertaken by the Royal Navy.

Despite the distance between the ship and land the Gazelle helicopters, LCUs and LCACs were able to transfer over 200 members of the ship's company ashore. Teams from the assault ship travelled over 30 miles along the Essequibo River to inland settlements to provide much-needed water storage and pumping equipment. Many people in these remote villages had not seen a doctor or a dentist for several years, and medical teams led by the PMO and the dental officer treated over 500 people. A large number of them were inoculated against measles, mumps, rubella and the deadly yellow fever, while 450 of the local people were treated for a variety of conditions, including malaria and glaucoma as well as bone deformities caused by incorrect setting after breakages. The ship's dentist, working from dawn to dusk, treated 400 villagers and extracted 1,000 decayed teeth in the process. In the capital Georgetown, which the working parties reached each day after enduring the long landing craft journey, a home for the elderly was repaired and refurbished, and assistance was also given to the Guyana Coastguard so that they could deal effectively with smuggling and illegal fishing. Their Georgetown base was refitted with redundant naval equipment, as well as £20,000-worth of material funded by the Overseas Development Agency. Two of their patrol craft, which were suffering from a lack of spare parts and maintenance, were taken in LCUs to *Fearless* where they were repaired in the dock. In one village, some 30 miles south of Georgetown, a team from the ship helped to complete the building of a school and repair a wind pump for the village's water supply. During the time spent off the coast Commodore Taylor remembers 'entertaining the President of Guyana, his entire Cabinet, the Commissioner of Police and the British High Commissioner whilst at sea. We received them using four Gazelles, fired a gun salute, paraded a guard and band, and generally did a cracking job entirely under way.' For the magnificent efforts of her ship's company in providing humanitarian aid *Fearless* was subsequently awarded the well-deserved 'Wilkinson Sword of Peace' for 1994.

With the aid package completed, on 15 July the assault ship departed for a three-day break at Trinidad and 'Exercise Cinnamon Fever', an amphibious operation on the island's north coast. During the passage between Trinidad and the island of Montserrat and on to Puerto Rico, the ship operated in conjunction with the US Coastguard, carrying out anti-narcotics operations. For the helicopters this meant overflying various islands to search for marijuana plantations. Arriving at Puerto Rico the ship was based at the massive US naval base at Roosevelt Roads where, for the enjoyment of most, there were beaches, bowling alleys and an enormous US Navy PX (US Forces equivalent of the NAAFI). Following this, on 29 July, she began a three-day visit to Tortola in the British Virgin Islands, where she anchored in Road Bay surrounded by

Flying operations whilst at sea. (Derek Fox collection)

unspoilt islands and beaches. On 31 July the assault ship left Tortola and, with *Oakleaf,* she made a four-day passage to Bermuda and the naval base at Ireland Island. *Fearless* was the last Royal Navy warship to visit the base before its closure and on 9 August, having handed over the duty of West Indies Guardship to *Broadsword,* she set course for home. After a ten-day Atlantic crossing, much of it into strong headwinds, she offloaded the embarked force in Plymouth Sound, before arriving in Portsmouth Dockyard on 20 August for leave and a dockyard assisted maintenance period.

It was on 22 November that *Fearless* put to sea again for a shakedown cruise in the Channel, and by the end of the month she was in Plymouth Sound carrying out her first amphibious embarkation for four months when she took on board men of 40 Commando. The first amphibious exercises took place on Scotland's west coast, in the Loch Fyne and Tobermory areas. On 6 December, at the end of the exercises, *Fearless* became the last big ship to navigate the narrows of the Kyle of Lochalsh before the completion of the Skye Bridge. Commodore Taylor remembers the event: 'In the days leading up to our passage, the Navigating Officer had to check daily with the bridge authorities to see if there was still room for us to pass. In the event, the bridge projected across the narrows at our bridge wing level and we had 30 feet or so on either side. A huge crowd of people gathered to watch us pass through.' The passage through the narrows was followed by a voyage to Den Helder where, between 9 and 12 December, elements of the First Battalion, Royal Netherlands Marine Corps were disembarked before *Fearless* returned to Portsmouth for leave and maintenance.

After leaving harbour on 25 January 1995, despite high winds, rain, snow and ice, the assault ship paid a goodwill visit to her affiliated port of Sunderland, the first major warship to do so since the north-eastern town had become a city. This was followed by a passage south to Plymouth where, over a period of five days at anchor in the Sound, elements of 40 Commando, their transport and equipment were embarked. Once again *Fearless'* amphibious exercises would take place in northern waters, and on 6 February she steamed north for the Sound of Mull to take part in 'Exercise Green Wader', which involved landings close to Tobermory. The second phase took place in Norwegian waters in the area of Andalsnes and Sognefjord. During this period, whilst operating in Laerdalsfjord, the dangers of navigating the ship in these deep, but narrow, waterways was highlighted, as Commodore Taylor remembers: 'We were steaming at ten knots up the fjord when we lost one boiler, the other was swiftly cross-connected. At this point we were approaching a particularly narrow part of the fjord and it seemed to be sensible to reverse course and seek more sea room. Good decision! Within five minutes or so the flame went out in the second boiler! The options were limited - we had three cables clear water in any direction and with 25 knots of wind, we were slowly edging onshore. As anchoring was not an option (water too deep) and as all the landing craft, except one LCVP, had been detached, there was little we could do other than await the best efforts of the Marine Engineering Department. The single LCVP was launched and it did what it could to push against the prevailing wind. The RMAS tug which had been detached from Rosyth for the duration of the winter deployment was unserviceable so our only other hope was HMS *Roebuck* - some 14 miles, or about an hour's steaming, away. *Roebuck* was ordered to prepare for towing aft. In the meantime the fjord sides were steep-to so there was no danger of grounding - we would have made a heavy alongside. All available fenders were prepared. However, after an hour or so Commander (E) advised that he had steam available in one boiler and I could sue 30 revs to crawl in the right direction. All was well! After the obligatory investigation it was discovered that the loss of both boilers was attributed to water in the fuel caused by a perforated diesel pipe which penetrated a ballast tank. The real mistake was the fact that both boilers were being fed from the same fuel tank, which was never repeated in my time.'

The main exercise, 'Green Wader', began on 20 February when *Fearless* rendezvoused with the UK task group, and amphibious operations continued in northern Norway until 9 March when the assault ship set course for Portsmouth, arriving in the Solent three days later. On 13 March, with the amphibious offload at Browndown having been completed, *Fearless* secured alongside Portsmouth Dockyard to begin a period of leave and maintenance. On 4 April 1995, whilst *Fearless* was alongside at Portsmouth, there was another change of command when Captain R. A. I. McLean OBE RN took over from Captain Taylor.

When the assault ship put to sea again and completed her shakedown cruise she headed south for 'Exercise Destined Glory' for which the rocky shores and the warmer weather of the Mediterranean provided a backdrop. Flying the broad pennant of the Commodore Amphibious Warfare, Commodore Paul Cantor, *Fearless* led a large multi-national amphibious task force, which included the US Navy's *Kearsarge, Nashville* and *Pensacola,* the Spanish ships *Castilla* and *Hernan Cortez,* the Italian *San Marco* and the Greek vessels *Krito* and *Samos*. The amphibious units and their escorts rendezvoused off Cape Teulada to begin a phased training exercise which was designed to fully integrate amphibious operations in NATO navies. It saw an imaginative programme of cross-operating between units of the seven nations involved, with landing craft of all shapes and sizes working from a range of ramps and well decks.

Some 41 helicopters were employed, including the giant US Navy CH46, and more valuable experience was gained operating from a variety of flight decks. The exercise ended with a night assault landing over four Sardinian beaches and the successful reinstatement of a 'deposed president'. For *Fearless* however, the deployment was marred somewhat by mechanical problems in the engine room, forcing her to put into Palma, Majorca for temporary repairs. On her return to Portsmouth the assault ship was dry docked for a few days in order that permanent repairs could be carried out, prior to her last major exercise before undergoing an assisted refit.

In June 1995, flying the broad pennant of Commodore Cantor, *Fearless* left Portsmouth to rendezvous with the destroyer *Gloucester,* the frigates *Brave, Brazen* and *Brilliant,* the mine countermeasures vessels *Berkeley, Brocklesby, Chiddingfold, Ledbury, Middleton* and *Sandown,* the RFAs *Argus, Fort Victoria* and *Orangeleaf* and the LSLs *Sir Geraint* and *Sir Tristram.* They were to represent the Royal Navy in JMC 952, exercises which were held three times each year to provide multi-national training. They were joined for the manoeuvres, which were held off Scotland's east coast, by surface units from the USA, Norway, Germany, France, Italy, Denmark and the Netherlands, with the nuclear-powered submarine *Triumph,* together with one German and two Norwegian submarines providing the underwater involvement. The exercise took place over a two-week period with air and sea attacks, together with a submarine phase and coordinated shore bombardment. The amphibious element, code-named 'Exercise Tartan Venture', brought the Royal Marines Logistics Regiment, embarked in *Fearless,* into their own with a landing on the beaches of Loch Ewe by LCUs, Chinook, Sea King and Gazelle helicopters, before the troops moved across country to the Moray Firth area. Witnessing the action from *Fearless* was the First Sea Lord, Admiral Sir Benjamin Bathurst, together with a party of Heads of European Navies - who quickly became known as the 'Hen Party'. After witnessing a steam-past and fly-past the senior officers disembarked to observe events ashore and at the end of the exercise *Fearless* set course for Portsmouth. During the passage, on 8 June, the ship's company gathered on the flight deck, as they had done every year since 1982, to commemorate the 13th anniversary of the deaths of six members of the crew of LCU *F4* during the Falklands Campaign. Next day, off Spithead, the LCUs were used to ferry 600 relatives and friends of the ship's company out to the assault ship for a Families Day of flying demonstrations and static displays, with a clown, Punch and Judy show and a bouncy castle for the younger guests. Finally, after a very busy programme, *Fearless* steamed up harbour to secure alongside and to prepare for an extended maintenance period which would keep her out of service for the remainder of the year.

Chapter Eight

HMS *Fearless* - Return To The Middle East 1995-2002

The refit on *Fearless* during the second half of 1995 was the largest work package undertaken by Portsmouth's Fleet Maintenance and Repair Organization since major refits ended in the dockyard some four years previously. The schedule during the assault ship's Docking and Essential Defects period was designed to keep her in service right into the twenty-first century, and it proved to be a formidable challenge that tested everyone's skills to the limit. Ten miles of heavy electrical cable were installed, together with 1,250 new pipes and 4,500 electrical components. The ship's galley was almost completely renewed, being converted from steam to electrical power and older electrical appliances being replaced with modern equipment. Likewise, the ship's laundry was converted from steam to electrical power. Perhaps the most formidable challenge was the overhaul of *Fearless'* main propulsion machinery, which was hampered by a badly corroded bulkhead, sub-zero temperatures during the winter months and, most seriously of all, in October 1995, by a fire in one of the boiler economisers. For their part in fighting the fire two of the Engineering Department's senior rates, CPOMEMs R. Renshaw and M. George, both received C-in-C's Commendations. At one stage in the refit it was rumoured that *Fearless'* corrosion problem would make it impossible for her to take part in spring exercises off the east coast of the USA, but these were quickly denied by the MoD whose spokesman declared that, 'The (rust) problems that have been uncovered are considered normal for a ship of *Fearless'* age.' Because of the unexpected problems work on *Fearless* fell behind schedule, but the delays were not sufficient to affect her commitments and by the end of February 1996 the refit was coming to an end.

On 6 March 1996 *Fearless* left Portsmouth to undergo a seven-day trials period, but this was marred by the death, on 12 March, of the ship's Weapons Engineer Officer, Lt-Cdr B. McClenaghan. The ship was at sea in the Channel at the time and although a Coastguard helicopter flew him to RNH Haslar, he was pronounced dead on arrival. After rectifying defects which had arisen during the trials period, on 23 March the assault ship left Portsmouth once again, this time for a work-up period and to prepare for the next deployment, which would take her to the east coast of the United States and the Caribbean. During the deployment she would carry an embarked force consisting of elements of 3 Commando Brigade and Sea King helicopters of 846 Squadron, together with personnel. *Fearless* was to play a leading role in 'Exercise Purple Star', which would bring together over 50,000 British and American service personnel in the largest mobilization of Anglo-American forces since the Gulf War of 1991. As well as *Fearless* the British maritime task force of 30 ships, led by *Illustrious* (flag Rear-Admiral Alan West), included the destroyers *Glasgow*, *Manchester* and *Southampton* and the frigates *Argyll* and *Cumberland,* while the smallest units to make the Atlantic crossing were the minehunters *Berkeley, Bridport, Chiddingfold* and *Cromer.* The submarines *Splendid* and *Trenchant* provided the task group with intelligence and conducted 'attacks' on opposing forces, which were made up of both RN and USN vessels. *Fearless* and the Royal Marines were involved in a dawn assault on the beaches of North Carolina, in conjunction with the US Marines, but unfortunately this particular part of the operation was marred by a mid-air collision between two US helicopters as they took part in an assault on beaches at Camp Le Jeune training base. The manoeuvres provided *Illustrious* and the carrier group with the first real chance to engage in deep water exercises for three years, after a long commitment in the Adriatic which had ended only two months earlier. The 25-day exercise was directed by Vice-Admiral Clark USN from the command ship USS *Mount Whitney,* and on its conclusion Admiral Clark showed his appreciation for the Royal Navy's contribution as follows: 'During the past three weeks, you, the men and women of the UK Task Group, distinguished yourselves in the most complex combined joint operation in recent history. The vigour with which you approached the months of planning, preparation for deployment and training in the Atlantic crossing was clearly evident as we joined forces. You brought considerable expertise to the exercise and we were all the better for it. Above, on and under the sea, your warfighting skills were magnificent. It was my distinct pleasure and honour to serve with you during this exercise. Well done, thank you, and fair winds and following seas as you proceed on duties assigned and transit home.'

For *Fearless* the 'duties assigned' meant a passage south to the Caribbean area for operations with US forces near the island of Vieques. In early June, whilst on passage from Vieques to Curacao for exercises with Dutch marines, a request for assistance was received from the US Coastguard. A Dutch merchantman, MV *Elizabeth Boye,* had recovered the wreckage of a speedboat close to Puerto

A fine aerial view of *Fearless* at sea. *(Official, courtesy of Maritime Books, Liskeard)*

Rico and although one of the occupants was dead, a second man, a St Lucian islander, was alive, but suffering from severe dehydration and delirium after drinking sea water for the 18 days that the boat had been drifting. Three other members of the boat's crew had been lost at sea. *Fearless* immediately set course towards the *Elizabeth Boye,* which had no medical facilities on board, and when she was within 200 miles of the ship, a Sea King helicopter made a night flight carrying the ship's PMO, Surg-Cdr Adrian Baker, who was winched down to the merchantman's deck. After stabilizing the seriously ill patient, both men were winched into the helicopter and flown back to *Fearless.* The Sea King then refuelled and flew the patient to hospital at Curacao. Five days later the Sea King was called upon to make a second mercy mission, this time to ferry a badly injured seaman to hospital in Trinidad from the MV *Francis Lee,* following an accident in which he had been hit by a flailing winch wire and had suffered serious lacerations to his arms and other parts of his body.

Following her involvement in 'Exercise Purple Star' *Fearless* led the LSLs *Sir Galahad, Sir Geraint* and *Sir Tristram* in a number of unit level training exercises codenamed 'Caribex 96', which culminated in 'Exercise Green Fever' in Belize. This was the execution of a large-scale evacuation plan following an 'earthquake', which had led to outbreaks of disease and civil unrest. It involved 3 Commando Brigade and also brought together more than 2,000 British service personnel and troops of the Belize Defence Force. Many ex-pat Britons and local Belizeans provided the 300 willing 'evacuees', some of whom had never seen a helicopter or warship before, and their participation added vital realism to the exercise. The task group was joined by the West Indies guardship HMS *Argyll* and its tanker *Gold Rover,* before anchoring close to the Guatemalan border off Punta Gorda. So that local people would not be alarmed by the large movement of troops, the LCUs and Sea Kings landed 42 Commando Group under cover of darkness. This also allowed the troops to establish themselves quickly and efficiently and once ashore the commandos, including the 4th Assault Squadron and members of the ship's company from *Fearless,* deployed with their vehicles into an area covering some 800 square kilometres. By first light they were ready to assist the 'evacuees', including children and elderly people, who had to be located before being moved to evacuation areas which was no easy task in a difficult terrain with a population spread over a wide area and with little in the way of communications. Assistance was also given by local officials who were able to provide details of British nationals and their last known whereabouts. The evacuees were gathered together in small settlements at the base of the Maya Mountains before they were moved to the coast, with Sea King helicopters providing the only means of transport in such inaccessible areas. Their crews were tested to the limit, having to contend with high temperatures and violent thunderstorms throughout. Nevertheless, the 300 civilian participants in the exercise were gathered together and moved to reception areas in the southern coastal towns of Punta Gorda and Independence. After registration the LCUs and helicopters transferred them to *Fearless* and *St Geraint,* and then at the end of the exercise it was back to school, work or service with the Voluntary Service Overseas organization, or in the case of some volunteers, 'Operation Raleigh'. The whole exercise, which was witnessed by senior officials from neighbouring countries, was judged to have been a great success and extremely realistic, despite the beaming smiles of some of the 'distressed' schoolchildren. At the end of June, after completing her three and a half-month deployment, *Fearless* returned to Portsmouth for leave and maintenance.

It was 14 October 1996 when *Fearless* left harbour again for three days of exercises in the Channel and on 21 October she sailed for ten days of manoeuvres before returning to Portsmouth to prepare for the next major deployment, which would take her east of Suez for the first time since May 1970. *Fearless* would spend seven months in the Middle and Far East in what was to be named 'Operation Ocean Wave', which would encompass the handover of Britain's last Asian Crown Colony, Hong Kong, to the Chinese Government. The 'Ocean Wave' task group was led by the aircraft carrier *Illustrious* (flag Rear-Admiral Alan West), with *Fearless* flying the pennant of Commodore Paul Stone, the Commodore Amphibious Warfare. Also included in the group were the destroyer *Gloucester,* the frigates *Beaver* and *Richmond,* the nuclear-powered fleet submarine *Trenchant,* and the LSLs *Sir Galahad, Sir Geraint* and *Sir Percivale,* with the RFAs *Fort Austin, Fort George* and *Olna* in support. In addition, during the deployment, the task group would be joined for periods of up to three months by the frigates *Chatham* and *Iron Duke,* the fleet submarine *Trafalgar,* and the survey ship *Herald.* One of the prime reasons for 'Ocean Wave 97' was to enable the Navy to maintain its experience of deployed carrier and task group operations. To achieve this the group would take part in several exercises, the two most important being 'Flying Fish', an air defence and anti-submarine exercise off Malaysia with forces from the Five Power defence agreement which covered South-East Asia, Malaysia, Singapore, Australia and New Zealand, and 'Exercise Setia Kawan'. The latter, which was to be an amphibious exercise with Brunei's armed forces, would be led by *Fearless*. The 'Ocean Wave' units would also exercise with a number of other regional navies and carry out hot weather trials of the Sea Harrier FA2s, the RAF GR7s, and Lynx Mk 8 helicopters.

On 10 December 1996, whilst *Fearless* was undergoing maintenance at Portsmouth, Captain M. S. Williams RN took command of the assault ship and four weeks later, on 14 January 1997 with Christmas and New Year leave over,

Fearless with Sea Kings on deck in Holland's New Waterway during September 1998. *(Mike Lennon)*

Fearless left harbour to steam down Channel for sea training before heading for Plymouth Sound where she embarked 300 Royal Marines from 40 Commando, together with their vehicles and equipment, and two Sea Kings from 845 and 846 Squadrons at Yeovilton. The crossing of the Bay of Biscay was bumpy, but by the time the assault ship reached Gibraltar, warm and sunny Mediterranean weather had taken over. The Greek port of Piraeus provided a four-day break for both ship's company and the embarked force, and many were able to take in the cultural sights of Athens before *Fearless* sailed south for Port Said. There was an historic day for *Fearless* when, on 1 February, for the first time since 25 September 1966, over 30 years previously, she sailed south through the Suez Canal. She had joined the royal yacht *Britannia* for the occasion, which saw the Navy's last two steam-powered surface ships working together. After anchoring in the Great Bitter Lake in order to allow a northbound convoy of ships to pass, *Fearless* completed her transit and once into the Red Sea maritime training was resumed. On 7 February there was a short stop at the barren French port of Djibouti, which has been described as being even more desolate than Aden. Here, in temperatures of 35°C (95°F) and stifling humidity, 40 Commando was able to go ashore for fitness training. After leaving Djibouti *Fearless* carried out an amphibious exercise, which was marked by severe thunderstorms, before she set course east for the fresher breezes of the Arabian Sea and the Indian subcontinent. During the 1,500-mile passage from North Africa to Goa, RAS exercises were carried out and while *Fearless* and two of the LSLs visited Indian ports, the RFAs headed west to meet the Carrier Task Group. On 16 February *Fearless* put into the former Portuguese colony of Goa on India's west coast for a four-day break, before setting course for Brunei on the north-west coast of the island of Borneo.

On 3 March *Fearless* anchored off the port of Muara, Brunei, where the Brunei armed forces were given landing craft training, and 40 Commando was disembarked to carry out jungle training in the steaming rainforests of Borneo. In the meantime *Fearless* made a short visit to the neighbouring Malaysian state of Sabah (formerly North Borneo), before returning to Brunei and then setting course for Singapore and the Sembawang Shipyard, which appeared little changed from the 1960s when it was the Royal Navy's dockyard and naval base. During the ten-day maintenance period at Sembawang a group of senior amphibious warfare officers joined the ship, and on 26 March *Fearless* set course for Brunei and the major amphibious exercise, 'Setia Kawan', which translated means 'Loyal Friend'. This was the first Far Eastern exercise in 25 years for the Royal Marines of 40 Commando and, after having honed their skills for a chilly war in Arctic climes, the saturating and debilitating heat of tropical rainforest made for a complete change of environment. The exercise ran for three weeks between 29 March and 19 April and joining *Fearless* and the three LSLs were *Illustrious*, *Gloucester* and other units. *Fearless* acted as the marines' headquarters afloat from where Brigadier Tony Milton and

97

In October 2000, with her ship's company and Royal Marines manning ship *Fearless* arrives in Malta's Grand Harbour, and ...

his staff directed the strategy. The part of the 'enemy' was played by the resident battalion of Gurkhas and men of the Brunei Army, and air mobile and amphibious landings were made in order to outflank the opposition, with 'battles' raging over most of Brunei, involving both conventional and guerrilla tactics. Meanwhile the LCUs of the 4th Assault Squadron used Brunei's rivers, the highways of the rainforest, to move men and supplies inland. For all those involved in operations ashore, Royal Marines, engineers or squadron air fitters, the constant high temperatures, with saturating and enervating humidity, made heat exhaustion a real problem. Nevertheless, despite all the difficulties, the exercise was a real success and on 22 April *Fearless* arrived back at Singapore's Sembawang Dockyard, where everyone could relax as the assault ship began a three-week assisted maintenance period.

It had been in September 1969 when *Fearless* last underwent an assisted period of dockyard maintenance at Singapore, and during those 27 years wide-bodied passenger aircraft and package holidays had helped to 'shrink' the world. On this occasion some 200 relatives of ship's company members were able to fly out to Singapore to make a holiday of the period spent alongside. On 15 May, however, it was back to business as *Fearless* left Singapore to take part in 'Exercise Muka Wave', which took 40 Commando back to the jungle regions where, in the 1950s, their predecessors had fought during the Malayan Emergency. This time the amphibious landings were staged off the east coast of Malaysia, following which *Fearless* called at Kuantan, with its beautiful unspoilt beaches. During the first two weeks of June the assault ship returned to the Brunei area, where 40 Commando and some ship's company members carried out advanced jungle training and survival courses. On 15 June, having joined *Illustrious*, *Fearless* made a four-day visit to Manila before steaming out into the South China Sea where the whole task force regrouped for exercises during the run-up to the handover of Hong Kong and the New Territories to the Chinese Government. Following the handover ceremonies, which took place during the evening of 30 June 1997, the whole task group formed two lines in the international waters off the mainland of China to greet the royal yacht *Britannia,* flying the Royal Standard of HRH the Prince of Wales and with the colony's last Governor embarked. As the royal yacht passed between the two lines all available hands were manning each ship to cheer her. With the steam-past over Prince Charles sent the following signal to the flotilla: 'I am enormously grateful to you all for the magnificent steam-past this afternoon. The sight of such a large and very obviously capable force together in such close company was both stirring and memorable. I send my heartfelt thanks to you all and wish you continuing success for the remainder of this important deployment and a safe return to your families. Splice the Main Brace.' Next day eight of the group's Sea King and Lynx helicopters, and five Harriers, performed a sunset fly-past.

With the handover of Hong Kong and the accompanying ceremonial completed, all that remained was for the task group to disperse. *Illustrious* and her battle group left for a high profile visit to Australian ports, while

...she secures alongside Laboratory Wharf, Carradino.
(*Both Michael Cassar, Valletta, Malta*)

Chatham and the Hong Kong Squadron sailed for Manila, and *Fearless, Sir Galahad* and *Sir Geraint* set course for Singapore. Once alongside at Sembawang the Royal Marines of 40 Commando disembarked for flights to South Africa, where they were to take part in training exercises, and on 7 July *Fearless* left Singapore to make her passage home. In the Indian Ocean severe gales and storms were encountered, and towards the end of July she made a short stop at Haifa. Finally, however, on Monday 4 August 1997, after an absence of seven and a half months, *Fearless* returned to her base port of Portsmouth. Dressed overall and, appropriately for a warm and pleasant summer's day, with the ship's company manning the flight and weather decks in their tropical white uniforms, the assault ship received a rousing reception as she proudly entered harbour before securing alongside. She had steamed some 27,000 miles and the 170 members of her Engineering Department had worked magnificently, often in unbearably hot conditions, to keep her elderly machinery running. Now, however, there was leave to look forward to and further maintenance to complete.

With the ship once again in dockyard hands, and with ever-increasing delays to the completion of the replacement assault ship *Albion*, it was becoming apparent that *Fearless* would have to soldier on for longer than had been originally envisaged. Rumours about the corroded state of *Fearless'* hull began to circulate and in one report *The Times* reported that the ship was, 'so badly corroded that there are fears it may not be able to return to sea.' However, these proved to be greatly exaggerated and at least with her sister *Intrepid* laid up at Portsmouth there was a ready source of spare parts upon which to draw, for it was unlikely that she would ever go to sea under her own steam again. As well as essential maintenance to her hull and machinery *Fearless* also underwent a notable improvement to the flight deck equipment when all the lighting was fitted with a revolutionary filter which made the lights almost invisible to pilots wearing night vision goggles. Previously flight deck personnel had to work in total darkness while at night flying stations, but once fitted the glass filters gave out a pale blue glow and suppressed all infra-red light. Another major task for the dockyard was the fitting of a new 42-ton stern gate to the assault ship, and new air-conditioning units were installed, as well as a 1007 radar aerial. In addition the ship's communications equipment was upgraded. Finally, in late January 1998, with all the work having been completed, *Fearless* was ready for sea once again.

During February *Fearless* carried out operational sea training, during which she operated from Plymouth Sound and landed elements of 40 Commando at Pentewan Sands near Mevagissey. This was followed by exercises 'Green Wader', 'Strong Resolve' and 'Destined Glory', the first of which took place in Scandinavia, in driving rain, gale force winds and heavy snowfalls. It was designed to test the Navy's ability to launch an amphibious assault in the Arctic region, and for *Fearless* it marked the return to the region after an absence of three years. In sharp contrast to the steaming rainforests of South-East Asia which had been encountered during 'Ocean Wave', 'Green Wader' took place well inside the Arctic Circle, close to the Norwegian town of Nesna, where the assault ship worked alongside her old friends, the LSLs *Sir Galahad, Sir Geraint, Sir Percivale* and *Sir Tristram,* as well as RFA *Argus,* using her landing craft, Sea Kings and Gazelle helicopters to help move more than 900 members of a combined force of Royal and Dutch Marines ashore. Although there were interludes of still weather, which revealed the majestic scenery of the Norwegian fjords, most of the exercise took place during stormy weather which tested everyone to their limits. The second exercise, 'Strong Resolve', saw *Fearless* sail directly from Norway to Quiberon Bay where the first landings were made in conjunction with FS *Foudre.* The final major exercise, 'Destined Glory', which began in late April, involved units from 25 countries, together with over 50,000 service personnel. *Fearless* and her group steamed south to Cartagena in southern Spain where the amphibious and maritime task groups rendezvoused. During this phase of the exercise the assault ship operated two Sea Kings from 845 Squadron, as well as two Gazelle and two Lynx helicopters from the Commando Helicopter Force, which meant six aircraft were competing for two spots on the flight deck. This was a real problem for the ship's aviation officer, and it gave him and his aircraft handlers a daily game of flight deck chess. During the transit south there was a naval gunfire support serial with the destroyer *Gloucester,* and also a minor panic in *Fearless* when the ship's refrigeration machinery broke down. This meant an early diversion to Cartagena before all the frozen food defrosted, but for the ship's company this provided an unexpected opportunity to spend two days sampling the Spanish 'culture'. On 5 May, with the refrigeration problem eased by the addition of two 40-ft portable food freezers to an already crowded flight deck, *Fearless* sailed for the amphibious landings, which began three days later. The helicopters undertook cross-training with USS *Wasp* and the Italian ship *San Marco,* as well as ferrying an Armed Forces Pay Review Body and a BBC film crew around the British fleet. It was said that the issue of 'flying pay' was discussed at 2,000 feet with the helicopter door open, and for *Fearless* there was a brief appearance on the 'Nine O' Clock News'. On completion of the amphibious phase the Task Group made an 'opposed' transit to Sierra del Retin on the south-west coast of Spain for the final exercises and a VIP day, both of which were hampered by thick sea mists. The exercise ended on 21 May, and it was followed by a three-day 'wash up' at Rota and a visit to nearby Cadiz. Two weeks later, in early June, *Fearless* returned to Portsmouth.

On 28 August 1998 there was a change of command, when Captain J. R. Fanshawe RN took over from Captain Williams, and *Fearless* took part in Portsmouth's International Festival of the Sea, which combined Navy Days with an extravaganza of tall ships and dockyard attractions. Prior to her autumn exercises the assault ship paid a visit to her affiliated town of Scarborough, and for the passage north from Plymouth Sound she was joined by 70 invited guests, including council representatives from the seaside town, children and their teachers from local schools and Sea Cadets. During the visit, as well as ferrying liberty men between the ship and shore, the landing craft crews rescued five members of a 'coxed-four' rowing boat which had capsized in a choppy sea. When she was opened to the public over 1,500 visitors made the journey out to *Fearless* at her anchorage which, once again, kept the landing craft crews very busy. The autumn of 1998 saw *Fearless* taking part, with the newly commissioned HMNLS *Rotterdam,* in the multi-national JMC 983, the biggest such exercise held off Scotland. The manoeuvres involved a total of 47 ships from 12 countries, with the Royal Navy's contribution including *Invincible, Fearless, Glasgow, Liverpool, Manchester, Lancaster* and *Westminster.* The amphibious force assembled at Faslane and included *Fearless, Sir Galahad, Sir Percivale* and *Rotterdam,* with Commodore Niall Kilgour flying his pennant in *Fearless,* and leading Task Group Two. This time the assault ship carried out landings at Loch Eriboll, and the 4th Assault Squadron took on an unusual duty when, after a request from a local farmer, they ferried a flock of sheep across the loch. With the exercise over and having dropped the embarked force at Plymouth Sound, *Fearless* returned to Portsmouth for her winter maintenance period.

On Wednesday 12 May 1999 *Fearless* left Portsmouth for what was to be a landmark in her long career, joint exercises with the newly completed, purpose-built helicopter carrier HMS *Ocean.* The new ship was a sign of government recognition of the importance of amphibious operations, but it also highlighted the fact that *Fearless,* at 34 years of age, was nearing the end of her operational life. During the exercises both *Fearless* and *Ocean* were put on standby for a possible diversion to the Adriatic, where a NATO-led force from European countries was undertaking peacekeeping duties in war-torn Kosovo. The manoeuvres culminated at the end of May in 'Exercise Aurora' off the coast of Devon, where *Fearless* led *Ocean, Sir Bedivere, Sir Galahad* and *Edinburgh* in a joint amphibious and helicopter landing, the like of which had not been seen since the days of the commando carriers *Albion* and *Bulwark.* At the end of the exercise, with *Ocean* fully worked up, *Fearless* paid a two-day courtesy visit to Hamburg where the German 'culture', including the Reeperbahn, was enjoyed by all. The assault ship's next major deployment, in the Mediterranean, had been programmed for September 1999, but with a possible role to play in military operations in the Adriatic, it was brought forward and in mid-August *Fearless* left Portsmouth for Plymouth Sound where she would take on board her embarked force. Over 20 warships and auxiliaries, including *Fearless* (pennant Commodore Niall Kilgour) and *Ocean* then left home waters for the Mediterranean, where they joined American, French and Egyptian forces for exercises which would end with a huge land, sea and air assault at El Alamein in Egypt. It was also the first major test of the Navy's new Amphibious Ready Group, of which *Fearless* was a vital part, which had been set up to enable a Royal Marines Commando force to be deployed anywhere in the world at immediate notice. After a spectacular departure from Plymouth Sound, *Fearless* and *Ocean,* carrying 40 Commando and a mixed force of Sea King, Gazelle and Lynx helicopters, together with *Edinburgh* and their RFA support ships, sailed for the eastern Mediterranean. Exercises were held en route with French, Portuguese and Spanish units, with port visits to Gibraltar and Naples, before they headed for the Aegean and 'Exercise Northern Approaches', which was held off the coast of Turkey at Saros Bay. Despite being the Navy's oldest, and last, operational steam-powered surface ship *Fearless* proved her credentials by acting as the command centre for the staff, as a refuelling platform for the amphibious task group helicopters and, with her landing craft, as one of the busiest beach units. At Saros the Royal Marines 'fought' alongside Turkish and American units during the beach assault and faced heavy opposition from Turkish infantry and armour during five days of non-stop action. During this period the opportunity was taken to assist the Turkish authorities in the wake of a disastrous earthquake, and almost 100 sailors and marines gave blood, which was the most urgent requirement. The exercises off Turkey were, however, the forerunners to the much larger, 'Exercise Bright Star', which involved 70,000 personnel from seven countries. First, however, there was a second visit to Naples by *Fearless, Ocean, Sir Galahad* and *Edinburgh,* which was marred somewhat by a small group of sailors in Sorrento who were involved in what the police described as a 'drunken rampage', which led to a ban on the sale of alcohol for 48 hours and some very unwelcome publicity.

The British contingent of the international flotilla involved in 'Bright Star', which was hosted by Egypt and involved a massive amphibious landing near the Second World War battlefield of El Alamein, included *Fearless, Ocean, Edinburgh, Cumberland,* three LSLs and four minehunters. The embarked forces in the amphibious ships included 1,242 men from 3 Commando Brigade, and following the landings, which were hampered by heavy surf, there was a live firing attack in support of land forces at El Alamein, with 500 Royal Marines using their full range of weapons. At the height of the exercise 540 fighter aircraft, bombers, tankers and reconnaissance aircraft were taking part, 135 of them from USS *John F. Kennedy.* In addition there were over 900 battlefield vehicles, from Egyptian, French, German, Greek, Italian, Jordanian, Kuwaiti, Dutch, US and UK forces, with the majority of British marines and their armour, together with the Egyptian main battle tanks, being landed from the Royal Navy's amphibious ships. After 'Bright Star' the amphibious task group split up for visits to Mediterranean ports, before undertaking more regional exercises with local forces. In November, having detached from the main group, *Fearless* steamed into the Black Sea to conduct exercises with Bulgaria and Romania, as well as staging an amphibious warfare demonstration off the Crimean port of Sevastopol. In early December, with her part in the deployment over, *Fearless* returned to Portsmouth. As a sign of the affection in which *Fearless* was held by those who served in her, Brigadier David Wilson RM remarked, 'She is an old lady but she is a real character and a happy character.' Commodore Niall Kilgour (COMAW) commented, 'She is well built and she is run extremely well. They have a very motivated ship's company and an experienced ship's company. We thrive on operating her old machinery.' Lieutenant Russ Strudwick RN, the Captain's Secretary, who had served in *Fearless* both as a senior rate and as a commissioned officer, summed up the feelings of the ship's company as a whole: 'There are a lot of people who feel a great sense of pride that they are serving in HMS *Fearless.*' He went on to say: 'I served in her between 1992 and 1994 as a senior rate before becoming an officer and I was surprised to see so many familiar faces when I returned. People love to come back. Once they have served in her she wins a place in their hearts, even if she is old and rusty.'

On 7 December 1999 Captain C. J. Parry RN took over the command of *Fearless* and the ship herself, now costing in the region of almost £25 million a year to keep operational, began another period of extended maintenance. On 26 January 2000, what could have been a serious incident was averted when, at about 08.15, sailors working in the ship saw smoke and the alarm was raised. Fortunately, a petty officer quickly extinguished the fire which had been started by stray sparks from a welding torch, and apart from five members of the ship's company and two dockyard workers being treated for smoke inhalation, there was little damage caused. On 10 July 2000, having spent over six months in dockyard hands, *Fearless* was once again back in business and carrying out her operational sea training, which included 'Exercise Fearless Dragon' - a landing at Lulworth Cove. The fact that the old lady had been prepared for sea in just six months was no mean feat and Captain Parry remarked: 'We were set a tall order, to prepare the ship to rejoin the fleet after six months alongside in half the time which most ships have. The ship's company has worked miracles over the last few weeks and the result is a tribute to their efforts. We are now ready for our forthcoming deployment and going out to do what we do best.'

Following her sea training she visited Scarborough

before returning to Portsmouth to prepare for her next operational deployment, 'Exercise Argonaut 2000', in the Mediterranean. Leaving Portsmouth on 14 September, *Fearless* embarked Royal Marines of 42 Commando in Plymouth Sound before heading south with *Ocean, Northumberland* and other units. Once again the 'Argonaut' exercises would put the amphibious task group through its paces in an exercise off Turkey, which involved a substantial number of ships and amphibious forces from a number of nations. It would also build on established relationships from previous goodwill visits to Mediterranean countries. The first exercise, 'Rock Wader', took place off Gibraltar where, in company with *Ocean* and HMNLS *Rotterdam*, a landing was made on the beaches of the Crown Colony. After spending the first two weeks of the deployment in the Gibraltar area, *Fearless* steamed east and, before commencing exercises off the coast of Turkey, she put into Malta's Grand Harbour with *Northumberland* to renew an acquaintance which went back to the mid-1960s with her last visit being made in 1978. As she had secured alongside Laboratory Wharf, Carradino, for security reasons the ship could not hold an open day, but for many members of the ship's company it was a chance to visit old haunts in Valletta and around the island.

On 5 October both ships left Malta and set course for the Aegean for a major exercise, 'Destined Glory 2000', the initial planning for which was conducted off Izmir before the task group sailed to Saros Bay, north of the Gallipoli peninsula, where the main landings took place. Afterwards *Fearless* paid an informal visit to the Turkish port of Antalya and on 29 October, whilst at the port, she was ordered to sail for Sierra Leone where the Royal Marines of 42 Commando would support the UN peacekeeping force which had been established in the troubled country. Leaving Antalya on 31 October *Fearless* set course to rendezvous with the remainder of the group, including *Ocean,* but at 04.15 on 2 November, when the ship was some 150 miles off Sicily, a fire broke out in the engine room. Although the blaze was extinguished by the ship's fire-fighting teams, nine members of the ship's company were treated for smoke inhalation and two for heat exhaustion. As a result the assault ship was withdrawn from the deployment to Sierra Leone and instead she limped into Malta where temporary repairs could be carried out. The enforced stop was limited to just a long weekend, and on 6 November *Fearless* set course for home. During the nine-day passage there was further drama when, 120 miles south of Ushant, she picked up fishermen's radio chatter indicating that a crewman on one of their vessels was in urgent need of medical treatment. Although the trawler was further out in the Atlantic the Lynx helicopter from the accompanying frigate *Montrose* was immediately launched, and after collecting *Fearless*' medical officer, Surg-Lt-Cdr Duncan Blair, the trawler was located. On a pitch dark night, with high winds and a heavy sea, in an operation which was extremely difficult and hazardous, the doctor was lowered onto the deck of the violently rolling and erratically pitching trawler. The patient was then stabilized before being flown back to *Fearless,* and on to hospital at Plymouth. As a result of his bravery Lt-Cdr Blair was awarded a C-in-C's Commendation. The assault ship herself limped into a Spithead anchorage during the morning of 15 November, and next afternoon she steamed up harbour to secure alongside Portsmouth Dockyard. This time, although she had been away for three months, for the first time the ship's company had been able to use new technology in the form of mobile telephones and e-mails to keep in touch with their loved ones. Nevertheless, there were emotional scenes as the assault ship returned to her base port. Once again she was to undergo an extensive maintenance period as she soldiered on as the Navy's only operational amphibious ship.

As well as essential repairs to her engine room, which at one stage during the fire had been flooded to a depth of some seven feet, the landing craft were refitted and her electrical and steam systems were overhauled. Despite the fact that her sister *Intrepid* was regularly raided for spares, the task of finding some replacement parts was becoming ever more difficult. The main task, however, was to get the engine room back into full working order. It was soon after the refit got under way that rumours began to circulate that *Fearless* was to be withdrawn from service before *Albion* was fully completed. With work on the new ship having fallen behind schedule, it was clear that *Fearless,* if she were kept in service, would be required to run on into 2003, a prospect which was looking increasingly unfeasible. The refit period was marred by the deaths of two of *Fearless'* officers, who lost their lives in tragic diving accidents whilst involved in training. On 4 April 2001 there was a final change of command when Captain T. A. Cunningham RN took over from Captain Parry and two months later, on 18 June, *Fearless* put to sea once more to begin sea trials prior to the final phase of her career.

With her sea training completed *Fearless* returned to Portsmouth to prepare for her deployment which, in the event, would take her to the troubled Middle East region again. She had been on active service there 33 years earlier as she assisted with the British 'withdrawal from Empire', helping to transfer the British military headquarters in the Middle East from Aden to Bahrain. This time, however, the political situation in the region had changed out of all recognition. *Fearless* was to form part of 'Exercise Argonaut 2001' Task Group, but instead of the Mediterranean its destination would be the Persian Gulf and Indian Ocean areas for a major joint-service exercise, code-named 'Saif Sareea', in Oman before joining in the 'war on terrorism' in Afghanistan following the terrorist attack on New York's World Trade Centre. Joining the LSLs *Sir Bedivere* and *Sir*

In May 2002 Fearless was towed to buoys off Gosport's Hardway where, prior to decommissioning for the last time, destoring was carried out. *(Lee Howard)*

Percivale and carrying the Royal Marines of 3 Commando Brigade, *Fearless* sailed via Cadiz and Gibraltar. After carrying out exercises off the Turkish coast and undergoing a seven-week maintenance period, which included boiler cleaning, at the Turkish port of Marmaris, *Fearless* set course for the Suez Canal. During her southbound transit of the waterway the upper gun decks were manned, as they were when she passed through the narrow Strait of Bab-el-Mandab at the southern end of the Red Sea. Once again the ship's engineers were faced with the most appalling conditions as high sea temperatures made the cooling of the elderly machinery very difficult, and the air-conditioning often struggled to keep living conditions comfortable. Sales of soft drinks and bottled water from the NAAFI rocketed, but as always the men and women on board the assault ship coped with all that came their way. This often included some bizarre situations, such as when the ship was at defence stations with the engineers dripping with sweat, the gunners baking in the heat of the upper decks and the commandos carrying out some gruelling training on the vehicle deck, while in the peace and quiet of the junior rates dining hall the Royal Marines Band rehearsed the Beatles' number, 'Yellow Submarine'.

With the men of 45 Commando embarked in *Fearless*, the exercises began with a period of amphibious training, followed by unit-level and brigade-sized tests. The main exercise lasted for eight days and it took place in the baking desert heat of Oman, in conjunction with the United Arab Emirates Marines. On completion of 'Saif Sareea' at the end of October it was announced that some 'Argonaut' units would remain in the area and be reassigned to 'Operation Veritas', Britain's contribution to the ongoing military action in Afghanistan, which had been triggered by the events in New York on 11 September 2001.

Although *Ocean* would return to the UK, of the amphibious task group *Fearless* was one of the units which would remain behind, along with *Illustrious*, which had been converted to an LPH role, and two LSLs. In addition HM Ships *Cornwall*, *Kent* and *Southampton*, as well as four supporting RFAs, remained behind in the Persian Gulf and Indian Ocean. During this period *Fearless* played a major part in interdiction operations in the region, checking shipping for smuggled goods and weapons which might be destined for the Al Qaeda terrorist organization in Afghanistan. *Fearless'* embarked force was reinforced by elements of 40 Commando and by Sea Kings of 847 Squadron and by mid-December Royal Marines from the assault ship had moved into Afghanistan and set up a base at Bagram airfield outside Kabul. For *Fearless* it was to be the last operational Christmas and New Year and, as in 1966, it was spent east of Suez. On 12 February 2002, however, *Ocean* left Devonport bound for the Middle East and at the end of the month she relieved *Fearless* on station. In early March *Fearless* steamed north through the Suez Canal and on Monday 18 March, flying her 518-ft paying-off pennant, she entered harbour for the last time. It was a blustery day in the Solent, with the last few miles being marked by gale force winds and heavy rain showers. On the flight deck the Royal Marines Band ran through its martial tunes, the drummer struggling to control his drum in the 40-knot gusts of wind. In the Solent her tiny landing craft bobbed around as a mark of respect, and overhead, first an RAF Jaguar, then a Hawk and finally the helicopters of the Commando Air Support Unit - a Lynx, Sea King and a Gazelle - zoomed past. The ship's company manned the upper deck, where some wag had prepared a banner reading, 'For Sale - One Careful Owner, Very Reliable - Some Spares', to hang over the guard rail. Finally, as friends and relatives greeted their loved ones on the jetty, *Fearless'* trusty boilers let off a final belch of smoke and steam which billowed over the 1,000 people waiting on the quayside, and the 'Grand Old Lady' secured her ropes for the last time. It had been a moving and fitting reception for a popular ship which had served her country well for 37 years.

Owing to the fact that the cost of keeping *Fearless* in service for another nine months would be well over £2 million, it had been decided that she would be withdrawn from operational service early. As a result a proposed summer 'farewell cruise', with visits to Liverpool, Newcastle upon Tyne and Scarborough, was cancelled. No sooner had *Fearless* paid off than attempts to preserve her began, which was a sign of the affection in which she had been held. However, as with all ship preservation the main problem was always going to be money for, as well as raising enough to purchase the vessel, over one million pounds a year would be required to run and maintain her. With *Fearless* on the disposal list there was serious interest from the Brazilian Navy, who needed to replace their ageing ex-US Navy amphibious ships, which dated back to the 1950s. They even sent a team to Portsmouth to survey and inspect *Fearless,* which they concluded was in far better condition than they had expected. Unfortunately, with an economic downturn affecting their economy, the prospect of a sale receded, and there is little chance that any other foreign navy would want her. Fortunately, a reprieve from the scrapyard came in the form of harbour training and, as this is written, she is due to take over from *Rame Head* as the harbour training ship in Fareham Creek. At least this will ensure that this 'grand old lady' remains part of the Portsmouth Harbour scene for a few more years to come.

HMS *Fearless* Commanding Officers

	Date Appointed:
Captain H. A. Corbett DSO DSC RN	30 June 1965
Captain M. W. B. Kerr DSC RN	29 May 1967
Captain J. R. S. Gerard-Pearse RN	3 April 1969
Captain B. J. Straker OBE RN	20 October 1970
Captain S. A. C. Cassels RN	22 March 1972
Captain J. B. Rumble RN	18 June 1973
Captain L. A. Bird MVO RN	13 August 1975
Captain W. R. S. Thomas OBE RN	24 August 1977
Captain E. S. J. Larken RN	4 May 1981
Captain R. Trussell RN	4 March 1983
Captain P. G. J. Murison RN	11 December 1985
Captain S. R. Meyer RN	6 February 1990
Captain S. Moore RN	18 December 1991
Captain A. J. S. Taylor RN	30 July 1993
Captain R. A. I. McLean OBE RN	4 April 1995
Captain M. S. Williams RN	10 December 1996
Captain J. R. Fanshawe RN	28 August 1998
Captain C. J. Parry RN	7 December 1999
Captain T. A. Cunningham RN	4 April 2001

HMS *Fearless*
Previous Ships

The first HMS *Fearless,* a purpose-built gun vessel, was launched at Gravesend in 1794 and she carried 12 guns with a complement of 50 men. She was wrecked in Cawsand Bay, Plymouth Sound, in January 1804. The next *Fearless,* which followed 11 months later again with 12 guns, saw action at Copenhagen in 1807. Five years later, in December 1812, she was wrecked near Cadiz. The third ship of the name was an ex-Post Office vessel, *Flamer,* which was built at Limehouse. In 1837 she was taken over by the Admiralty when they became responsible for the Packet Service. She was a wooden paddle wheel survey vessel and she served until June 1875 when she was broken up by Admiralty Order.

The fourth *Fearless* was a torpedo cruiser of 1,580 tons, armed with four 5-inch guns and three torpedo tubes. She was built by the Barrow Shipbuilding Co, which later became Vickers Armstrong and she was launched on 20 March 1886. She was commissioned at Portsmouth, serving in the Mediterranean and, in 1899, at the Cape of Good Hope. In 1900 she was paid off, but in November 1902 she was recommissioned at Sheerness for service on the China Station. She was finally sold in 1905.

The fifth *Fearless* was a four-funnelled, 3,440-ton unarmoured Active-class cruiser which was built at Pembroke Dock, and launched on 12 June 1912. She carried ten 4-inch guns, four 3-pounder guns and two torpedo tubes. During 1913 and 1914 she served with the Home Fleet, seeing action off the Dutch coast on 18 August 1914 when she engaged the German light cruiser *Rostock*. Ten days later, off Heligoland, she was present at the sinking of the German destroyer *V187*. Two years later she was in action at the Battle of Jutland and she subsequently became attached to the 12th Submarine Flotilla. Present at the 'Battle of May Island' in the Firth of Forth in 1918, she was sold in November 1921.

The sixth *Fearless* was an F-class destroyer of 1,375 tons, which was built at Birkenhead and launched on 12 May 1934. She was armed with four 4.7-inch guns and eight 21-inch torpedo tubes. She was involved in the Spanish Civil War in 1937. In 1940 she was teamed up with HMS *Brazen* when, in waters which would become very familiar to her successor, she sank *U49* off Harstad. The following year, again with other ships, she helped to sink *U38* west of Cape Trafalgar, only to suffer torpedo damage a month later while screening *Ark Royal* in the Mediterranean. *Fearless* caught fire, lost all power and, on 23 July 1941, when judged to be too damaged for further towing, she was sunk north of Bone by HMS *Forester*.

The fourth *Fearless*, a torpedo cruiser armed with four 5-inch guns. She served the Royal Navy between 1886 and 1905. *(Maritime Photo Library, Cromer, Norfolk, No 1089)*

The fifth *Fearless* was a four-funnelled cruiser of the Boadicea class. She was launched in 1912 and was armed with ten 4-inch guns. In the First World War she earned distinguished battle honours, and was finally sold in 1921. *(Maritime Photo Library, Cromer, Norfolk, No 1124)*

The sixth *Fearless* was a handsome F-class destroyer armed with four 4.7-inch guns. In July 1941 she was lost in the Mediterranean. *(Maritime Photo Library, Cromer, Norfolk, No 1929)*

HMS *Fearless*
Battle Honours

Explicit nomen
(The name explains itself)

Heligoland 1914	Malta Convoys 1941
Jutland 1916	Mediterranean 1941
Norway 1940	Falkland Islands 1982

Part Two

HMS *Intrepid* 1967-1991

HMS *Intrepid* - First Commission 1967-1968

It was in May 1962 that the second assault ship was ordered from the Clydebank shipbuilder John Brown and Company who had provided the second lowest tender at £8,005,360, and the first keel plates were laid on 19 December that year. She was the last warship to be constructed by this renowned company of shipbuilders, ending a connection with the Royal Navy which could be traced back to 1884 and the cruiser HMS *Scout*. Work on the ship did not proceed as fast as had been hoped, and it was the summer of 1964 before she was ready for launching. The ceremony was carried out on 25 June 1964, when Lady Audrey Elworthy, the wife of Air Chief Marshal Sir Charles Elworthy, the Chief of the Air Staff, named her *Intrepid* and sent her down into the waters of the River Clyde. Unfortunately, owing mainly to the delay in receiving the detailed drawings and plans from Harland & Wolff, work on *Intrepid* had fallen further behind schedule, and with the workforce having to complete the fitting out of the passenger liner *Kungsholm* as well as *Intrepid* and given the late delivery penalties for which the shipbuilder would be liable, work on the passenger liner took priority. The situation was not helped by a series of industrial disputes in the shipyard, but in July 1966 her first commanding officer, Captain J. A. R. Troup DSC RN, was appointed to the ship and he joined other key personnel who were standing by the vessel at Clydebank. He had already had some experience of life on board an assault ship when, in February that year, he had flown out to spend the day aboard *Fearless* on passage between Plymouth Sound and Southampton Docks. In October 1966 *Intrepid* left the fitting-out berth under her own steam to carry out builder's trials in the Firth of Clyde, before returning to Clydebank for another five months.

On 6 March 1967, as work on fitting out neared completion, the main body of the ship's company arrived on board and, once settled in, they began storing and cleaning up in earnest. John Higgins remembers the journey north: 'We travelled from Portsmouth on a special train, and our first stop was Edinburgh where we were accommodated overnight in an Army barracks. Next morning we made the rest of the journey to Glasgow in coaches. I remember clearly our arrival at John Brown's shipyard where on the slipway next to *Intrepid*, which was in the fitting-out berth, was the hull of the giant liner *QE2*. When we arrived *Intrepid* was almost ready for sea and about a week later we steamed down the Clyde and out to sea.'

On Saturday 11 March, with Air Chief Marshal Sir Charles Elsworthy and Lady Elsworthy as guests of honour, the Commissioning Service took place on the tank

In October 1966, with much of her fitting out still to be completed, *Intrepid* is at sea for her builder's trials.
(Maritime Photo Library, Cromer, Norfolk, No 3549)

With fitting out almost completed *Intrepid* lies alongside John Brown's Clydebank shipyard shortly before commissioning.
(Glasgow Herald)

deck. Two days later, at 11.10 on the forenoon of Monday 13 March, the mooring ropes were slipped and the Clyde tugs *Strongbow* and *Vanguard* hauled the assault ship away from her berth before she set course downriver. By 11.42 she had passed the Erskine Ferry and 14 minutes later the tugs left her to complete her passage to the Tail of the Bank. At 13.00 *Intrepid* passed Gourock and after initial trials in the Firth of Clyde she anchored off Greenock. That evening she weighed anchor to carry out a three-hour full-power trial, which also saw her set course south for Portland. At 06.35 on Tuesday 14 March *Intrepid* was accepted into naval service and an hour later she anchored in Weymouth Bay. Not only was *Intrepid* late entering service, but she was also due to relieve *Fearless* in the Middle East, so it was imperative that she complete her trials and work-up as soon as possible, and less than an hour after arriving at Portland she was at sea again carrying out machinery trials. On 15 March, whilst in the Channel, there were problems with both main engines and at one stage she suffered a complete power failure but the engineers managed to rectify both, although during the first few days *Intrepid* was reduced to one engine. During the forenoon of 16 March the ship was flooded down for the first time and, having collected the LCMs from Poole, the stern gate was opened so that they could be docked. Further trials followed in the Channel, between the Isle of Wight and Plymouth Sound, and during the forenoon of 18 March *Intrepid* steamed up the Hamoaze to secure alongside Devonport Dockyard's No 9 wharf, better known as the Coaling Wharf. During her eight weeks alongside, like her sister *Fearless* before her, *Intrepid* proved to be a source of great interest to personnel of all three services, with the first VIP visitors being the C-in-C Plymouth, Admiral Sir Fitzroy Talbot, and the Admiral Superintendent, Rear-Admiral Wildish. Among the Army visitors were officers and men from the Royal Artillery, the Welch Fusiliers, the 13/18th Hussars, the Argyll and Sutherland Highlanders and the Durham Light Infantry, who would form the first embarked force. Meanwhile the ship's company and the dockyard staff were still hard at work, putting the finishing touches to the ship's radio and radar equipment.

On Monday 22 May *Intrepid* left Devonport to continue her trials and work-up which, on 27 May, included the first deck landing by a Whirlwind helicopter. There were RAS trials with RFA *Brown Ranger* and further engine tests at full power, as well as a mini amphibious landing on the beaches at Eastney, which enabled one member of the Royal Marines, who happened to be coxswain of an LCM, to get home for lunch. For most members of the ship's company, however, there were just frequent and frustrating views of a distant Southsea seafront. The trials continued for the rest of the month, and by early June *Intrepid* had reported to Portland to begin her work-up under the watchful eye of the Flag Officer Sea Training. For the whole of June, often in company with the frigate *Dido, Intrepid* underwent the gruelling exercises and evolutions of her work-up, and on 1 July with the last manoeuvres having been successfully completed, she returned to Devonport for a spell in No 5 dry dock. By mid-August *Intrepid* was alongside the sea wall again, and at the end of the month she took part in her first Navy Days, attracting over 27,000 visitors.

With *Intrepid* having suffered more than the usual amount of mechanical teething troubles for a new ship, the dockyard staff, representatives from the builders and the ship's own engineering personnel, toiled to rectify defects in the main engines. By 25 September the work had been completed and during the day some 511 officers and men of the Durham Light Infantry, plus personnel of the Royal Horse Artillery were embarked, which gave the ship's company some idea of the meaning of 'overload', when applied to assault ships. The trial embarkation afforded Devonport Dockyard, as well as passengers on the Torpoint Ferry and those on the numerous harbour sightseeing tours, the unusual spectacle of soldiers doing PT en masse on *Intrepid's* flight deck. On 6 October, having embarked men of 43 Commando, elements of 29 Commando Light Regiment, Royal Artillery, Wessex helicopters of 707 Squadron, and Sioux helicopters of the Royal Marines, *Intrepid* sailed for Scotland by way of the Irish Sea. Not long after leaving Plymouth Sound, however, when she was off The Lizard, there were more problems with the main engines and the assault ship returned to Cawsand Bay, where she spent eight hours at anchor while the engineers sorted out the loss of vacuum in the main condensers. At 01.00 on 10 October she weighed anchor and once again set course for the north, this time without any problems. After steaming via the Pentland Firth, during the afternoon of 11 October the assault ship anchored off Barry Budden in the Firth of Tay. The amphibious exercise lasted for 48 hours and included a night landing exercise, using both landing craft and helicopters, before the troops were re-embarked and *Intrepid* steamed south by way of the North Sea, bound for Portsmouth. With the passage marked by choppy seas and strong winds the ship's company had their first experience of how a soldier's normally ravenous appetite dropped off when the ship began rolling and pitching more then usual. During the afternoon of 13 October the assault ship went to the aid of a merchantman which, it had been reported, required medical assistance. In the event no help was required and during the early hours of the next day there was some relief for the troops when *Intrepid* anchored at Spithead and the army personnel were disembarked. Later in the day the assault ship moved up harbour to secure alongside South Railway Jetty for what should have been a three-day visit prior to leaving home waters for the Middle East. The weekend alongside was devoted to the 250 Pompey men of the ship's company, with wives and families being invited on board to see the ship. On the morning of Tuesday 17 October, when *Intrepid* had been due to leave harbour, not only were severe gales blowing, but a steam valve to one of the main engines jammed, which took two days to repair - much to the delight of the Pompey natives. Finally, however, at 13.45 on Thursday 19 October, *Intrepid* left Portsmouth Harbour to set course down Channel for a non-stop passage to Cape Town.

As well as stores and equipment for her east of Suez deployment, because of labour troubles at London Docks, *Intrepid* was also carrying 1,000 bags of Christmas surface mail for members of all three services who were serving in the Middle and Far East. For the first few days of the voyage she was accompanied by a Soviet trawler which showed great interest in her and shadowed her as far as Gibraltar. The delayed sailing from Portsmouth meant that a proposed visit to St Helena had to be cancelled, but Crossing the Line was marked by all the usual ceremony. On 2 November, with the ship just 24 hours out of Cape Town, speed was reduced in order to allow all departments to paint and clean ship and next morning at 08.00 the pilot was embarked off Robben Island. After firing a 21-gun National Salute *Intrepid* secured alongside No 7 berth in Cape Town's Duncan Dock. For the younger members of the ship's company the overwhelming hospitality of the people of the city came as a pleasant surprise, while many 'old hands' were able to renew former acquaintanceships. All too soon, however, the visit came to an end when, at 09.00 on 7 November, *Intrepid* put to sea for a fast passage to Aden. As she steamed north there was just time to wave at the ships on the Beira Patrol and to carry out training as everyone became familiar with their assault stations. After ten days at sea, at 08.00 on Friday 17 November, *Intrepid* anchored in Aden's Outer Harbour. Already at anchor was her sister ship *Fearless,* together with other units of Task Force 318, which included the fleet aircraft carrier *Eagle,* the commando carrier *Albion,* the destroyers *Barrosa* and *London* and the frigates *Ajax, Minerva* and *Phoebe*. During the four days which followed her arrival large quantities of stores and equipment were transferred from *Fearless* and on 20 November Rear-Admiral E. B. Ashmore, the Flag Officer, Second in Command, Far East Station, and the

On 13 March 1967, still flying the Red Ensign, *Intrepid* leaves the Firth of Clyde for her acceptance trials.

(*Maritime Books, Liskeard*)

Two Wessex helicopters of 848 Squadron join *Intrepid* in home waters. *(John Vitti)*

Commander of Task Force 318, which had been specially formed for the British withdrawal from Aden, hoisted his flag in *Intrepid*. At 09.00 on 21 November, having handed over her duties to *Intrepid*, *Fearless* weighed anchor and set course for home. For the remaining five days of British rule over Aden and the surrounding territories *Intrepid* was to act as the headquarters ship of the Task Force, from where the final withdrawal of the Royal Marines of 42 Commando, who were providing the rearguard units, the air defences provided by *Eagle* and operations at sea were all coordinated. During this period *Intrepid* operated the remaining Wessex helicopters of 78 Squadron RAF, who, with *Albion's* 848 Squadron, would be responsible for the final airlift of troops from the defensive perimeter which had been established around the airfield of RAF Khormaksar. For the ship's company this was an extremely busy period, with the only light relief coming in the form of deck hockey tournaments and 'shark-free' swimming in the assault ship's flooded down dock. With terrorist activity on shore at its height security on board was tight and John Higgins remembers that he spent his nineteenth birthday carrying out sentry duty on *Intrepid's* flight deck, armed with a self-loading rifle, complete with five rounds of live ammunition, a brass whistle and a buff-coloured card giving instructions on how to challenge anyone acting suspiciously and when to shoot. Fortunately, he did not have to use the rifle.

On Saturday 25 November all units of TF 318 were dressed overall for a review by Aden's last British High Commissioner, Sir Humphrey Trevelyan, who embarked in the minesweeper *Appleton* to sail between the lines of assembled warships and auxiliaries. Following this he transferred to *Intrepid* for an impressive fly-past of *Eagle's* Sea Vixens and Buccaneers which had, by that time, taken over the air defence role from the RAF. The last full day of British rule in Aden came on Tuesday 28 November, with 78 Squadron's six Wessex helicopters carrying out 18 patrols over the former colony. Meanwhile, with the withdrawal almost complete, *Intrepid* embarked the men and armoured cars of the Queen's Own Hussars and at 22.25 on Wednesday 29 November she weighed anchor and, in company with *Minerva* and RFA *Olna*, set course for the Persian Gulf. Five days after leaving Aden *Intrepid* arrived off Dubai where the last few helicopters of 78 Squadron were flown off (most of the squadron's remaining helicopters and stores had been transported by *Fearless*). Two hours later, at 09.00 on 4 December, *Intrepid* anchored off Dubai where she docked down to disembark the personnel and vehicles of the Queen's Own Hussars. Two days later *Intrepid* sailed for Bahrain, where she arrived on 7 December to disembark the remainder of the stores and army equipment.

For most of those on board *Intrepid* the two days spent in Bahrain were quite long enough, and as soon as all the stores had been unloaded there were sighs of relief as she sailed for Singapore and the Far East Station. During the passage, on the forenoon of 11 December when the assault ship was in the Arabian Sea, a request for medical assistance was received from the Liberian oil tanker *Dona*. As there were no helicopters aboard, *Intrepid* steamed for four hours, before locating the tanker at 15.45. Within minutes the seaboat carrying the Medical Officer had been

The passage south to Cape Town was marked by some heavy seas. Here *Intrepid* demonstrates her rolling abilities. *(John Vitti)*

launched and a member of the merchantman's crew was treated for diabetes. At just after 17.00, with the seaboat and doctor having been recovered, *Intrepid* resumed her voyage and eight days later, at 07.40 on 19 December, she commenced her passage up the Strait of Johore. At 08.00 the assault ship stopped to disembark her LCMs and LCVPs, which were to follow in her wake as she steamed up harbour with full ceremony, to secure alongside Singapore Naval Base. *Intrepid* had arrived in Singapore just in time for the ship's company to become acclimatized to the sweltering heat and humidity, and to get used to the local 'Tiger' beer before Christmas and New Year were upon them. On 15 January 1968, with the festivities well and truly over, *Intrepid* sailed for the local exercise areas in the South China Sea to carry out various manoeuvres, ranging from Seacat firings to the ditching of an old 3-ton army truck. During the afternoon of 17 January three Wessex helicopters of 848 Squadron were embarked, and night flying exercises continued into the early hours of the following morning. There was a 'Vertrep' exercise with RFA *Retainer* and the helicopters and, after a night at anchor off Pulau Tioman, on 19 January the helicopters flew off to Sembawang while *Intrepid* steamed round to Singapore's south coast where she anchored in the port's busy Outer Roads which, for liberty men, meant an easier journey into Singapore City. During the six days at anchor, men of a Gurkha Regiment and the Life Guards, together with all their equipment and transport, were embarked. Phil Gormley remembers the Gurkhas in particular and the fact that they slept in all sorts of unusual corners of the ship, including the main passageways where, when going on and off watch, one had to be very careful not to tread on them. On 25 January *Intrepid* weighed anchor to set course for Hong Kong where, four days later, she secured alongside the dockyard's West Arm. For nine days the ship's company was able to sample the 'delights' of Wanchai and San Miguel beer before, on 7 February the ship sailed for 'Exercise Cherry Blossom' off Hong Kong. After landing her embarked force *Intrepid* returned to Hong Kong Harbour, but on 15 February she was at sea once again for the return passage to Singapore. During the forenoon of 17 February, whilst closing to replenish from RFA *Retainer*, *Intrepid* collided with the auxiliary and was forced to haul off to starboard where damage could be assessed. Fortunately, this was confined to upper deck fittings and was superficial on both ships, which allowed the RAS to resume. Next day, at 18.00, *Intrepid* secured alongside Singapore Naval Base, where she immediately began to prepare for her next amphibious exercise.

For two days the men, transport and equipment of Headquarters 3 Commando Brigade were embarked for an exercise which was code-named 'Amphibex 1', which took place in the Penang and Kedah States of Malaysia. Leaving Singapore during the forenoon of 21 February, *Intrepid* steamed north to land the embarked force on Penang Island for what had originally been planned as an exercise for the Brigade Administrative Area, but whose scope was increased to include exercises for No 1 Raiding Squadron, SBS, a close-support exercise and the operation of RAF helicopters from both *Intrepid* and the LSL *Sir Lancelot*. It also served to give *Intrepid's* 'Supporting Arms Coordinating Centre' practice in air support procedures, the control of low-level airspace and in naval gunfire, which was interspersed with the helicopter air sorties. On 25 February, having re-embarked her troops, *Intrepid* set course south for Singapore's Outer Roads where all the

On 19 December 1967 *Intrepid* arrived at Singapore Naval Base for the first time. *(John Vitti)*

men, equipment, transport and the RAF helicopters left the ship. Three days later she sailed for the Middle East and another spell in the Persian Gulf.

On Friday 8 March, after a ten-day passage from Singapore, *Intrepid* anchored off Dubai to begin embarking the infantrymen of the Lancashire Fusiliers, before sailing for her next exercise. On 11 March the first anniversary of commissioning was marked and Leading Airman John Vitti remembers that the 'celebration' of milestones had led to some intense, but friendly, inter-departmental rivalry. As John remembers, it all began when the Fleet Air Arm personnel celebrated, in customary fashion, the 1,000th deck landing. As always there was a cake to cut and the champagne corks popped as senior officers, the lucky pilot and the flight deck party alike, enjoyed a light-hearted break from flying stations. Watching the proceedings were 'groups of seamen, stokers, cooks, marines and even the odd "pongo", looking somewhat puzzled at this strange soirée. Then, over the weeks that followed, there was a proliferation of "commemorative" events throughout the ship, all a direct response to the Air Department's celebration. The cooks celebrated their 7,000,000th spoon washed in the galley and the 30,000th sausage eaten. The engine room celebrated the amount of fuel used and the 100,000th pressure gauge polished. The seamen calculated how many times the ship's bell had been rung and had a cake baked for that. The list became endless, with the Writers calculating how many pay days had passed by as all the departments tried to outdo each other. There was tremendous rivalry, but it was all in good fun and it gave a refreshing insight into our ability to laugh at ourselves.'

With the Lancashire Fusiliers having embarked *Intrepid* weighed anchor to set course for the beaches of Qatar where, as part of 'Exercise Gold Leaf', the troops were landed at dawn on 12 March. There was also a visit from the British Political Resident in the Persian Gulf, which indicated the importance of this oil-rich area to government planning. Having completed her role in 'Gold Leaf' *Intrepid* returned to Dubai, where she prepared for her next exercise, code-named 'Gold Dust'. This time the LCMs made a night assault on the nearby beaches of Yas Island off the Trucial coast. Unfortunately there were some unforeseen delays caused by the assault ship's beach armoured recovery vehicle (BARV), which was virtually a Centurion tank chassis with the gun turret removed, and with the whole machine waterproofed. Although it was capable of operating in six feet of water and was fitted with an engine capable of pulling or pushing a craft or vehicle which was stuck, often it became a victim of the soft sand. On this occasion the BARV had to be rescued from Yas Island, which delayed *Intrepid's* return to her Dubai anchorage. On 26 March she left Dubai to set course for the head of the Persian Gulf and the Iranian port of Abadan. As she was behind schedule the 'clean and paint ship' was confined to just the starboard side which, as she would be starboard side to, was all that would be seen. As John Vitti remembers, 'It was decided to concentrate on that side of the ship and working parties set to with paintbrushes and polish. Soon brightwork began to gleam, the awnings were scrubbed white and the paintwork glistened - but only on the starboard side.' At midday on

116

Intrepid prepares to go alongside at Hong Kong as she arrives for her first visit. *(John Vitti)*

In May 1968, shortly before leaving Hong Kong for Tokyo, *Intrepid* operated with an RAF Whirlwind helicopter from 78 Squadron. For the visit to Japan she had also embarked a Humber staff car, an SRN5 Hovercraft and two naval buses. The mixed assortment can be seen on the flight deck. *(John Vitti)*

Wednesday 27 March the pilot was embarked and *Intrepid* began a three-hour passage up the Shat al Arab Waterway, to secure alongside Abadan's No 3 Jetty. During the visit there were the usual official functions, visits from Iranian VIPs and a popular children's party. During the afternoon of 29 March the ship was opened to the public and the Royal Marines Band played on the flight deck. As John Vitti remembers: 'The unpainted sections were roped off so that the people could not compare port and starboard sides, but as the afternoon wore on long queues formed on the jetty and, as those already on board were reluctant to leave after they had looked round, people on shore started to get very bad tempered. The situation became even uglier when the Iranian naval police arrived and promptly waded into the crowd, striking out at people indiscriminately with their batons. It was not a very nice sight.' Next day, at 06.30, *Intrepid* slipped her moorings to set course for Singapore.

On Tuesday 9 April *Intrepid* arrived back at the naval base on the north shore of Singapore Island to spend the rest of the month, and the first week of May, carrying out maintenance. It was on 8 May that she put to sea again, this time for hovercraft trials. On 15 May she sailed for Hong Kong, arriving alongside the dockyard's West Arm five days later. On 24 May, FO2 FES, Rear-Admiral Ashmore, hoisted his flag in *Intrepid* and three days later, in company with *Caprice, Euryalus* and RFA *Tidespring*, the assault ship sailed for a goodwill visit to Japan. After a four-day passage, *Intrepid* arrived alongside Tokyo's Harumi Pier at 12.00 on Saturday 1 June for a six-day visit to Japan's capital city where, according to one member of the ship's company, 'even the grubbiest in our midst developed a new interest in bathing'. On the day after her arrival the ship was opened to the public and, as a measure of the keen local interest, in the space of four hours some 3,500 people visited her. On Wednesday 5 June, the Queen's official birthday, the Royal Marines and their band paraded for a ceremonial Sunset at the British Embassy, a very popular event which 'brought the house down'. Shortly before *Intrepid's* arrival Captain Troup had addressed the ship's company about their conduct ashore, and he stressed that he did not want the ship or the British Embassy involved in any legal wrangling with the city's police. In the event everyone's behaviour was exemplary, with just one incident involving the police. John Vitti takes up the story: 'An invitation had been extended to the ship for an athletics team to take part in a meeting against Tokyo University at

Intrepid ballasted down and operating her LCMs. *(John Vitti)*

the city's Olympic Stadium. A team was organized and they travelled to the stadium in one of the single decker buses we were carrying. A very enjoyable afternoon was had by all, and at the end of this cordial meeting thanks were exchanged and *Intrepid's* party set off back to the ship through the heavy and almost chaotic rush-hour traffic. As the bus drove through the city it was involved in a minor collision with a car, and as details were being exchanged a police car drew up. An officer asked in broken English who was in charge and the Padre, who had organized the outing, said, "I suppose I am". Without any ado the police immediately bundled him into the police car and drove him off to the police station where he was detained. It took deputations from both the ship and the Embassy to secure his release from jail. Everyone, including the Padre, found the whole incident very amusing, but it showed just how the local police acted first and asked questions later.' The two buses, which had made the passage to Japan on *Intrepid's* flight deck along with a car, a hovercraft and Sioux helicopters, also ran some popular trips to Mount Fuji and other tourist attractions. On Friday 7 June *Intrepid* sailed from Tokyo to make a three-day passage to the port of Maizuru on the west coast of the island of Honshu, making the journey by way of the Inland Sea and the narrow waterway of Shimonoseki, which separates Honshu and Kyoto. The two buses, meanwhile, made the overland journey to meet the ship again at Maizuru. Although the port did not have the glitter of Tokyo there was a warm welcome, with the Japanese Defence Force doing all it could to make the ship's company feel at home. On 14 June, however, the visit to Japan ended and *Intrepid*, again in company with *Caprice* and *Euryalus*, set course for Singapore where, seven days later, she arrived alongside the naval base.

On 23 June, having disembarked Admiral Ashmore and embarked nine Sioux helicopters, *Intrepid* sailed for 'Exercise Lath' which began with a landing at Marang on Malaysia's east coast. As well as the amphibious operations, trials were carried out with an SRN6 hovercraft, and on 27 June *Intrepid* arrived back at Singapore. In early July the assault ship was dry docked at the naval base and the ship's company moved ashore into the more spacious and comfortable accommodation at HMS *Terror*. There was now the opportunity for station leave, which took some 'up country' into Malaysia, while one group of enthusiastic volunteers spent many long hours helping to refurbish the Cheshire Home for the Disabled in Johore Bahru. The ship's team did well in the Navy's Athletics Championships and on the football field *Intrepid's* team played many a fierce game of soccer. That *Intrepid* became a feature of the naval base's landscape became apparent when a mynah bird built her nest in the ship's starboard navigation light. By mid-August, however, with the refit completed and the ship back alongside the sea wall, the ship's company had moved back on board.

On Monday 19 August, Rear-Admiral A. T. F. G. Griffin, the new FO2 FES, hoisted his flag in *Intrepid* and seven days later the assault ship sailed to carry out post-refit trials and a mini work-up. The latter, which took place off Pulau Tioman, included night docking exercises with the LCMs and deck landing practice for Sioux and Whirlwind helicopters. By 30 August the assault ship had returned to Singapore Naval Base, where she received a brief visit from the First Sea Lord, Admiral Sir Michael Le Fanu. Early September saw *Intrepid* carrying out a local exercise, code-named 'Quick Look', with *Albion*, but after five days she returned to the naval base to prepare for her next big exercise and the final leg of the commission, which would take her to Australia. On 20 September, with the Headquarters 3 Commando Brigade and 13 of the Brigade's Sioux helicopters and personnel embarked, *Intrepid*, in company with *Albion* and *Triumph*, left Singapore to take part in 'Exercise Coral Sands', the biggest amphibious exercise in the Far East since the end of the Second World War, which was virtually a re-enactment of a Japanese plan for the invasion of northern Australia which, fortunately, did not come about. *Intrepid* sailed by way of the South China Sea, through the Balabac Strait and the Sulu and Bismarck Seas to George's Channel, the narrow waterway which separates the islands of New Britain and New Ireland. On 25 September she and *Albion* rendezvoused with a force which included *Hermes*, which was still operating as a conventional aircraft carrier, *Defender*, *Diana*, *Euryalus*, *Glamorgan*, *Puma* and HMAS *Parramatta* and *Vendetta*. The exercise began in earnest on 30 September, with an opposed passage of the Solomon Sea and a night encounter exercise with the 'Orange Force'. This was followed by a fleet replenishment exercise, with phase two being an opposed transit of the Coral Sea. On Saturday 5 October, the amphibious force, which included *Intrepid*, *Albion*, *Triumph* and HMAS *Sydney*, escorted by the destroyer *Glamorgan*, was quiet as preparations for the main assault took place and the force formed up for a passage through the Capricorn Channel to Queensland's Shoalwater Bay. However, as John Vitti remembers, this massive exercise had its amusing moments, such as when Australian Ministry of Agriculture officials flew on board to exchange all the field rations for the Australian equivalent, and to steam clean the undersides of all the vehicles which would be going ashore. On 6 and 7 October, with the main landings in full swing as the troops, in full battle kit, waded ashore from the LCMs and LCVPs onto the beaches of Shoalwater Bay to start a four-day 'battle' for Queensland, the same Ministry officials suddenly appeared out of nowhere to line the heavily laden 'invasion' troops into orderly queues to step through trays of disinfectant. Once the routine was complete they were then allowed to, 'tear up the beach John Wayne style, to continue the invasion.' Clearly, war or no war, the Ministry of Agriculture was not taking any chances with

Exercise 'Coral Sands' was a re-enactment of a Second World War plan for the invasion of northern Australia, and it took place in September and October 1968. In this photograph *Intrepid* is operating a Westland Sioux helicopter, and forming up in line astern are the commando carrier *Albion*, *Triumph* (hidden by *Albion*) and four RFAs. *(John Vitti)*

Intrepid refuelling from RFA *Tidespring* with *Triumph* closing to refuel on the RFA's port side. *Albion* can be seen in the background. *(John Vitti)*

foreign pests and diseases which might be lurking on a commando boot or vehicle tyre. For four days, whilst *Intrepid* was at anchor off Broome Head, the 'battle' raged ashore, but on 12 October the Royal Marines were re-embarked by LCM, hovercraft and helicopters, before *Intrepid* sailed for Brisbane and what everyone agreed was by far the best run ashore of the commission.

At 15.30 on Tuesday 15 October *Intrepid* entered the Brisbane River and two hours later she had secured alongside Brett's Wharf in the city. For everyone on board Queensland's Gold Coast lived up to its name, offering sun, surf, girls and a beer garden by day, and girls, a beer garden and nightclubs by night. During the weekend of 19 and 20 October, when some 8,000 visitors swarmed over the assault ship, it was no longer safe for the few people left aboard, usually just the duty watch, to wander from the mess deck to bathroom wearing only towels and flip flops. Each day the invitations from the people of Brisbane to the ship's company flooded in and at 10.30 on Friday 25 October, when the time came to leave Australia, to everyone's delight strong westerly winds were blowing and sailing was delayed for 24 hours. For those with girlfriends, and for those who just enjoyed the run ashore, there was the opportunity to enjoy a second farewell in this very hospitable city. At 08.00 on 26 October, when *Intrepid,* in company with *Albion,* finally did sail, there were cheers and tears from the shore as she steamed down the Brisbane River.

The return passage to Singapore was made by way of the Great Barrier Reef, with a 14-hour overnight stop off Wyburn Reef to await the high tide before the passage resumed through the Adolphus and Prince of Wales Channels, and the Torres Strait. Steaming by way of the Java Sea *Intrepid* arrived off the Johore Shoal Buoy in the early hours of 5 November, where she anchored for seven hours. At 09.00 that forenoon, flying her paying-off pennant, with the ship's company and embarked force manning ship and with the landing craft in formation astern, the assault ship weighed anchor to steam the short distance to the naval base. Overhead the 13 Sioux helicopters clattered by in a farewell fly-past, but as *Intrepid* approached the C-in-C's saluting dias on the port shore the Royal Marines bugler sounded the 'Alert' and all on board came to attention. Suddenly, between the ship and the saluting platform, a speedboat appeared towing a water skier who began to perform some 'clever' tricks. John Vitti remembers the incident: 'As it drew level with the ship's bow the water skier began performing clever tricks and was clearly showing off. Knowing that the Admiral was watching the ship on this, the final curtain call of the commission, we remained rigidly at attention. No one moved a muscle, although we all watched the silly antics of the clown on water skis who seemed determined to spoil our entry into harbour. Suddenly, as he hit the ship's wake, he was catapulted into the air and, as he lost his tow, he cartwheeled over the water with legs and skis seeming to point in all directions. Finally, he hit the water in one huge ungainly splash, and at this there was a spontaneous roar as everyone manning the port side collapsed in uncontrollable laughter. I'm sure the C-in-C must have been just as amused as the rest of us.'

Within days of her arrival at Singapore *Intrepid* had paid off, and most members of the ship's company were flown home for leave and for new drafts. For *Intrepid* there was the prospect of recommissioning, with a new complement.

During 'Exercise Coral Sands' *Intrepid* replenishes stores by jackstay and helicopter from RFA *Tarbetness*. (*John Vitti*)

Intrepid alongside Bretts Wharf, Brisbane, during her 11-day visit to the city. *(John Vitti)*

With the embarked force manning the flight deck, and with cheers and tears from the shore, *Intrepid* leaves Brisbane. *Albion* is also preparing to follow the assault ship downriver. *(John Vitti)*

Chapter Ten

HMS *Intrepid* - Withdrawal From The Far East 1968-1972

On 5 December 1968, four weeks after *Intrepid* returned to Singapore from Australian waters, her new commanding officer, Captain J. H. F. Eberle RN, joined the ship and over the days which followed almost all the ship's complement was changed. Most of the officers and men who would make up the new ship's company were flown from RAF Brize Norton, via the Indian Ocean island of Gan, to Singapore, and at 10.30 on Saturday 14 December 1968 *Intrepid* was recommissioned, the occasion being marked with a small service attended by senior officers of the Far East Fleet. With the ship undergoing a short period of self-maintenance there was little opportunity for acclimatization to the hot and humid weather conditions of Singapore before, on Thursday 19 December, *Intrepid* slipped her mooring ropes to put to sea for familiarization exercises in the South China Sea. Two days later she anchored off Pulau Tioman - an island which is familiar to anyone who has served east of Suez - and after 34 hours there, which included a few banyans, on 23 December *Intrepid* returned to the naval base. During the following week sports teams were formed and throughout the commission all of them, particularly the soccer, rugby and hockey teams - the latter led by Captain Eberle - were always well supported by the ship's company.

On 30 December 1968, with the Christmas celebrations over, *Intrepid* left harbour to rendezvous with the destroyer *Dainty* for exercises in the South China Sea which were to last for four days. During this period the Assault Squadron were put through their paces and the engineers practised main machinery breakdowns. On 4 January 1969 there was time for some relaxation when *Intrepid* anchored off Singapore's south coast for a week, before she steamed back round to the naval base where she arrived alongside on 11 January. During the weekend which followed the first embarked force was taken on board and on Monday 13 January the ship sailed for Penang where the amphibious landing of the commission would take place. On the flight deck the Sioux helicopters of the Commando Air Squadron vied for space as up to 13 machines at a time operated there. One aircrew member described the situation thus: 'Only 13 pieces are required for flight deck chess, and the object is to park as neatly as possible, taking up the minimum amount of deck space then, having achieved it, start all over again.' On 17 January, with this exercise over, *Intrepid* returned to Singapore to disembark her troops and to take on board a second force, ready to repeat the amphibious exercise the following week. In early February *Intrepid* joined up with the aircraft carrier *Albion* for the amphibious phase of 'Exercise FOTEX 69' which, once again, took the assault ship into the Strait of Malacca. In the second half of February, flying the flag of Admiral W. D. O'Brien, the C-in-C Far East Station, *Intrepid* carried out a series of amphibious landings along the Malaysian coast of North Borneo, with runs ashore at Labuan and Kota Kinabalu. On 25 February, after leaving the latter port, *Intrepid* set course for Hong Kong, where she arrived on the first day of March for what many considered to be the first good

Looking aft from *Intrepid's* tank deck as the ship docks down and sea water floods in. *(Frank Stockton)*

Deck hockey, a fast and furious game, is played on *Intrepid's* flight deck during a period of relaxation.
(Frank Stockton)

run ashore. During exercises off the colony an LCM from *Intrepid*, which contained the ship's BARV, ventured very close to the border with China and a helicopter and two police launches were sent to turn her back. Fortunately the warnings were in time and no violation of territorial waters occurred. By early May, however, it was time for the assault ship to head back home for a major 12-month refit, which she did by way of the Persian Gulf, Durban and St Helena, where the ship's company had an unusual run ashore in the capital, Jamestown.

In early June 1969, following her return to Devonport, *Intrepid* began her first major refit, which would last for almost 12 months. As well as undergoing a complete overhaul, the assault ship became the first ship of the Royal Navy to be fitted with a satellite communications system, operated via the Skynet satellite from a stationary orbit over the Indian Ocean. For most members of the ship's company the highlight of the refit came as it neared an end in June 1970 when, at midday on Thursday 11 June, all work in the dockyard came to an abrupt and unscheduled stop. Normally such a state of affairs was only brought about by a strike, or by a visit by a member of the royal family, a head of state or a political leader, but on this occasion it was the arrival of six glamorous girls who formed the popular dancing group Pan's People, whose destination was *Intrepid's* 24 Mess, the home of the ship's Amphibious Detachment. The marines had written to the girls to ask if they would be their mess mascots, to which they had agreed and sent some autographed photographs. These were quickly framed and displayed in a prominent position in the mess, whose members then invited the girls to visit *Intrepid*, an invitation which they accepted. Accompanied by a BBC 'Top of the Pops' film crew, the girls arrived on board to film a dance sequence in and around *Intrepid*, much to the delight of the ship's company who provided an appreciative audience. Frank Stockton, who was in charge of the auxiliary machinery watchkeepers, remembers all those on watch vacating the machinery spaces, leaving him alone with generators and evaporators. Eventually he went to search for his staff to find them all on the forecastle watching the dance routines, along with the rest of the ship's company from the Officer-of-the-Day downwards. After much effort he managed to coax the watchkeepers below once again. The filming took most of the afternoon, with only a break for tea, with the day being rounded off with a meal and drinks ashore for 24 Mess before the group returned to London. Frank remembers seeing the Top of the Pops programme, featuring the assault ship and Pan's People, a few days later.

In late June 1970 *Intrepid's* refit came to an end and she left Devonport for her trials, which included the debut of the Navy's first operational satellite communications system. Following this the assault ship left home waters to steam east once again, this time via Casablanca and Cape Town. Once into the Indian Ocean *Intrepid* steamed north-east to Mauritius, the Seychelles and the island of Gan, before heading for the naval base on Singapore's north-east coast. After returning to the Far East Station the ship's first amphibious exercise was 'Summer Frolic' in Brunei, which also acted as her work-up. After embarking Headquarters 3 Commando Brigade, which consisted of the men of 42 Commando, the assault ship sailed for the landing area, arriving off Brunei's coast during the early hours of 7 September. As far as 42 Commando was concerned, after the ship-borne passage, operations ashore involved counter-insurgency exercises, with the 'enemy' being provided by the Royal Brunei Regiment and the Gurkha Rifles, who were stationed at Seria. At 06.00 on 7 September Wessex helicopters were airborne with the first wave of troops, and over the following three days operations ashore were conducted in heavy rain over a very muddy terrain. The exercise ended at 09.30 on 10 September and, despite the fact that a number of vehicles had become bogged down in thick mud, by 15.00 the unit had been re-embarked and the ship was able to return to Singapore. During this leg of the commission, as well as carrying out amphibious

Some very popular visitors to *Intrepid* during the refit period at Devonport in June 1970 were the girls of the dancing group Pan's People. Here Babs (Barbara Lord) is piped aboard with full ceremony from the Officer-of-the-Day and all the gangway personnel.
(Frank Stockton)

Babs poses for a photo shoot on one of *Intrepid's* Seacat missile launchers. The girls recorded a dance routine on board which was later broadcast on BBC Television's 'Top of the Pops' programme. *(Frank Stockton)*

exercises, there were visits to South Korea and Japan. In Korea *Intrepid* visited the port of Chinhae, west of Pusan, where exercises were engaged in with the Republic of Korea's Marines. *Intrepid* then steamed through the Shimonoseki Strait into the Inland Sea, bound for Hiroshima. Here the Peace Museum was visited by most members of the ship's company and, as an indication of the Royal Navy's popularity, when she was opened to the public long queues formed on the quayside. There were visits to a brewery, and it was said that sales of saki in the city's bars increased dramatically. In mid-October, in company with *Triumph,* and with 40 Commando and elements of 48 Gurkha Brigade embarked, *Intrepid* took part in 'Exercise Far Fling' in Hong Kong's New Territories. During the manoeuvres she also operated the Wessex helicopters of 847 Squadron and the Whirlwinds of the RAF's No 28 Squadron, but in the event the exercise was cut short by the threatened approach of 'Typhoon Joan', which had rampaged across the Philippines and was thought to be heading for Hong Kong. Although it passed clear and never came closer than 300 miles, its pressure was felt in Force 8 gales, which were enough to halt boat operations. With most of the troops embarked, both *Intrepid* and *Triumph* rode out the storm at sea, and by 23 October they had returned to Singapore Naval Base.

As Christmas approached *Intrepid's* ship's company was looking forward to Christmas 'down under' in Sydney, but it was not to be for in mid-November a tragedy in the Bay of Bengal was to interrupt her schedule. During the night of Friday 13 November 1970 cyclonic storms with 120 mph winds swept across the region and hit southern districts of low-lying East Pakistan (Bangladesh). With the winds came huge tidal waves, at least one of which was over 20 feet high, that struck the offshore islands of Hatya and Bhola in the Ganges Delta, cutting them off from the mainland and sweeping thousands of people and their livestock into the sea. The city of Chittagong, some 135 miles south-east of Dacca, and the Ganges Delta towns of Barisal and Khulna were severely damaged by the hurricane-force winds. It was a disaster on a mammoth scale, with at least 12,000 people dead and over two million more rendered homeless in flooded areas, which were also polluted with mud and raw sewage. In London the government immediately announced that one and a half million pounds were being set aside for humanitarian aid, and that both *Intrepid* and *Triumph* would load relief supplies and sail for the Bay of Bengal, where *Intrepid* would act as the headquarters ship for the international

127

When *Intrepid* returned to the Far East Station in autumn 1970, another use for the LCMs was ferrying the ship's company ashore for banyan leave at Pulau Tioman in the South China Sea.

(Frank Stockton)

relief effort which was getting under way. In addition to the depot and assault ships, the LSL *Sir Galahad* and the survey ship *Hydra* were both diverted to the area. Between them the naval units would be able to operate 14 helicopters which, with heavy seas and high winds still affecting the area, would be the most effective way of delivering aid.

After loading relief supplies, embarking units of 40 Commando and Wessex helicopters of 847 Squadron, *Intrepid* left Singapore at 16.00 on Friday 20 November, to be followed by *Triumph* some six hours later on 'Operation Burlap', the mercy mission to East Pakistan. Both vessels were carrying tons of food, medicines and supplies of all kinds, including three tons of clothing which was donated by families of service personnel in Singapore, for what was the biggest relief operation since the end of the Second World War. It was in the early hours of Tuesday 24 November that *Intrepid* and *Triumph* arrived off the coast of East Pakistan but, owing to uncharted and shifting sand banks, they anchored some 30 miles south of the nearest land, which was the coast of Patuakhali. No sooner had they come to rest than the mercy mission began to swing into action, with sailors and marines in landing craft, inflatables and helicopters landing large quantities of stores and equipment, and evacuating people from the worst hit areas. Within 24 hours *Intrepid* and *Triumph* had landed over 400 tons of food, medical supplies and clothing, as helicopters flew day and night on the relief work. In addition, on board *Intrepid,* the Skynet satellite system underwent its biggest operational workout so far as it kept up constant communications links between the Navy's flotilla lying off the coast of the Ganges Delta, the naval base at Singapore and Whitehall. One of the Royal Marines who was involved in the helicopter operations recalls his experiences: 'At a hundred feet the stench of death was unforgettable. Huddled in little groups, always close to a red flag which showed help was needed, the survivors waited anxiously for food and water. Our pilot wisely landed away from the pathetic groups, as only two days before starving islanders had jumped at an American Bell helicopter and pulled it out of the sky. Three people were injured as the helicopter crashed to the ground. Within seconds of landing, the crowds reached us and, despite our efforts to keep them back, they quickly ripped open the sacks of rice and many of them began to eat it raw. Later, when I had time to talk to some of the people, I learnt that on this particular island, Rangunbau, only 2,000 of an original 12,000 survived. Most, I was told, had been swept out to sea. I saw no women or children under the age of about seven. Only a few palm trees remained standing, and on one of them I was shown the waterline which was fully 15 feet from the ground.'

The fact that the relief ships were anchored some 30 miles from the nearest land stretched communications and the supply operation to the limit. The Navy's helicopters flew up to 16 hours a day, while *Intrepid's* landing craft ran a shuttle service between ship and shore, as they ferried thousands of tons of supplies into four major distribution centres one of which, for the LCMs, was a small island at the southern tip of the British relief area code-named 'Daffodil'. Over 120 marines from *Intrepid* were based ashore at Patuakhali, from where they were able to control the distribution of food. They also had to control the people who gathered round and sometimes put themselves in danger by standing too close to the whirling blades of helicopters, and on the dropping zone when supplies were parachuted down. *Intrepid's* Assault Detachment, using 17-ft glass fibre Dorys, powered by outboard motors, waterplaned along the main channels carved out by flood waters, carrying food, blankets and clothing to villagers. One of the marines told of his experiences: 'I saw the bodies of four children. The youngest was about 18 months old, the oldest about four. They were lying on driftwood. The villagers were always pleased to see us and made us welcome. There was always a big crowd when we arrived.' Another remembers the scene below as he flew back to *Intrepid*: 'At one point, where large numbers of dead cattle littered the fields, we could smell the rotting carcasses at 200 feet and travelling at nearly 100 mph. But we saw that some of the people had begun to rebuild some rough shelters.' *Intrepid's* role in the relief operations came to an end on Friday 11

December, when the last LCM returned to the assault ship's dock and she set course for Singapore. With their role having been taken over by civil aid agencies such as the British Oxfam team, the Navy's task was at an end. During the period spent offshore some 2,850 tons of supplies had been landed, two schools had been built, a hospital, jetties and buildings had been repaired and three wells had been sunk. Commodore Derek Napper, who had been in charge of the naval units, summed up the feelings of all who had taken part: 'Every single man felt he was doing a worthwhile job. The operation has been a great success and we have done what we came to do.'

On *Intrepid's* return to Singapore there was a change of command when Captain W. D. M. Staveley RN took over from Captain Eberle, and Christmas was spent at Hong Kong before *Intrepid* returned to Singapore where, in January 1971, she was recommissioned. Once again, most of the ship's company was changed, with the new complement being flown out to Singapore to replace the men who flew home. On Friday 15 January, just a few days after her new complement had reported for duty, there was an important event in the assault ship's career when the Prime Minister, Edward Heath, who was in Singapore for the Commonwealth Conference, hosted a dinner party in the wardroom on board. He invited four other Prime Ministers and one ex-Prime Minister to the function, namely Sir Keith Holyoak of New Zealand, Lee Kuan Yew of Singapore, Tun Abdul Razak of Malaysia and John Gorton of Australia, as well as the former British Prime Minister, Sir Alec Douglas Home who, at that time, was the Foreign Secretary. After the formal dinner, at which the wardroom chefs excelled themselves with a menu of Vichyssoise sole, spring chicken, fruit salad, brandy snaps and, it was said, a very smooth brandy, the guests watched the Royal Marines Beat Retreat on the floodlit flight deck. Ten days after the visit, on 25 February 1971, *Intrepid* sailed to carry out a mini work-up in local waters and to take on two Wessex helicopters of 847 Squadron, which would work closely with the assault ship for two more months.

On 10 March 1971, with *Intrepid* having completed her maintenance period and work-up, and having embarked 400 men of 40 Commando, their equipment and transport, she left Singapore in company with the LSLs *Sir Galahad* and *Sir Lancelot* for 'Exercise Summer Frolic'. The exercise, which took place at Marang on Malaysia's east coast, was really a mini work-up for the ship's company before a major SEATO exercise in the Philippines. The main landing began on 12 March, and was preceded by a recce troop who went ashore in Gemini dinghies to secure a beach and footbridge across a nearby lagoon. The rifle companies followed in Wessex helicopters and by LCVPs, and it had been intended to land the vehicles by LCM, but with heavy surf crashing down onto the beaches this operation had to be abandoned. By midday the troops had been established ashore, together with a small Commando Headquarters, and next morning the re-embarkation in *Intrepid* took place. This was completed by midday and during the afternoon the assault ship headed back to Singapore, where she arrived during the forenoon of 14 March. Eight days later, on Monday 22 March, having once again embarked men of 40 Commando and their vehicles, *Intrepid* sailed for Manila Bay, where she anchored four days later. Also taking part in the exercise, code-named 'Subok', were the LSLs *Sir Galahad* and *Sir Lancelot* and the US Navy's amphibious warfare units, *Iwo Jima* and *Cleveland*. During the weekend at anchor off Manila, whilst the pre-exercise briefings were being held, most members of the ship's company and the embarked force were able to fit in at least one run ashore before, on Monday 29 March the whole task force, under the command of Rear-Admiral Gaddis USN, weighed anchor and set course for the exercise areas. The rehearsal landing took place in Subic Bay on the last day of March, and 24 hours later the force returned to Manila Bay for a wash-up, but this time no leave was granted. During the evening of 1 April the ship's divers

'Operation Burlap', the international relief effort in the devastated areas of cyclone-hit East Pakistan, involved both *Intrepid* and the depot ship *Triumph*. Here a landing craft delivers food supplies.

(Frank Stockton)

Royal Marines of 40 Commando unload food, clothing and 40-gallon drums of fresh water for the survivors in the areas which were devastated by cyclonic storms and tidal waves and...

...the LCMs land 3-ton trucks to assist with the distribution of supplies to the worst hit areas.
(Both Frank Stockton)

arrested two Filipino swimmers who had strayed too close to the ship and brought them on board for interrogation, which added some realism to the 'Operation Awkward' exercise. During the afternoon of 2 April the fleet put to sea again for the main exercise, which started with a three-day opposed passage and an amphibious landing on the palm-fringed beaches of Lingayen Gulf. While the helicopters of 847 Squadron landed the supplies and equipment, the LCMs and LCVPs ferried 40 Commando Group ashore, together with all their vehicles, which took five hours. During the three days spent ashore the Royal Marines 'fought' their battles and, with time left for 'hearts and minds' work, helped to renovate a local school. On the afternoon of 8 April, with the force having been re-embarked, *Intrepid* weighed anchor to set course for Singapore where she arrived four days later and whilst entering harbour, the helicopters of 847 Squadron, who were leaving for home, staged a farewell fly-past.

Intrepid's stay in Singapore was limited to just 24 hours for, at 10.15 on 13 April, she left harbour to set course for an official visit to Bangkok. Two hours later, however, having suffered mechanical problems in her main engines, the assault ship was back alongside the naval base where the dockyard carried out repairs. On 15 April *Intrepid* left Singapore for engine trials, and to carry out manoeuvres with the Australian frigate *Parramatta* in the Tioman area of the South China Sea. By 19 April, however, she had returned to Singapore and next day the ship's company moved to the shore accommodation at HMS *Terror*, as the ship prepared for dry docking. During her period in dockyard hands the C-in-C Far East Station, Vice-Admiral Troup who, less than three years earlier, had been *Intrepid's* first commanding officer, flew his flag in his old ship for a week. It was on 22 May 1971 that the ship's company moved back on board and eight days later *Intrepid* left the naval base to undergo three days of trials before returning to harbour to prepare for her next series of exercises and visits to ports in Australia. On Friday 4 June, having embarked elements of 1/2nd Gurkha Rifles, *Intrepid* left Singapore to set course for Fremantle, where she arrived six days later. As always, during the four-day visit the ship's company took full advantage of the overwhelming hospitality, and one of the LCMs, manned by Royal Marines and sailors, took part in, and won, a 'time trial' on the Swan River. Competing against all manner of boats the win earned the crew a Pennant of the Royal Yacht Club and, in the clubhouse, several jugs of beer. From Fremantle *Intrepid* steamed across the Great Australian Bight and the Bass Strait to secure alongside Melbourne's Station Pier for a six-day visit. On 24 June, after leaving Melbourne, *Intrepid* set course for Adelaide, where she arrived alongside in the port's inner harbour the next day, this time for a seven-day visit. Once again the hospitality from the people of the city was tremendous and when the ship was opened to the public almost 10,000 people flocked aboard, with the most popular visitor being the local beauty queen. After leaving Adelaide during the forenoon of 2 July *Intrepid* made her way back to Fremantle from where, after a nine-hour refuelling stop on 6 July, she set course for Singapore.

After disembarking the Gurkhas off Singapore's south coast, *Intrepid* steamed into the South China Sea to Pulau Tioman where the Assault Squadron practised landings by LCM and LCVP before, on 14 July, the assault ship returned to the naval base. During her five days alongside preparations were made for the Operational Readiness Inspection, which began on 19 July when, with units of 40 Commando embarked, the assault ship left Singapore for Malaysia's east coast. The amphibious assault began on 21 July at Marang and, three days later, *Albion* joined her off the coast. The re-embarkation of the Royal Marines was filmed for a Navy recruiting programme and by 22.15 it had been completed. Next day both *Intrepid* and *Albion* made their way back to Singapore, arriving on 29 July to disembark the men of 40 Commando. For *Intrepid* most of August was spent alongside the naval base undergoing maintenance, which was long enough for one officer to get married in the dockyard church, then on 27 August, the assault ship put to sea to carry out deck landing practice with two Wessex helicopters before setting course for Hong Kong. On Wednesday 1 September *Intrepid* arrived off Junk Island, and later in the day she secured alongside the dockyard's north arm to prepare for two exercises. The first amphibious assault, code-named 'Quick Flip', simulated a landing in the New Territories in order to 'quell a local rebellion'. The second exercise began after embarkation of troops of the 51st Infantry Brigade when, during the afternoon of 3 September, *Intrepid* sailed to spend the night at sea, anchoring in Port Shelter Bay the following forenoon. Once at anchor the assault got under way using the landing craft and the Wessex helicopters of A Flight, 848 Squadron. With the first exercise having been completed, the embarked force was exchanged for the 1st Battalion Irish Guards, and in the early hours of 6 September *Intrepid* made the short passage from Port Shelter Bay to Lantao Island for 'Exercise Quick Flip II', where she anchored two hours later for the amphibious assault. The object of this exercise was to land the Army force in order to 'rescue a VIP held by local guerrillas', but for many journalists on the scene the dawn assault became known as the 'Battle of Lantao'. Both assaults were directed from *Intrepid's* Amphibious Operations Room, with the minehunters of Hong Kong's 6th Mine Countermeasures Squadron also taking part. On conclusion of the exercises the assault ship returned to the colony's dockyard during the evening of 7 September and secured alongside the north arm.

With the commitment in Hong Kong over *Intrepid* was scheduled to visit Korea and Japan, and on 14 September, after embarking 55 personnel of the Irish Guards, she sailed for Chinhae. Once at anchor off the South Korean port she embarked a force of 278 men from the Republic of Korea Marines for exercises in the Pusan area. The landing, code-named 'Exercise Foam Lift III', took place on 20 September and after leaving the South Korean marines to march back to their barracks, *Intrepid* set sail for Japan's Inland Sea and the port of Kobe where she arrived the following day. The visit to the Japanese port lasted for six days, during which time there was a full programme of social and sporting activities, but on 27 September the assault ship left for Singapore. During the return passage there were exercises off Pulau Tioman and on Tuesday 5 October the assault ship arrived alongside Singapore's Naval Base which, in early November, was to be handed over to the Government of Singapore as Britain withdrew its military presence from the Far East base. *Intrepid*, however, would not be involved in this final withdrawal as, on 8 October, she left Singapore and set course for Mombasa. Eight days later, in the Indian Ocean, a traditional Crossing the Line ceremony was held, where the official 'defaulters' included Captain Staveley, the Executive Officer, Commander A. J. Marx, and, most popularly, the Master-at-Arms. Four days after the ceremony, on 20 October, *Intrepid* secured to buoys in Mombasa's Kilindini Harbour for a seven-day stay in the Kenyan port. By this time, however, the assault ship's long tour of duty east of Suez was drawing to a close, and for the final phase of the deployment *Intrepid* would steam north for the Persian Gulf where, as in the Far East, Britain was shedding its military commitment. Unlike the departure from Aden four years earlier, however, British forces were leaving in an atmosphere of goodwill.

On 27 October *Intrepid* left Mombasa to head north for Dubai where, on 2 November, she anchored just long enough to refuel and to embark the last Commander British Forces Persian Gulf, Major-General R. C. Gibbs, who hoisted his flag. It was appropriate that the assault ship's command and control facilities should act as an operational headquarters during what was politically a very sensitive time, when it was important that direct and secure communication be maintained with the British Political Resident in the Persian Gulf and with the Government in London, so that everyone could be kept in touch with what

Intrepid and USS *Cleveland* together in early April 1971 during 'Exercise Subok' off the Philippines.
(Fleet Air Arm Museum, Yeovilton)

seemed to be a rapidly changing situation in the area. Bahrain itself was gaining independence from Britain and, happily, nothing occurred to mar either the progress of the rundown or the attainment of independence. For three weeks *Intrepid* underwent a maintenance period in the port, and at the end of November she carried out exercises and manoeuvres with the frigate *Minerva* and the LSL *Sir Galahad*. So smoothly did the rundown of the forces go that in early December Captain Staveley was given permission for *Intrepid* to leave the Persian Gulf before the end of the year, which was welcome news for the ship's company. During the second and third weeks of December efforts were directed towards the official farewells to the rulers of the Gulf States and other civic authorities in the area. The Wessex helicopters of 848 Squadron's B Flight were kept busy flying General Gibbs to and from his official visits and, on 11 December, flying members of the Military Coordination Committee Persian Gulf to their final meeting, which was to be at sea on board *Intrepid*, as the assault ship carried out four days of manoeuvres off Bahrain. After the meeting, as he left by helicopter, the British Political Resident was given his final salute from a unit of the Royal Navy. On 17 December, with *Intrepid* back alongside Bahrain's deep water jetty, the Royal Marines Detachment mounted a ceremonial guard for General Gibbs, whilst the ship's company provided a side party as the last Commander British Forces Persian Gulf struck his flag and was towed away in a Land Rover by the wardroom as he relinquished his command. Two days later, at 14.30 on Sunday 19 December, came the time for *Intrepid's* departure when she had the melancholy distinction of being the last naval unit to leave the Persian Gulf Station. For the ship's company there was the satisfaction of bringing a page of Imperial history to a successful conclusion, and the anticipation of the passage home.

Steaming via the Cape of Good Hope *Intrepid* spent Christmas Day at sea, crossing the equator during the morning watch, as she steamed south off the coast of Somalia. Six days later, during the forenoon of 31 December, the assault ship secured alongside No 4 quay in the South African port of East London, where the ship's company was able to celebrate the New Year in style. Shortly before leaving harbour, as a foretaste of things to come as part of the Dartmouth Training Squadron, 39 junior electrical ratings who were under training at HMS *Collingwood* and who had flown out from the UK, joined the ship for the passage home via Gibraltar. During their time on board the juniors joined various ship's departments to gain valuable experience for their future time at sea. Finally, in late January 1972, having spent 19 months away from home, *Intrepid* closed a 150-year chapter in the Royal Navy's history when, as the last major unit of the Far East Fleet, and in pouring rain and gale force winds, she returned home to Devonport, to be greeted by families and friends who were waiting on the jetty to welcome her.

On 8 April 1971, as *Intrepid* entered Singapore Naval Base, the Wessex helicopters of 847 Squadron, which was returning to the UK, staged a farewell fly-past over the ship.
(Fleet Air Arm Museum, Yeovilton)

Early morning amphibious landings in the South China Sea
(Frank Stockton)

Chapter Eleven

HMS *Intrepid* - Redundancy 1972-1981

Following her return from the Middle East in January 1972 *Intrepid* was taken over by Devonport Dockyard for an assisted maintenance period which would keep her out of service until the summer. This included a five-week period in dry dock, during which her ship's company was accommodated ashore, many in the nearby Royal Sailors Rest but some in lodgings in the Devonport area. Although the long leave periods reduced the numbers on board, some 285 ratings still found themselves looking for accommodation. On 5 April 1972 there was a change of command when Captain J. F. Kidd RN took over from Captain Staveley. Mr E. Shrimpton remembers the day that the new commanding officer arrived on board: 'As he arrived on the gangway, a pre-arranged signal went to Petty Officer Flags who immediately hoisted the Jolly Roger at the masthead. Like the rest of us Captain Kidd thought it was amusing and he took it all in good part.' By June that year the ship was back at sea and undergoing trials and a work-up in the Portland area. These included berthing trials by two SRN 6 Mk II hovercraft from the Royal Corps of Transport which, in an operation that some thought reminiscent of a classic comedy film, ran up the assault ship's lowered tailgate and disappeared into the dock area.

In July, following the successful conclusion of her work-up, *Intrepid* set out on a series of 'Meet the Navy' visits, which took her from Devonport to Spithead where students from Peckham Grammar School, with which the ship had links, were welcomed on board. After leaving the Solent the assault ship steamed up Channel and into the North Sea to Harwich, where juniors under training from nearby HMS *Ganges* were able to tour the ship. During a four-day visit to Antwerp Belgian hospitality was enjoyed, after which *Intrepid* headed for the River Mersey and the city of Liverpool. On passage a Wasp helicopter of *Scylla's* flight, which was temporarily embarked in *Intrepid*, flew to Bude, where 400 children in a local school watched it land on their sports field to drop representatives from the ship and collect mail. The same helicopter, carrying Captain Kidd, also made the landmark 2,000th deck landing onto the assault ship. During her stay in Liverpool some 10,000 people, including two local beauty queens, were welcomed on board and the city provided what all agreed was a good run ashore. From Liverpool *Intrepid* steamed north for Oban, her Scottish port of call. During the passage *Intrepid* rendezvoused with her sister *Fearless*, for the first meeting of the two sisters since the withdrawal from Aden in 1967. *Fearless* was on a similar 'Meet the Navy' cruise, and was on passage between Swansea and Rosyth, so the opportunity was taken to hold an inter-ship sports day. Competitors from *Fearless* transferred to *Intrepid* by light jackstay for a hectic afternoon of deck hockey, 'marathon' running and tug-of-war. By a very narrow margin the overall victory went to *Intrepid* and at the end of the day the two ships went their separate ways. From Oban *Intrepid* steamed south again, calling at the Isle of Man before returning to Devonport for maintenance, leave and, during August, the port's Navy Days.

On Tuesday 12 September, with summer leave having been taken and the maintenance period completed, 60 midshipmen were embarked, together with 22 personnel of 40 Commando, and *Intrepid* left Devonport. As part of the Dartmouth Training Squadron, much of her tank deck was occupied by temporary Portakabin classrooms and on this occasion two of her LCMs were still in dockyard hands. After carrying out machinery trials the Assault Squadron staged a mini-landing at Dorset's Ringstead Bay, which saw the BARV stuck in reverse gear and jammed against a rock face on the shore. After much hard work it was finally recovered and *Intrepid* steamed to Torbay to rendezvous with her missing LCMs, which had made a successful passage from Plymouth. During *Intrepid's* weekend at anchor off Torquay she received a surprise visit from a party of nine GPO telephone exchange 'hello' girls. They had actually been invited on board the minesweeper *Kedleston,* but misunderstanding their boarding instructions they had arrived at Torquay's Princess Pier to find one of *Intrepid's* boats alongside whose crew, obligingly, took them out to the assault ship where, although no party had been planned, something was soon under way. Meanwhile, at the other side of Torbay, alongside Brixham's harbour quay, *Kedleston's* ship's company waited in vain for their visitors. When they realized what had happened the signal, 'Give us our girls', was made to *Intrepid,* but the assault ship politely refused to part with their unexpected visitors.

Following the weekend in Torquay *Intrepid* weighed anchor to set course for Gibraltar where, with calm seas, blue skies and plenty of sunshine, hundreds of 'white knees' made an appearance as everyone changed into tropical whites. At Gibraltar 40 junior seamen from the boys' training establishment HMS *Ganges* joined the ship, and it was not long before she was heading east for Malta. Prior to starting her official visits to Mediterranean ports the assault ship steamed from Grand Harbour to Sicily's Golfo di Castellammare where, during a fine weekend at anchor, there was a 'paint ship' which involved most of the ship's company and all the men under training. The *Ganges* juniors showed off their athleticism by being lowered over the ship's sides in bosun's chairs, with almost as much paint being applied to flesh as to the hull. At the end of the weekend, with the ship looking spick and span for her official visits, she set course for Trieste where, with 50 knot winds blowing, she berthed alongside. On leaving Trieste the LCMs became floating classrooms for midshipmen's manoeuvres, as they made their way independently to Venice, *Intrepid's* next port of call. With cheap wine and plenty of sightseeing Venice was always a popular run ashore, but on leaving harbour it was back to serious business with long periods at Action Stations and Action Messing. There was a rendezvous with the US Navy's aircraft carrier *Forrestal* for joint exercises and manoeuvres, while off Cyprus preparations were put in hand for the ship's Sea Inspection, which inculded Abandon Ship trials. Mr E. Shrimpton remembers these: 'Commander King, the Executive Officer, wanted the ship's company to test life jackets by jumping over the side from the forecastle. Unfortunately, many of those who took the plunge got rather a surprise when, on hitting the water, their life jackets burst. The Commander, leading the exercise in his swimming trunks, was the first to experience the bursting life saver which amused everyone.' Whilst off Cyprus the Assault Squadron carried out a night landing exercise, which ended when they returned with elements of 41 Commando for a major NATO exercise off the island of Corsica.

On 18 November, having successfully completed her Admiral's Inspection off Malta, *Intrepid* rendezvoused with her sister *Fearless* outside Grand Harbour to carry out depth charge trials with helicopters and to prepare for 'Exercise Corsica 72', which for *Intrepid* would mean the amphibious landing of 41 Commando on Corsica's west coast. As well as the two assault ships, also taking part in the exercise were the commando carrier *Bulwark,* the fleet carrier *Ark Royal,* the frigate *Arethusa* and four RFAs. For the amphibious force the main part of the exercise was an 'opposed' landing, with the defence being provided by the French Foreign Legion's 'Green Scorpion' Battalion. Following the exercise both *Intrepid* and *Fearless* visited Toulon, and from there they steamed to Gibraltar from where they would make their way home. After a short delay *Intrepid* left the colony to make the final leg of the deployment, arriving home in plenty of time for Christmas.

In early January 1973, with the winter holiday over, *Intrepid* embarked 130 midshipmen and 20 sub lieutenants under training, followed by personnel of 845 Squadron, together with two of their Wessex helicopters, and the Royal Marines Band from *Ark Royal* which was about to leave for exercises in the Mediterranean. Finally, with a midshipmen's guard paraded, the band playing and with the ship's company manning ship, *Intrepid* left Devonport and a distinctly cold south coast to make a ten-day Atlantic crossing. The assault ship's destination was Bermuda, with the passage being made through heavy seas and high winds. The four-day stop at Ireland Island naval base was intended as an opportunity for a 'paint ship' programme, but even more severe weather meant that only one day was spent smartening up the ship. From Bermuda *Intrepid* set course for the port of Jacksonville in north Florida where, despite being dogged by bad weather once again, most of the ship's company were able to enjoy the warm hospitality of the city. Many were able to visit the Cape Kennedy Space Centre and even Disney World. As always the ship was opened to visitors but the Band's ceremony of Beating Retreat had to be cancelled because of torrential rain. Before leaving the port, *Ark's* band left for a temporary attachment to *Bulwark* which was visiting Charleston, and *Intrepid* steamed south for the Bahamas where she finally left the rain behind her.

On 3 February, with the assault ship in the Caribbean, duties began with midshipmen's manoeuvres, which meant that the young officers virtually took over the LCMs for navigation exercises. On one occasion these were disrupted by an engine room fire in one of the vessels, but prompt action by the crew members and an accompanying LCM quickly prevented what could have been a nasty incident. The next port of call was Nassau which, as always, was very expensive and on leaving the Bahamian capital *Intrepid* carried out a series of amphibious landings which were a rehearsal for an Anglo-American exercise which was to take place at the end of the month. These were followed by the biggest replenishment operation the assault ship had carried out for some time, with 60 loads being embarked by vertical replenishment and 100 by jackstay. No sooner had it been completed than the ship began refuelling and once she was fully stored and fuelled she steamed south to the Windward Islands and the island of St Vincent, where assistance was required to airlift building materials to the lip of the 3,000 ft active volcano, Mount Soufriere. The volcano had last erupted in 1902, a year which had seen disastrous volcanic activity in the region, and on that occasion it was with such violence that thousands of people had lost their lives. Although it had been largely dormant since the early part of the twentieth century, there were signs that magma pressure was building up once again, and a small seismic station which would house scientific instruments was to be built on the lip of the mountain. The crater of Mount Soufriere had very steep sides and 500 feet down, reflecting the colour of the blue sky and looking disarmingly idyllic, was a large, placid lake. However, only a few years earlier the water temperature had risen to near boiling point, while an evil-looking smoking island of

A very smart 'Procedure Alpha' turnout as *Intrepid* leaves harbour in the summer of 1972.
(*E. I. Shrimpton*)

In July 1972 *Intrepid* and *Fearless* met at sea for the first time since the withdrawal from Aden.
(E. I. Shrimpton)

black slag appeared ominously in its centre. Although nearby residents were quickly evacuated, on that occasion nothing more had happened and as the water temperature cooled the people slowly drifted back to their homes. It was this incident which had led to the decision to build the scientific station, but the St Vincent Government required help in getting the building materials to the top of the mountain. As *Intrepid* was in the area and carrying midshipmen under training, it was considered that this would be a valuable evolution for them and official approval was given for the airlift to be organized. Camps were set up at the base and the lip of the volcano and the Wessex helicopters, carrying loads of 1,000lb each trip, ran a shuttle service between the camps. At the summit, midshipmen and marines fetched and carried, while local people began the job of building the station. Meanwhile, back at the ship, various 'expeds' and banyans were run for the ship's company, but without doubt the Navy's assistance on Mount Soufriere was the highlight of the visit and it was much appreciated by the islanders.

After leaving St Vincent there was a one-day stop at Antigua, before the ship moved on to the US Naval Base at Roosevelt Roads, Puerto Rico, for 'Exercise Rum Punch' with the US Navy. The joint exercise was commanded by Commodore R. W. Halliday, Commodore Amphibious Warfare, who was flying his pennant in *Intrepid,* and it provided an opportunity for the ship's Assault Squadron to carry out joint operations with the dock landing ship USS *Plymouth Rock*. With the exercise over, Tuesday 13 March saw *Intrepid* at Bridgetown, Barbados, and, with a Royal Guard paraded on the flight deck, the ship received an unofficial visit from Princess Margaret who inspected the 'British Week' trade displays on the tank deck. Two days later the ship's company put on a military tattoo which was watched by a crowd of 30,000. All sorts of events were held including a Field Gun Competition for young seamen, while a fire engine on display was manned by multi-coloured clowns. The two helicopters of 846 Squadron gave a display of precision flying and the Assault Squadron staged a mini amphibious assault using both helicopters and LCMs. Finally, as 'Sunset' was played by *Ark Royal's* band, which had rejoined the ship, the helicopters flew past dropping the White Ensign and Barbados National Flag. It was a fitting finale to *Intrepid's* display and her first Caribbean deployment. From Bridgetown the assault ship sailed for home, and whilst off Ushant and only a few hours steaming from Plymouth Sound, she went to the assistance of a merchant tanker which was on fire while under tow to Brest. Damage control teams from *Intrepid* soon extinguished the blaze and her arrival in Plymouth Sound was delayed by only one day.

With seasonal leave over far too quickly for most members of the ship's company, and having embarked a contingent of midshipmen, Headquarters 3 Commando Brigade and a troop of Centurion tanks of the 13/18th Royal Hussars, on 1 May 1973 *Intrepid* slipped from C buoy in Plymouth Sound and set course for Gibraltar. For this deployment she was primarily in her amphibious role and after a calm passage across the Bay of Biscay and down the Portuguese coast, the assault ship secured alongside Gibraltar's south mole. During the weekend at the colony each of the ship's departments entered a team for the race to the top of the Rock, with the midshipmen, not surprisingly, taking the first prize. From Gibraltar *Intrepid* steamed east to Cyprus, where the Commando Brigade was landed in readiness for 'Exercise Double Bass'. Whilst they were ashore the ship sailed north for a more enjoyable time experiencing the delights of Istanbul, but when the sojourn came to an end she steamed back to Cyprus where the brigade was re-embarked. It was not long, however, before

137

Intrepid at Gibraltar in autumn 1972.
(*Mike Lennon*)

they were once more deposited ashore, this time in southern Cyprus for 'Exercise Spring Double', which also involved *Bulwark* and the Royal Marines of 41 Commando. During this exercise *Intrepid* received a visit from a Government Defence Minister and a group of MPs, who were there to watch the assault ship being put through its paces. For them the highlight of the day was a trip up the beach in the BARV. At the end of the exercise, between 2 and 7 June, *Intrepid* and *Bulwark* made a five-day visit to Piraeus, where they anchored in Phaleron Bay. Some members of the ship's company went off to view the ancient ruins of Athens, whilst others chose to seek out the more modern bars of Piraeus and so, one way or another, when the two ships sailed for 'Exercise Dawn Patrol' there were many empty pockets and aching heads. The exercise was a major NATO undertaking involving a huge multi-national task force, and on its conclusion *Intrepid* sailed for Naples for the exercise wash-up and another enjoyable run ashore. There were trips to Rome including, for one group, an audience with the Pope, as well excursions to Pompeii and Vesuvius. The LCMs ran banyan trips to Capri and Sorrento and members of the Royal Marines Detachment enjoyed 'expeds' into the Italian countryside. By the last week in June the assault ship was back in Gibraltar and on the last day of the month she left the colony, bound for home.

After arriving in Plymouth Sound during the late evening of 4 July, the next morning saw the start of 'Families Day' with the relatives of over half the ship's company embarking by tender. As soon as the last passengers were aboard the ship weighed anchor and put to sea to give a demonstration of *Intrepid's* capabilities, with the day finishing at 16.00 when the ship arrived back in Plymouth Sound and the guests were disembarked into MFVs. Once the families were ashore again *Intrepid* set course up the Channel and North Sea for Newcastle upon Tyne where alongside at Wallsend the 24th Air Portable Brigade was embarked for the next exercise, code-named 'Harsh', in Scapa Flow. With heavy mist hanging over the whole area the LCM and LCVP crews faced a real challenge as they journeyed from ship to shore in 'nil' visibility to meet their opposition in the form of the Royal Greenjackets. With the exercise completed 24 Brigade was re-embarked and returned to Wallsend where, with Force 9 gales sweeping across the river and sailing delayed for 24 hours, the ship's company got an extra night's shore leave. Finally, with Tynemouth receding into the distance, *Intrepid* set course for Rosyth and 'Exercise Sally Forth', which involved the largest force of HM ships and RFAs seen together for a long time. This demonstration of British maritime capability was closely observed by Defence Ministers from NATO countries, members of the NATO Council, senior officers from all three services and the Secretary of State for Defence. The exercise began with mine hunting and fishery protection manoeuvres, followed by a simulated submarine hunt by helicopters and an attack on HMS *Bristol* by the submarine *Otter*. With the Navy awaiting the outcome of the Government's deliberations on a maritime version of the Harrier, one of the highlights of the exercise was a demonstration by two of the RAF's planes which landed and took off from *Bulwark's* flight deck, while *Intrepid's* landing craft showed off their capabilities, as they operated with SBS units and divers. At the end of the demonstration, with the LCMs back in the dock and the LCVPs in their davits, the assault ship sailed

A traditional ship's company photograph on the flight deck at Trieste. (E. I. Shrimpton)

for Spithead where, on 26 July, there was a second 'Families Day', this time off the Isle of Wight. The day ended with *Intrepid* securing alongside Portsmouth's Middle Slip Jetty for the start of the summer leave periods, and during Navy Days at Portsmouth the ship was one of the main attractions, with more than 30,000 visitors over three days.

On 4 September 1973, with leave over, *Intrepid* left Portsmouth for Gibraltar and her autumn cruise in the Mediterranean for her last deployment before a major refit. From Gibraltar she steamed east to Malta where she went alongside in Grand Harbour, and from there she sailed on to Dhekelia in Cyprus in preparation for her next amphibious exercise starting on 25 September. Also at anchor in Dhekelia's outer harbour was the commando carrier *Bulwark,* together with the destroyer *Devonshire* and the LSLs *Sir Galahad* and *Sir Lancelot*. The amphibious section of the exercise, code-named 'Deep Furrow', would be led by Commodore D. T. Smith, Commodore Amphibious Warfare, who was flying his pennant in *Intrepid,* and it was designed to test the capabilities of the forces on NATO's southern flank. It involved some 54 ships and supporting units, with over 50,000 soldiers, sailors and airmen from the USA, United Kingdom, Greece, Turkey and Italy. The naval escort force assembled off south-west Turkey to carry out anti-submarine, gunnery and carrier operations, while the amphibious assault force, which included *Intrepid* with 3 Commando Brigade embarked, and USS *Mount Whitney,* steamed north to Saros Bay in north-west Turkey where they would carry out a landing in support of the Turkish Army. Before the assault, Allied aircraft delivered strikes on the 'defending' force and provided air cover over the beachhead for the Royal Marines and US Marines ashore. Whilst most of *Intrepid's* embarked personnel were landed by helicopter, the LCMs and LCVPs took the bulk of the transport and heavy equipment. Finally, on completion of the exercise most of the fleet, including *Intrepid* and *Bulwark,* put into Istanbul for the wash-up and a run ashore. Upon leaving the ancient city and passing through the Dardanelles, a wreath was laid on the water in memory of the assault

Intrepid at Venice in October 1972.
(Ron Slater)

ship's predecessor which had been lost in 1943 near Leros. At Malta the men of 41 Commando were disembarked and the opportunity was taken to carry out some maintenance. From Grand Harbour *Intrepid* visited Cannes and Genoa, before making her way home via Gibraltar. En route all manner of evolutions were practised in preparation for the Operational Readiness Inspection which, for some inexplicable reason, was staged immediately before the ship's major refit at Portsmouth, when she would be paid off and most of the ship's company would be dispersed to other ships.

On 21 February 1974, with the ship well and truly under refit, there was a change of command with Captain N. J. S. Hunt MVO RN taking over from Captain Kidd. A year later, in February 1975, the refit was coming to an end and *Intrepid* was preparing for sea once again, which meant plenty of hard work for all departments. By March *Intrepid* was undergoing her post-refit trials and her Basic Operational Sea Training off Portland. In the following month, at Portsmouth, she took over the Dartmouth Training role from *Fearless,* when all personnel and equipment were transferred to *Intrepid.* At the same time almost all conceivable forms of sport were played between the two ships' teams, and many an old acquaintance was renewed. By May *Intrepid* was fully operational once again, and on 10 May she left Plymouth Sound for Rotterdam where she embarked 280 men who made up two companies of the Royal Netherlands Marine Corps, before setting course for the Mediterranean. The spring deployment would see the assault ship, with *Bulwark* which had 41 Commando and 848 Squadron embarked, taking a leading role in the NATO exercise, 'Double Bass', off Corsica. With political considerations limiting the numbers of men ashore *Intrepid* took on a monitoring role, but for the assault ship's small Brigade HQ who did get ashore the rugged terrain and the excellent 'enemy', provided by the French Foreign Legion, made for a useful exercise. Following these manoeuvres *Intrepid* spent an eight-day maintenance period at Malta, where the marines left for training on the island. On 13 June, with the troops re-embarked, *Intrepid* left Grand Harbour to take part in 'Exercise Dawn Patrol', a major NATO naval, air and amphibious exercise involving some 25,000 personnel. Its aims were to demonstrate NATO solidarity and to exercise the forces of the organization's southern flank in operating together. Once again *Intrepid* operated with *Bulwark,* but the exercise also involved units from the USA, Italy and Turkey. The amphibious fleet met in Taranto Bay on 19 June to commence the transit phase which was an opposed passage round southern Sicily, before a rendezvous with RFAs, which had steamed through the Strait of Messina. After two days of mine clearance and reconnaissance operations, on 23 June the main amphibious landing took place off Cape Teulada, followed by two days of hectic activity for the landing force. Opposing them were two mechanized companies of an Italian tank battalion and a company of American paras, but the day was carried and the landing force soundly 'defeated' the 'enemy'. During her nine-week deployment in the Mediterranean *Intrepid* exercised with units of the Portuguese, Italian, Turkish and

US Navies and embarked companies of Italian and Dutch marines as well as men of the French Foreign Legion. In mid-June, however, after returning the Dutch marines to Rotterdam, *Intrepid* returned to Portsmouth.

In early September 1975, with leave and maintenance over, *Intrepid* returned to the Mediterranean for 'Exercise Deep Express 75', which saw her operating with *Bulwark, Hermes, Ashanti,* and the LSLs *Sir Galahad* and *Sir Tristram*. This was the major southern flank exercise of the year, involving the deployment of NATO reinforcements to Turkey to counter 'aggression' by Warsaw Pact forces. Having left the UK in early September the Royal Navy's amphibious force and their escorts stopped off in Malta for work-up exercises and for shore leave. Embarked in *Intrepid* were Headquarters 3 Commando Brigade and a Signal Squadron, with 40 Commando Group in *Bulwark* and 41 Commando Group in *Hermes,* while the two LSLs carried the Commando Logistics Regiment. The exercise also involved the land and air elements of the Allied Command Europe Mobile Force, 32 Marine Amphibious Unit US Marine Corps, the Italian San Marco Tactical Group and the 3rd Battalion Turkish Naval Infantry, all of whom were embarked in their own naval vessels.

The combined amphibious task force met up at Antalya in southern Turkey on 18 September when, at a pre-sail conference, final orders were given to the commanding officers of the landing force units. The whole force then set course for Daganby Bay in the Aegean Sea for a rehearsal landing on 22 September, before they sailed to Saros Bay in Turkish Thrace for the main exercise which took place between 24 and 28 September. The scenario for the exercise was a situation in which, after a period of increasing tension, Warsaw Pact forces had invaded Turkish Thrace with the aim of securing ports on the northern shore of the Aegean Sea and around Istanbul, thus isolating the Black Sea. The task of the NATO amphibious force was to recapture terrain already secured by the enemy, which was depicted as a Warsaw Pact motor rifle regiment, a brigade-sized force and a battalion of tanks. In reality, the 'enemy' was actually a Turkish Army mechanized battalion. During the four-day exercise the Royal Marines' landing force advanced some 60 miles inland, securing numerous objectives, with the helicopters of 845 and 848 Squadrons leapfrogging up the main axis of advance in order to maintain the momentum of operations. It was said that the Turkish 'enemy' was surprised by the speed of their movement. Meanwhile, at sea, a small Turkish minesweeper got too close to *Hermes*' overhang and had her mast carried away. Lieutenant Colin Mitchell, *Intrepid*'s DWO, remembers the incident: 'The Turkish minesweeper then followed the carrier round like a kicked dog slinking after its master - "too frightened to go home", we all said - until Admiral Eberle took pity on the CO and ordered the ship to *Intrepid* for us to make good the damage. It was said that Captain Hunt had been boasting of the excellence of his technical departments and had been invited to prove it. Needless to say we rose to the occasion and after some very basic engineering with heavy hammers and araldite bandages, we gave the grateful minesweeper captain a reconstructed mast, complete with navigation lights, communications and radar. My radar artificer claimed that the Turkish officers were amazed by the picture on their radar screen - it was the first they had seen and didn't know what to do with it.'

With all the units re-embarked the amphibious force put into Istanbul for a post-exercise wash-up and, for the ship's company and embarked force, a welcome run ashore. There were fascinating trips to the Topkapi Palace, Suliman's Mosque and, for many, a stop at the nearest nightclub which boasted a veiled belly dancer. During the deployment there were also visits to Naples and Venice, Malta for maintenance and then, shortly before her return to the UK, *Intrepid* was diverted back to Malta in case she was required to steam to the coast of Lebanon to evacuate British nationals from Beirut, where the fragile fabric of life in the elegant capital was being ripped apart by a vicious civil war. In the event her services were not needed and *Intrepid* returned to Portsmouth for leave and for maintenance.

The new year of 1976 saw *Intrepid* in her Dartmouth Training role with midshipmen and other officers under training occupying embarked force mess decks, and Portakabin classrooms on the vehicle decks. When employed in this role many of the ship's officers were required to act as Divisional Officers to classes of midshipmen, which meant, in addition to their normal duties, marking journals and completing individual reports, as well as attending to their charges on watchkeeping duties. At the start of her spring cruise *Intrepid* crossed the Atlantic in January bound for Bermuda and the Caribbean. Other ports of call included Cartagena, Colombia, where Royal Marines and sailors marched through the city with bayonets fixed as part of a wreath-laying ceremony at the Simon Bolivar Memorial. There was a five-day call at the American port of Corpus Christi, Texas, where the assault ship had to pass under the city's road bridge with only a few feet to spare. On the day that she was to be opened to the public in the afternoon, queues started forming at 07.00 and at one stage they stretched for three-quarters of a mile. In all over 18,000 enthusiastic Americans toured the ship and, as always, the hospitality shown to the ship's company was almost overwhelming. During the stay the assault ship received a visit from the C-in-C Fleet, Admiral Sir John Treacher, who also called on HMS *Glamorgan,* which was part of the same deployment and was visiting San Diego. During her homeward passage *Intrepid*'s ports of call included Vera Cruz and Bermuda, before she returned to Portsmouth.

Intrepid, with a Wessex helicopter landing on, leads *Bulwark* and *Ark Royal* during 'Exercise Corsica 72' in the Mediterranean. *(Ron Slater)*

On 27 September 1973, shortly after leaving the Dardanelles, a wreath-laying ceremony was carried out by Lt-Cdr John Bloom and MEM Rodney Philips in memory of *Intrepid's* immediate predecessor which had been lost in 1943 near Leros.

(E. I. Shrimpton)

Intrepid's final cruise before being laid up in Reserve was to northern waters, which combined midshipman training with amphibious exercises on a reduced scale. Visits to Bergen, Kristiansand and Oslo in Norway, Aarhus in Denmark and to Gdynia in Poland were included. During the four-day visit to Bergen hillwalking proved popular, and the ship spent a day in Sognefjord, Norway's largest fjord, transiting to Ardal some 80 miles from the open sea. She then steamed north to the Lofoten Islands, inside the Arctic Circle, which earned all on board their 'Blue Nose' certificates. In Kristiansand full use was made of the Joint Services Outward Bound Centre, where all the officers under training and even some adventurous members of the ship's company went hillwalking, rock-climbing, canoeing and sailing. Colin Mitchell remembers that in his capacity as a midshipmen's Divisional Officer he had the '...pleasure of panting up mountainsides as my class carried out their exped duties. We even camped for the night above the snowline.' At Gdynia many sightseeing tours were organized, but these were still Cold War times and as Colin Mitchell remembers: 'Shore leave as we normally understood it just didn't exist. Anyone leaving the ship was either on duty or participating in an organized trip or sports event.' Colin also recalls numerous security briefings being held on board and, '...shore telephones being brought on board by four Polish naval officers, a commander, two captains and a vice-admiral. The admiral was most insistent that he had a very special telephone for our captain's cabin, and he was most upset when we accepted only one for the ship's exchange. There were also video cameras "hidden" behind screens and they filmed everyone who crossed our brow.' Colin also remembers

Manoeuvres in the Mediterranean in the autumn of 1975.
(E. I. Shrimpton)

In February 1979, during her post-refit sea trials, *Intrepid* visited Torbay. Here she is at anchor off Torquay. *(Neil Segger)*

'...the grey lifeless buildings and wide, deserted and dismal streets, with no colour and little sign of life. One had a constant urge to take a walk to see what lay behind those main streets. I also remember the almost continuous "bottoms up" vodka toasts at the Polish official reception. We thought our hosts might actually be drinking water, until they started falling over. I remember that all the organized trips, whether sightseeing or sporting, included a visit to a Second World War concentration camp, which was always a horrific experience. I also remember the final wardroom cocktail party when we were all aware that it would be the last one before paying off, and it was even rumoured that the old girl might never sail again. Our Polish guests happily made their "bottoms up" toasts with gin and tonic. My final memory is of the band of the Royal Armoured Corps Beating Retreat on the flight deck and playing for the Sunset ceremony to finalize the cocktail party. They had already performed to rapturous audiences ashore and they pulled out all the stops for this final performance - it was marvellous.' In mid-June, following her visit to Gdynia, *Intrepid* steamed to Rosyth to carry out a final amphibious exercise before setting course for Devonport where she transferred her Dartmouth Training role to *Fearless*, which was about to recommission. At the end of June there was a 'Families Day' at sea off the Isle of Wight before she secured alongside in Portsmouth Dockyard to pay off.

In July 1976 the process of 'preservation by operation' began, with all the upper deck equipment being encased in plastic sheeting, while all the main passageways and ladders were protected by hardboard sheets and then with most of the ship sealed off and dehumidified, she was placed in Reserve. Her ship's company was reduced to five officers and about 80 ratings, and in November that year she spent a period in dry dock before being secured alongside *Bulwark* in No 3 basin. Colin Mitchell recalls life on board during the early weeks of 1977: 'By the new year we were sharing duties with the officers and men of *Bulwark*, with one officer and a fire party between the two ships each night. By day we worked from a Portakabin on the flight deck. I inherited the job of Unit Security Officer which meant every non-cash safe on board had to be opened, checked and relocked with one combination setting. It was only then that I realized just how many safes there were on board, including one in every cabin, and the strange items which had been left in some of them. What a grand occasion it was when one took a turn as night duty officer - accommodated in *Bulwark's* Flag Cabin, with no heating, ventilation or water, but with one's own personal oil drum to pee in. Meals consisted of pre-cooked, and often congealed, food in cardboard containers which were sent down from some galley in the barracks. After a busy and enjoyable commission it was sad to see the locked compartments and shut-down equipment.' In May 1977

Colin left *Intrepid*, and in autumn that year the ship was taken in hand for a refit. Once back in dry dock it was not long before the assault ship was surrounded by scaffolding, as the whole of her hull and superstructure underwent a full survey. Internally, her main propulsion machinery was completely overhauled and her 39 ballast tanks, the huge compartments which, when flooded, increased the ship's weight from 11,000 to 17,000 tons ballasted, were surveyed and repainted. On 5 June 1978 *Intrepid's* new commanding officer, Captain D. H. Morse RN, was appointed to the ship and by the end of the year, when the ship's own catering facilities took over from the elderly barge which had been acting as a floating galley for eight months, it was clear that the refit was coming to an end.

On 5 January 1979 the first of *Intrepid's* LCMs, *T1*, was embarked when, for the first time since the summer of 1976, the assault ship ballasted down, lowered her stern gate and allowed *T1* to sail into the dock. On 16 January the ship was visited by the C-in-C Fleet, Admiral Sir Henry Leach, who toured the different departments. On 19 February, two weeks after the first of the LCVPs had arrived from Poole, *Intrepid* carried out five days of sea trials, which included the rescue of a small yacht by *T8* and a short visit to Torquay, where Captain's Divisions were held on the flight deck. That same day the ship weighed anchor to undergo four more days of trials before returning to Portsmouth for defect rectifications.

It had been intended to hold the Rededication Service on the flight deck, but Friday 9 March 1979 saw gale force winds and driving rain sweeping across the Solent so, apart from the Royal Marines Honour Guard who stayed in the rain to salute the VIPs, everyone transferred to the tank deck. Among the guests was the MP for Winchester, the city with which *Intrepid* was affiliated, Rear-Admiral Morgan Giles, together with the city's mayor. The cake-cutting ceremony was performed by Mrs Jill Morse, wife of the commanding officer, assisted by the ship's youngest rating MEM Karl Jones. On 19 March, ten days after the ceremony, *Intrepid* sailed once again to conduct more trials and to begin her work-up at Portland. On 30 April the assault ship left Portsmouth and set course for Plymouth Sound to embark 150 midshipmen and 50 marine engineering apprentices, before setting course for the Azores on the first leg of a Caribbean training cruise. After refuelling at the Portuguese islands *Intrepid* continued her Atlantic crossing heading for Bermuda, where everyone was able to get ashore. Here many took to mopeds as the best form of transport across the islands, and during the ship's passage between Bermuda and Charleston T-shirts proclaiming, 'I survived a Bermuda motorbike' were much in evidence on board. As the ship steamed past the Fort Sumter national monument and into the mouth of the Cooper River 'Procedure Alpha' in tropical white shorts proved quite an ordeal, as it lasted for some ten miles of

Intrepid alongside Portsmouth's South Railway Jetty in August 1975. *(Don Smith)*

At speed and looking her best. *Intrepid* in 1982. *(Neil Segger)*

At sea in the Channel during the later years of her career. *(FotoFlite, Ashford, Kent)*

Intrepid taking part in amphibious exercises in Scandinavian waters during 1988.
(Official, courtesy of Maritime Books, Liskeard)

Carrying out prewetting trials. *(Neil Segger)*

wide open and windy areas of river, but finally *Intrepid* arrived at the US naval base. The next destination on America's east coast was Annapolis where the LCMs were used to ferry the midshipmen to the US Naval Academy to meet their American counterparts. There then followed a short journey upriver to Baltimore, where the assault ship secured opposite the oldest American warship still afloat, USS *Constellation*, a veteran of the 1812 war. Conveniently the berth was only 200 yards from the city centre, and many took the opportunity to visit Washington. From Baltimore *Intrepid* steamed north once again, this time to Boston where the 32 members of the Assault Squadron marched through the city. The occasion was the day on which the Honorable Artillery Company of Massachusetts held its annual parade, which involved a cathedral service and two march pasts, covering a distance of four miles. Also representing *Intrepid* were the Junior Band of the Queen's Division and 30 midshipmen under training, all of whom received warm applause from the people of Boston. When she left the port the US Marine Corps Air Squadron performed a fly-past of four Skyhawks and four 'Huey' helicopters, over the assault ship. Canada was the next stop where the port of Halifax NS, compared to the US visits, seemed very quiet. On leaving Halifax *Intrepid* made her eastbound crossing of the Atlantic, arriving in Plymouth Sound on 25 June when the midshipmen and apprentices were disembarked.

With all the trainees having left the ship *Intrepid* returned to her amphibious role and after embarking 18 vehicles and personnel of the Commando Logistics Regiment, she sailed for the Solent and the amphibious work-up on Browndown Beach. With all sections of the Assault Squadron having been put through their paces the ship returned to Plymouth Sound to prepare for her first major amphibious exercise for over three years. Code-named 'Whisky Venture', the exercise began with the embarkation of 3 Commando Brigade, which included 98 vehicles and trailers, four 105mm light guns and five Scout helicopters. With the embarkation having been completed in less than four hours it was clear that the ship was operating at peak efficiency as she sailed for Scottish waters and the first of a number of amphibious landings. The second phase of the exercise took place in Denmark, after which there was a visit from the C-in-C Fleet, Admiral J. F. H. Eberle, who, only nine years before, had been *Intrepid's* second commanding officer. The next stop, in mid-July, was Barry Budden at the mouth of the Firth of Tay where there was another amphibious landing, followed by a passage via the Western Isles to Plymouth Sound where the embarked force was landed. After an overnight passage to Spithead a 'Families Day' was held, before the ship secured at Portsmouth Dockyard for some much-anticipated leave.

In August 1979 *Intrepid* took part in Portsmouth's Navy Days, before embarking a force of midshipmen and apprentices for her autumn training cruise to the Mediterranean. The deployment began at Gibraltar on 20 September when the ship was dry docked for maintenance to her hull, which gave an opportunity to hold the Rock Race. As often happened on a training cruise the midshipmen's and the apprentices' teams took first and second places respectively, with the Royal Marines being pushed into third place. After leaving Gibraltar with a freshly painted hull *Intrepid* set course for Athens where the ship's teams ran a mini-marathon which, appropriately, started at the town of Marathon, and once again the midshipmen came in first. The next stop for the assault ship was Istanbul where, with the city under martial law, some activities were limited. However, haggling in the Grand Bazaar and visiting the fine mosques and palaces made for an interesting run ashore. During the passage between Istanbul and Alexandria the ship underwent her Sea Inspection and next day she berthed alongside a jetty in the Egyptian port. For the Royal Marines the first appointment on the agenda was an Honour Guard and, after boarding an Egyptian Navy bus, they were driven across the city to the Memorial to the Unknown Soldier by an Egyptian sailor who, according to one marine, 'was hell-bent on either homicide or suicide'. The ceremony included the laying of a wreath by Captain Morse and a march past in company with an Egyptian Navy Honour Guard. As a run ashore Alexandria was quiet, but there were organized trips to the Pyramids and to Luxor, which was a 650-mile round trip. After leaving Alexandria *Intrepid* set course for Palermo, where she arrived on 2 November for the last Mediterranean visit of the deployment. On sailing from the Sicilian port the assault ship steamed into some heavy weather which meant that a RAS with RFA *Stromness* was carried out in marginal conditions. During the passage to Gibraltar one of the LCVPs broke free from its davit, and although it was not lost overboard it was left hanging precariously. In order to secure it and prevent further damage, at 23.30 on 6 November *Intrepid* put into Gibraltar where a crane lifted the offending landing craft into the dock for the remainder of the passage and one and a half hours later *Intrepid* was back at sea. Five days later the assault ship arrived at Portland where two LCMs were exchanged with two from *Fearless* then *Intrepid* continued her passage north, arriving off the Norwegian naval base at Ramsund during the forenoon of 17 November. Here the two borrowed LCMs, and one of *Intrepid's* own, were left behind ready for an exercise the following year. Next the assault ship sailed north to Narvik where freezing temperatures and only four and a half hours of daylight made quite a contrast to the eastern Mediterranean ports, and there were more than a few sighs of relief when main engines were rung on and *Intrepid* sailed for Portsmouth and Christmas leave.

The new year of 1980 started in a routine way for

In spring 1979, whilst in the Mediterranean, *Intrepid* met the Soviet helicopter carrier *Moscow*.
(Neil Segger)

Intrepid and *Bulwark* replenish fuel and stores during 'Exercise Cold Winter' in March 1980.
(Neil Segger)

Intrepid when, with a full complement of midshipmen on board, the ship sailed for a much-anticipated spring cruise to the Caribbean. Leaving Portsmouth in early January, she set course for Madeira where there was a short stop in the picturesque port of Funchal. However, on 18 January, when *Intrepid* was in mid-Atlantic, she was ordered to Gibraltar. Continued tensions and civil strife in Lebanon meant that *Intrepid* would spend the remainder of January and most of February in the eastern Mediterranean. After leaving Gibraltar the assault ship set course for Cyprus, where she anchored off Akrotiri. This was followed by a mini-amphibious exercise for the Assault Squadron, helped out by a helicopter from 845 Squadron, and followed by a banyan weekend at Cephalonia. From here the LCMs set out independently, via Patras and the Corinth Canal, for Athens where they arrived a day before the ship. From Piraeus *Intrepid* called at Izmir and the last day of February saw her back in Gibraltar as she made her way home to Portland where the midshipmen were disembarked. From Portland *Intrepid* steamed north to Trondheim where, in her amphibious role, she embarked Headquarters and Signal RM and sailed north to Tromso for an amphibious landing in Malangen Fjord. Despite a damaged LCM, which grounded during operations in an ice-bound fjord, operations went well and after re-embarking her troops at Tromso *Intrepid* sailed for Plymouth Sound to land the embarked force, and then proceeded to Portsmouth for seasonal leave.

On 1 April 1980 there was a change of command when Captain P. G. V. Dingemans RN took over from Captain Morse. During the last week of April *Intrepid* left Portsmouth, but only for local waters and the Solent where the new Assault Squadron personnel practised their skills on Browndown Beach, before the ship sailed for Portland and nearby Warbarrow Bay, close to Lulworth Cove. During exercises at the latter location *Intrepid* embarked main battle tanks for the first time for five years in the form of seven Chieftains, and in addition she loaded four CVR Scimitar light tanks, all of which belonged to the 17/21st Lancers. According to one marine, 'It was pleasant to see the tank and lower vehicle deck filled with military equipment rather than the perennial, rather lost looking, midshipmen.' After leaving home waters *Intrepid* set course, once again, for the Mediterranean where, after Gibraltar, she called at Sicily for banyans, Trieste and Marseilles. One of the LCMs, however, carrying out a navigation exercise, sailed independently from Trieste to Marseilles, by way of San Remo and Toulon. In mid-June there was a fun weekend at sea which began with Divisions and ended with an 'It's a Knockout' competition, deck hockey, deck soccer and other sports tournaments. By the end of the month, however, the ship was back at Portsmouth.

Intrepid's autumn deployment began at the end of August 1980, when she left Portsmouth to head for the Dorset coast to carry out landing craft evolutions in preparation for 'Exercise Teamwork 80', in which she would participate for four weeks. On 2 September, in Plymouth Sound, she embarked 3 Commando Brigade, together with HQ and Signals Squadron and the Brigade Air Squadron with their six Scout helicopters, and set course for Norway. During the passage a rendezvous was made with *Bulwark,* and the LSLs *Sir Bedivere, Sir Galahad, Sir Lancelot* and *Sir Tristram*, for landings in Norway during which the BARV got stuck in seven feet of mud and had to be left behind. A run ashore at Rosyth followed, after which the amphibious force sailed to Cape Wrath to rendezvous with other NATO units and to carry out practice landings in preparation for the final part of the exercise. With the rehearsals completed it was back to Norway for further landings and an ASW exercise with *Bulwark* which took both ships into the North Sea. Following the final withdrawal from Norway, during which *Intrepid* embarked a large number of vehicles, both wheeled and tracked, the six Scout helicopters, two Wessex helicopters of 845 Squadron and two bowsers, she departed for Plymouth Sound. Once secured at C buoy the Commando Brigade, vehicles and aircraft were disembarked and the ship made a quick change to her training role as 147 midshipmen boarded, together with the Band of the 1st Battalion, the Queen's Regiment. This time, after leaving Plymouth Sound *Intrepid* was bound for warmer waters as she set course south down the coasts of Spain and Portugal.

The first port of call on *Intrepid's* Mediterranean deployment was Gibraltar where she arrived on 3 October, but instead of just a brief visit the assault ship was dry-docked for a 12-day maintenance period, which gave the ship's company a chance to relax on the first run ashore for five weeks. On leaving the colony the ship began nine days at sea by towing a splash target for *Invincible's* Sea Harriers. During the deployment there were calls at Cyprus, Naples and the Spanish port of Cartagena, but the highlight was a four-day visit to the port of Haifa. Few of the ship's company had been to Israel so they made the most of 12-hour coach tours which took in Nazareth, Jerusalem, Bethlehem and the Sea of Galilee. During the homeward passage the Flag Officer Third Flotilla, Rear-Admiral J. M. H. Cox, hoisted his pennant and took passage from Naples to Lisbon, which was the final port of call before *Intrepid* returned to her base port for Christmas leave.

On 6 January 1981, with Christmas and New Year leave over, *Intrepid* left Portsmouth bound for the Caribbean and with the ship in her training role she had on board a full complement of midshipmen, while ten members of the Assault Squadron took the opportunity to make the passage as far as Barbados as volunteer crew in the Royal Navy's yacht *Chaser*. For those members of the ship's

Leaving the Solent for the Caribbean on 6 January 1981.
(Mike Lennon)

company who had been on board the previous year there was a sense of relief when the ship actually made it to the Caribbean, and on 19 January *Intrepid* arrived at St John's, Antigua, the first port of the training cruise. The passage between St John's and Bridgetown, Barbados, saw the midshipmen begin their navigation exercises as they took the LCMs independently between ports, while others manned the yacht *Chaser*, which stayed close to the assault ship during the deployment. For the ship's company Barbados provided plenty of golden beaches and warm Caribbean sea and sun, not to mention discos, steel bands and cheap rum for evening entertainment. The next navigation exercise took *Intrepid* to the island of Bequia, where she anchored in Admiralty Bay close to Port Elizabeth, the island's only settlement of any size. As well as a day-long banyan for the ship's company, working parties from the ship helped to repair hurricane damage in the area. It was here that LCM *T4* and its crew spent an afternoon removing the wrecked and half-buried hull of a yacht from a nearby beach. Surf caused by the wreck had been eating away at sand in front of local houses, so with the help of the LCM the two halves of the boat were towed out to sea and sunk, after which the grateful residents plied the *T4's* crew with rum.

From Bequia *Intrepid* rendezvoused with the Dutch destroyer *Rotterdam* and set course for Aruba where, on 3 February, she anchored off Arashi Beach. During the two days at anchor over 100 Dutch marines of the 23 Infantry Company were embarked for an amphibious exercise. After spending the night on camp beds on the tank deck they were landed by the Assault Squadron for a two-day exercise. Following this *Intrepid* secured alongside in Orangestaad, Aruba, for a four-day visit, during which time all on board were able to enjoy more sun, sand and surf. During the visit Divisions were held and the Royal Marines Band gave an excellent evening display of Beating Retreat on a floodlit jetty. Meanwhile, the crew of LCM *T6* earned themselves a few beers when they went to the rescue of the ship's whaler which had ended up beached and stranded during a senior rates' banyan. The next stop was St Thomas, one of the US Virgin Islands, which offered a good run ashore, although muggings on one or two members of the ship's company marred the visit somewhat. It was in St Thomas that Rear-Admiral Cox visited the ship and toured all departments on board. On 16 February the assault ship anchored off Tortola where the ship's rugby team played and beat the British Virgin Islands side and four days later, steaming via Roosevelt Roads where she refuelled, *Intrepid* arrived at San Juan, Puerto Rico, the final port of the deployment. On 23 February she set out on her voyage home and on 4 March, in the vicinity of the Azores, she stood by in case she was required to refuel a Sea King which was answering a distress call from a Portuguese trawler. Two days later she arrived at Portland where the midshipmen were disembarked and the ship underwent a fast role-change as she prepared to exchange the heat of the Caribbean for the sub-zero temperatures of northern Norway. On 8 March, after embarking HQ Brigade Signal Regiment, *Intrepid* sailed for 'Exercise Cold Winter', which saw her operating with *Bulwark* for the last time. Also involved in the exercise were the US Navy's ships *Guam*, *Barnstaple County* and *Austin*, as well as the LSLs *Sir*

Geraint and *Sir Tristram.* As well as a night exercise in Lyngenfjord, where the SBS provided the opposition, there were brief visits to Trondheim and Tromso, before *Intrepid* returned to Portsmouth on 24 March.

On 28 April 1981, having embarked personnel of the 9/12th Lancers, together with four of their Chieftain tanks and ten Scorpion light tanks, *Intrepid* sailed for 'Exercise Arish Mell', at the location of the same name in Warbarrow Bay, Dorset. Following this operation she reverted to her training role and steamed north through the Irish Sea, hugging the coast and sailing via the Western Islands and the Pentland Firth for a 48-hour visit to Hamburg, which coincided with celebrations of the anniversary of the port's founding. Escorted by the destroyer *Norfolk,* the assault ship called at the Danish port of Aarhus, which attracted the attention of a Soviet Kotlin-class destroyer and an East German corvette. There were further calls at Stockholm, the small Swedish town of Harnosand and Kristiansand in Norway, where Captain Dingeman's father, an RNR Surgeon Captain, joined the ship for the passage to Spithead, where she arrived on 18 June. Next day there was a major amphibious exercise when the LCMs transported 1,300 guests out to *Intrepid* for a 'Families Day'. During the day at sea with *Norfolk,* which also had families embarked, there were demonstrations by hovercraft and Wessex helicopter flying displays, as well as a jackstay transfer between *Norfolk* and *Intrepid.* Finally, both ships steamed up harbour to secure alongside.

During the period alongside at Portsmouth, whilst most of the ship's company were on leave, a Government Defence Review was published which announced that *Fearless* would finally pay off in 1984, but for *Intrepid* the end was to come much earlier, at the end of November 1981. Suddenly, the assault ship was at the end of her career, with only five months of active service left. In the short-term, however, the commission continued as scheduled and on 24 August she left Portsmouth for a short shakedown cruise in the Channel before embarking 470 Royal Marines of 42 Commando, together with their vehicles and four Scout helicopters for 'Exercise Amber Express' in Danish waters which provided an opportunity for a run ashore in Copenhagen. The exercise lasted for ten days, but by 26 September the ship was in Plymouth Sound to disembark the Royal Marines and to embark 128 midshipmen and 67 apprentices under training. After leaving home waters *Intrepid* set course for the Mediterranean and her final deployment. Whilst en route through the Bay of Biscay an emergency signal was received from an Italian yachtsman competing in a mini-transatlantic yacht race whose boat had foundered. He was the third competitor of the 26 who had set out from Penzance on 26 September, whose yacht had sunk. Fortunately a Wessex helicopter of 845 Squadron was launched from *Intrepid* and the man was rescued safely, to be landed at Gibraltar three days later. On 12 October *Intrepid* put into Palermo for four days, following which the assault ship and her RFA *Green Rover* took part in a convoy escort exercise with the Italian Navy, during which she met her near-namesake ITS *Intrepido,* a 34-knot destroyer. During the exercise *Intrepid,* RFA *Green Rover* and ITS *Stromboli* acted as merchantmen, with air cover being provided by the Italian Air Force and *Intrepid's* two Wessex helicopters, while opposition was by an Italian submarine and an armed hydrofoil of the Italian Navy. After a night rendezvous ten miles south of the toe of Italy the 'convoy' carried out NATO procedures to defend itself, with Captain Dingemans acting as the convoy commander. The convoy route took the ships within ten miles of Taranto, following which on 19 October, with the exercise over, *Intrepid* put into Naples for a four-day visit. This was followed by calls at Akrotiri in Cyprus and the Dodecanese island of Leros where, upon leaving, Ceremonial Divisions were held over the spot at which the assault ship's predecessor had been sunk in 1943. There was a three-day visit to Piraeus and to Alexandria, before the assault ship began her passage home, calling at Gibraltar for two days and finally, on 20 November, at Cadiz. On Friday 27 November 1981, flying a 350 ft-long paying-off pennant, with the ship's company manning her upper decks and her LCMs and LCVPs following her in formation, *Intrepid* steamed into Portsmouth Harbour. Overhead two Wessex helicopters of 845 Squadron, which had only recently left the ship, clattered overhead in a farewell fly-past before the assault ship secured alongside. On the bridge 'Finished with Engines' was rung and *Intrepid's* active career with the Royal Navy was over - or so it seemed at the time.

On 27 November 1981, with her ship's company manning the decks and her paying-off pennant proudly flying, *Intrepid* enters Portsmouth Harbour for what was thought to be the last time. *(Michael Cassar, Valletta, Malta)*

Chapter Twelve

HMS *Intrepid* - An Unexpected Reprieve 1981-1991

When *Intrepid* returned to Portsmouth Dockyard on 27 November 1981, it was to pay off for what was thought to be the last time and to begin a de-storing process which was expected to last until early April 1982, when the last members of her ship's company would disperse. The Government's 1981 Defence Review proposed the withdrawal from service of some 17 ships, including *Hermes, Fearless, Intrepid, London, Glamorgan, Norfolk* and a number of frigates. The biggest blow, however, came with the news that negotiations were being conducted with the Australian Government over the sale of the aircraft carrier *Invincible*. There is no doubt that the proposed defence cuts were as swingeing as those of the mid-1960s but, in fact, they continued a process which had been carried out by all governments since the end of the Second World War which paralleled the shedding of Britain's worldwide colonial commitments. In 1981, although the Government's defence of its decision cited 'changing operational requirements and the introduction into service of new ships' which had made it possible to withdraw the vessels, this ignored the fact that the country still had overseas commitments, some of which were the subject of long-standing sovereignty claims. One such commitment, far away from home in the South Atlantic, were the Falkland Islands and their Dependencies.

Another consequence of the 1981 Defence Review was the decision to withdraw the Royal Navy's sole representative in the South Atlantic, HMS *Endurance*, at the end of her 1981-82 deployment. This was a proposal which had been opposed by the Foreign Secretary on the grounds that the sovereignty dispute with Argentina was far from settled, and that any reduction in Britain's commitment to the islands would be interpreted by Argentina as a sign that the country was unwilling to defend them. His exhortation was in vain, and on 30 June 1981 the decision to withdraw *Endurance* was confirmed in Parliament - with the predicted result. Although the attitude of successive British governments had been to declare the Falkland Islands British, a status they would retain for as long as the inhabitants wished, behind the scenes various options for sharing or transferring sovereignty to Argentina had been considered, including a 'leaseback' option. These negotiations had led to concern in the islands, where the residents were also becoming increasingly alarmed by the number of overflights by Argentine military aircraft.

Meanwhile, at Portsmouth, December 1981 saw *Intrepid* rapidly being stripped of stores and ammunition. On Monday 8 March 1982, however, the Secretary of State for Defence, who just a few months previously had visited *Fearless* in the Solent, announced in Parliament that both assault ships would be reprieved and would continue to take turns with each other in order to provide both an amphibious capability and the Dartmouth Training role. For the Royal Marines this was welcome news, but in the Royal Navy there was a mixed reaction, since most senior officers would have preferred to keep *Invincible,* and it was apparent that to retain *Fearless* and *Intrepid* they would

HMS *Antrim's* Sea King helicopter operating from *Intrepid* during the passage south to the Falkland Islands.
(Fleet Air Arm Museum, Yeovilton)

155

Intrepid closes to fuel from RFA *Plumleaf* during operations in the South Atlantic.
(G. Mortimore/ Action Photos, Isle of Wight)

probably have to sacrifice other ships, including destroyers and frigates. It would not be long, however, before events in the South Atlantic would intervene in the political manoeuvrings of Whitehall.

In December 1981 the Argentine naval ice breaker, *Almirante Irizar,* had made an unauthorized visit to the British Dependent Territory of South Georgia, ostensibly to land an Argentine scrap metal dealer who had purchased derelict equipment at the old whaling station at Grytviken. A subsequent diplomatic protest to the Argentine Government was summarily rejected and later that month Captain Nick Barker of HMS *Endurance* reported that his ship's company had received a very 'cold' reception at the Argentine port of Ushuaia, and that he was aware of an order not to fraternize with his sailors. In March 1982 events in the South Atlantic took a more sinister turn when the scrap metal dealer made an unauthorized visit to Grytviken, having been taken there in the Argentine naval support vessel *Bahia Buen Sucesco.* Members of the British Antarctic Survey Team, who were responsible for law enforcement on the island, reported that a sizeable party of Argentine civilian and military personnel had also disembarked, gunshots had been heard, the Argentine flag had been raised and a notice warning of unauthorized landings had been defaced. Although the vessel eventually left Grytviken, a further illegal landing was made at nearby Leith Harbour and it was apparent that the activities were being deliberately carried out under the Argentine Navy's guidance. It was becoming clear that what appeared to be trivial incidents were being deliberately exaggerated by Argentina, and the Foreign Secretary in London reported that the dispute had developed to the point where '...an early confrontation with Argentina might need to be faced.'

With *Endurance* having been ordered to South Georgia to oversee the departure of the Argentine naval party on the island, on 25 March information was received in London to the effect that Argentine warships were being dispatched to prevent her from carrying out the task. Meanwhile, at Leith, a second Argentine naval ship had arrived and military landing craft and a helicopter were operating in the harbour. Over the days which followed the diplomatic situation continued to deteriorate and on 26 March an Argentine fleet left for what were supposed to be anti-submarine exercises with the Uruguayan Navy. However, accompanying the 'anti-submarine' fleet was the tank landing ship, *Cabo San Antonio,* and the Type 42 destroyers *Santissima Trinidad* and *Hercules,* together with two frigates, all of which were carrying troops. In addition, another frigate and the submarine *Santa Fe,* carrying marines and commandos, set course for South Georgia. With the aircraft carrier *Veintecinco de Mayo*[*] and escorts also at sea, the situation had become very dangerous indeed. By 29 March the Ministry of Defence in London had been alerted to the situation which had developed in the South Atlantic and already moves were in hand to form a Task Force which could be sent south, but it would be

---

[*] *Veintecinco de Mayo* was the ex-Royal Navy light fleet carrier HMS *Venerable*. See 'The Colossus-Class Aircraft Carriers 1944-1972'. FAN PUBLICATIONS 2002.

three weeks before the first units arrived in the area. Next day it was clear that the Argentine fleet was actually intending to invade the Falkland Islands and, although nothing could be done to prevent it, the First Sea Lord, Admiral Sir Henry Leach, was confident that he could '...put together a task force of destroyers, frigates, landing craft and support vessels' which would be led by the aircraft carriers *Hermes* and *Invincible,* and which would be ready to leave in 48 hours. In the early hours of Friday 2 April 1982 Argentine forces invaded the Falkland Islands and, with a force of 2,800 men backed up by armoured vehicles, they overwhelmed the tiny garrison of some 68 Royal Marines, but only after a spirited defence of Government House at Stanley where they suffered more casualties than they had expected. At home, although many people had to reach for their atlases to find out exactly where the Falkland Islands were, there was shock and indignation at this unprovoked aggression.

Although the Navy was quick to react and start assembling the Task Force, it was not initially thought that *Intrepid,* which was now well and truly out of commission, would be required. On 3 April, however, with Commodore Amphibious Warfare, Commodore Michael Clapp, pressing for her inclusion it was calculated that at least 14 days would be required to prepare her for sea. From COMAW's point of view *Intrepid,* together with *Fearless,* with their helicopter landing decks, their troop-carrying facilities and with their landing craft, would be vital additions to the Task Force which, it was envisaged, would be carrying out an amphibious landing on the South Atlantic Islands. By Monday 5 April it had been decided to include *Intrepid* for service with the Task Force and as preparations went ahead to reverse the de-storing and de-ammunitioning work of the previous three months, at Poole her LCUs and LCVPs were made ready and her Beach Unit was formed. Next day *Fearless* left Portsmouth bound for the South Atlantic, and on 8 April *Intrepid's* landing craft left Poole to sail in formation to Portsmouth. Meanwhile, in the dockyard civilian staff worked night and day to reverse all the preparations for transferring the ship to the Reserve Fleet. Finally, on 21 April, commanded by Captain Peter Dingemans RN, *Intrepid* left Portsmouth bound for Portland where she would carry out a brief work-up. On Monday 25 April, with the ship's company manning the upper decks, she sailed from Portland for Plymouth Sound where she embarked men of the 2nd Battalion Parachute Regiment, before leaving the following day for a fast passage to Ascension Island. During the voyage *Intrepid* joined the converted merchantman *Atlantic Conveyor,* which was acting as an auxiliary aircraft carrier and carrying a full load of Sea Harriers, Wessex and Chinook helicopters. Both ships arrived at Ascension on 5 May, where *Intrepid* was able to join other units of the amphibious force, including *Fearless.* Her arrival was much welcomed by Commodore Clapp, for with all diplomatic efforts having failed it was obvious that the Argentine forces would have to be evicted from the Falkland Islands and South Georgia by force.

Two days after *Intrepid's* arrival at Ascension Island her sister *Fearless* sailed for the second leg of her voyage south and next day, during the forenoon of 8 May, *Intrepid* followed her. By 9 May she had caught up with the amphibious fleet and in the early hours of 10 May the two assault ships rendezvoused with the troop transport *Canberra, Norland, Atlantic Conveyor, Europic Ferry* and the escorts *Ardent* and *Argonaut.* During the afternoon of 11 May, with the amphibious force some 930 miles north-west of Tristan da Cunha, there was a submarine alert when a lookout in *Intrepid* reported sighting a periscope. For an hour the force zigzagged at 16 knots, but at 15.30 conditions were relaxed, with the sighting thought to have been a whale spouting. Although it was a false alarm the incident reminded everyone that the Argentines were very interested in their passage south and had submarines which were capable of ranging the Atlantic Ocean. During the forenoon of 13 May a company of 45 Commando was transferred from the comfort on board *Canberra* to *Intrepid.* Three days later the force rendezvoused with the five LSLs of the amphibious force, *Sir Galahad, Sir Geraint, Sir Lancelot, Sir Percivale* and *Sir Tristram,* and their escorts *Antrim* and *Plymouth.* This meant that the amphibious force consisted of 19 ships and with their position just 650 miles east-north-east of Port Stanley, they were now approaching their destination. During the afternoon of 19 May, when they were some 230 miles from Port Stanley, the troopship *Canberra* stationed herself off *Intrepid's* port quarter for the transfer of the men of 3 Para by LCU. That forenoon 40 Commando had transferred from *Canberra* to *Fearless,* now it was 3 Para's turn. Fortunately the operation was completed without any mishaps just before darkness fell, with the last LCU returning to *Intrepid* at 16.15. Like her sister *Fearless, Intrepid* was now in 'mega-overload', with hardly room to move on board as marines and paras took what rest they could in the packed mess decks, cabins, dining halls and passageways. On the tank deck men worked steadily on their vehicles, securing canvases and mounting additional machine-guns. During the day 11 Harrier aircraft had flown over from *Atlantic Conveyor* to *Invincible,* and closer to shore the naval bombardment and air attacks on enemy targets continued.

'D-Day' was fixed as Friday 21 May, with the amphibious landings taking place at San Carlos Water to the north of East Falkland Island. By 20.00 on 20 May the amphibious force had passed the point of no return and the fleet formed into three waves with *Intrepid* and *Fearless* leading the way in 'Wave One'. The first ships to enter Falkland Sound, between East and West Falkland, were *Antrim* and *Ardent,* and they were closely followed by

With *Intrepid* in the foreground, the Amphibious Task Force lies at anchor in San Carlos Water. (*PO Pete Holdgate, courtesy Maritime Books, Liskeard*)

On 14 July 1982, with her hull and superstructure rus-streaked and weather-beaten, *Intrepid* returns to Portsmouth Harbour following her service to liberate the Falkland Islands. *(Mike Lennon)*

A very smart 'Procedure Alpha' entry into San Juan Harbour, Puerto Rico, in July 1986. The ship's company and Assault Squadron are manning the upper decks.
(Royal Marines Museum, Eastney, No 14/2/10 - 515)

Fearless and *Intrepid,* both of which would need additional time to dock down. The second wave, escorted by *Plymouth,* would consist of *Canberra, Norland* and *Stromness* and finally came the five LSLs and *Europic Ferry.* With the amphibious force making the last 100 miles or so of their passage under cover of darkness, *Intrepid* anchored in Falkland Sound at 23.37 on 20 May and it was not long before the LCUs and LCVPs were ferrying men and equipment ashore. The first enemy troops to be encountered were at Fanning Head and, in a firefight which lasted several hours, they were dealt with by units of the SBS. It was men of 3 Para from *Intrepid* that encountered 40 enemy troops who soon fled the scene to meet up with the survivors of the Fanning Head engagement, and during the forenoon of 21 May, as the troops dug in ashore, the Argentine Air Force launched the first of a series of air attacks on the shipping in San Carlos Water and Falkland Sound, but by the end of the day all troops and large quantities of stores, ammunition and equipment had been landed. However, the frigate *Ardent* was repeatedly hit by bombs and she later sank, with the loss of 22 members of her ship's company. Fortunately, for the operation as a whole, none of the troop transports, LSLs or the two assault ships was damaged.

During the days which followed, as the British forces gradually built up their strength and began their long march on Port Stanley, *Intrepid* and her sister *Fearless* became two of the longest-serving inhabitants of the San Carlos anchorage, which became known as 'bomb alley'. On board there was a hectic pace of activity as they provided vital support for the forces ashore and anti-aircraft fire. Although she had practised for the role many times in the past, she had never had to continue under pressure for such a sustained period of time. *Intrepid* acted as depot ship, air warfare controller, and base for vast numbers of weary troops who, when circumstances permitted, were able to obtain their first hot food and showers for some days. She provided a base for four Sea King helicopters of 846 Squadron, and provided a landing platform for the occasional Harrier which needed refuelling. Most importantly, she contributed her share of the curtain of bullets and missiles fired to meet attacking aircraft with every available weapon, including small arms, which resulted in the destruction of a number of Argentine aircraft.

During the night of 5/6 June, in order to speed up the land battle, *Intrepid* embarked men of the Scots Guards and carried them round to the vicinity of Lively Island at the entrance to Choiseul Sound. With *Penelope* as her escort she sailed at 16.30 on 5 June, and made the passage without incident so that at 22.30 her fully laden LCUs were on their way towards Bluff Cove, where they arrived safely after a very difficult trip. By 06.30 she was safely back at her anchorage in San Carlos Water. Next night *Fearless* took units of the Welsh Guards to the same area. During the night of 10/11 June *Intrepid* left San Carlos Water again, this time to deliver ammunition to troops at Fitzroy and to pick up two of *Fearless'* LCUs which had

Intrepid approaches Portland Harbour in 1987 to begin her operational sea training. The ship is in 'Procedure Alpha' for a ceremonial check by the Flag Officer Sea Training. *(Official, courtesy Commodore A.J.S. Taylor)*

The LCUs and LCVPs begin an amphibious assault during 'Exercise Dragon Hammer 88' in the summer of that year.
(Royal Marines Museum, Eastney, No 14/2/10 - 520)

been working long hours in the area. Once again the operation was completed successfully and the assault ship returned to her anchorage in San Carlos Water. Despite the fact that the LSLs *Sir Galahad* and *Sir Tristram* were bombed and seriously damaged causing heavy casualties, by 12 June the final assault on the town of Stanley had begun and during the evening of 14 June, with the Argentine forces having surrendered, the fighting was over. What had begun at the end of March with diplomatic failure had ended, against all the odds, in a military triumph. Although *Intrepid* remained in San Carlos Water for another week, by the last week of June both she and *Fearless* carrying Royal Marines, gunners of the Royal Artillery and personnel of 846 Squadron, were on their way home. On Tuesday 13 July *Intrepid* and *Fearless* arrived in Plymouth Sound to drop off the troops and Fleet Air Arm personnel. Next day, to a tumultuous welcome, both assault ships arrived in Portsmouth Harbour and it was not long before *Intrepid* was once again reduced to the Reserve Fleet. The campaign in the South Atlantic had well and truly highlighted the vital role of amphibious assault ships in the Navy of the late twentieth century. It ensured a further period of service for *Intrepid* and the need for successors to be built and commissioned to replace both her and her sister *Fearless*. It also ensured that all three Invincible-class aircraft carriers would remain in the service of the Royal Navy.

On 26 September 1983, over a year after arriving home from the South Atlantic, and under tow by the Admiralty tug *Robust, Intrepid* slipped almost unnoticed from Portsmouth Harbour. She was bound for Devonport where she arrived two days later to begin a major, 19-month, refit. On 8 January 1985 her new commanding officer, Captain A. G. M. A. Provest RN, was appointed to the ship and soon afterwards her ship's company was brought up to strength. In December 1984, at Poole, 6 Assault Squadron of the Royal Marines had been formed, and after six weeks of hectic specialist training, on 19 February 1985 they, together with their LCUs and LCVPs, joined *Intrepid* at Devonport. On board the assault ship the refit had included an overhaul of the hull and all machinery, and modifications to enable her to operate the larger Sea Kings as well as Wessex and Scout helicopters. In the light of the Falklands campaign she was also fitted with new 20mm 'Gambo' anti-aircraft guns. The refit ended on 29 March and was followed by Harbour Acceptance Trials, when all the ship's systems were tested whilst alongside her berth. Then came Sea Acceptance Trials and basic Operational Sea Training, still known to most as the work-up, at Portland. This was followed by an amphibious work-up and by Flag Officer Sea Training's final inspection. In early June *Intrepid* took over the Dartmouth Training role from *Fearless*, and the two ships took part in joint manoeuvres before, on 5 June, having embarked 140 midshipmen and 90 apprentices, *Intrepid* sailed for the Mediterranean. After a rough passage south, in the Western Mediterranean the assault ship rendezvoused with HMS *Naiad* and many of the midshipmen transferred to the frigate for a day to carry out various evolutions. Later both ships headed for Palma, Majorca, for long weekend visits which, according to one member of the ship's company, '...was a great run ashore, notably for the numbers of sailors and marines who had to be assisted up the gangway as they returned to the ship.' For *Intrepid* the next port of call was Villefranche on the French Riviera and from there the ship steamed to Cape Teulada off Sardinia, where the Assault Squadron got ashore for amphibious training. The final visit on the cruise was to Lisbon, which was enjoyed by all, and on 12 July there was a Families Day off the Isle of Wight. The event included air displays, a SAR demonstration and music from the Royal Marines Band of FOF3, who had embarked for the deployment. It was an opportunity for everyone to relax with families and friends for the day, after which *Intrepid* steamed up harbour to begin a three-week assisted maintenance period as well as the summer leave periods.

On Tuesday 6 August 1985, at the end of the maintenance period, the opportunity was taken to rededicate the ship, with the ceremony taking place on the flight deck. During the ceremony the C-in-C Fleet, Admiral Sir Nicholas Hunt, inspected the ship's company at Divisions, and Royal Marines from the Assault Squadron formed an Honour Guard. Also present at the ceremony was the Commodore Amphibious Warfare, Commodore Jeremy Larken, who had commanded *Fearless* during the Falklands campaign. After the religious service the rededication cake was cut by Mrs Pauline Provest, wife of the commanding officer, and she was helped by JA Ck K. Canham, who was the youngest member of the ship's company, and who had also had a hand in icing the cake.

In early September *Intrepid* left Portsmouth to embark elements of 3 Commando Brigade and Sea King Helicopters of 846 Squadron, before sailing north round the tip of Scotland to the Kyle of Lochalsh, where she rendezvoused with the Townsend Thoreson ferry, *Dragon*, which was carrying men and equipment of 45 Commando. There then followed amphibious exercises in Loch Eriboll which were code-named 'Rolling Deep' and for four days, in thoroughly wet and windy weather, the marines were landed from Cape Wrath in *Intrepid's* landing craft, all the while being supported from the ship as they advanced inland. In mid-September, after disembarking 3 Commando Brigade in Plymouth Sound, *Intrepid* returned to Scottish waters where she embarked half of 45 Commando, the other half having boarded the ferry *Dragon*, for 'Exercise Highland Reprise'. Both ships then spent two days at sea before a helicopter and surface assault took place in Holland, on the island of Schouwen, which attracted a good deal of attention from local people who turned out in force to watch. The exercise ended on 12 October, with a four-day visit to Amsterdam, where some members of the ship's company visited Arnhem and other tourist sights, while others sought out less reputable local attractions. For *Intrepid* the exercise was followed by a three-week maintenance period at Gibraltar, before she returned to Portsmouth for Christmas leave.

The early weeks of 1986 saw *Intrepid* embarking 539 Assault Squadron for an annual winter exercise in Norway, where she landed the hovercraft before sailing south in atrocious weather, with wind speeds of 75 knots and 50ft seas. The severe storms delayed the ship by 24 hours, which did not leave much time for sprucing up the paintwork before an important visit to Belfast. It was the Royal Navy's first 'big ship' call at the city for some years and *Intrepid* secured alongside a berth which was not far from where her sister *Fearless* had been built. On board for the visit was the C-in-C Fleet who hosted a reception for 250 local civic and military dignitaries. Following the visit *Intrepid*, carrying Headquarters 3 Commando Brigade, returned to the Harstad area of Norway where the Royal Marines were undergoing the winter training exercise. *Intrepid* operated in company with the ferry *Dana Anglia* and code-named 'Anchor Express 86' the manoeuvres were designed to test a landing force under severe winter conditions. However, on 5 March everything was cut short when an avalanche of soft and unstable snow killed 16 Norwegian soldiers. This led to a rapid rethink by Brigade HQ in *Intrepid* and two days later an improvised and more limited exercise, 'Westward Shift', began. Men of 42 Commando were flown ashore to the Lofoten Peninsula where they successfully conducted a formation exercise in the wintry conditions, all under the watchful eye of the Secretary of State for Defence, who had embarked in *Intrepid*. As far as the assault ship was concerned, in order to practise both 539 Assault Squadron and the merchant ships which had been taken up from trade, two amphibious landings were undertaken and the final stages of the exercise saw the ship in Vagsfjord, close to Harstad, from where, on 12 March, Headquarters 3 Commando Brigade was re-embarked and returned to Plymouth Sound.

Following Easter leave and maintenance, *Intrepid* took on her Dartmouth Training role and, in company with *Glamorgan* and RFA *Plumleaf*, left Portsmouth with a full complement of midshipmen and apprentices for a nine-week deployment to the Caribbean and the east coast of the United States. Leaving Plymouth in late April, during the transatlantic crossing there was a short refuelling stop at Ponta Delgada in the Azores where, during her four-hour stay, a few managed to get ashore only to find everything was closed. During the crossing the embarked Wessex helicopter was kept busy carrying out training flights, and during the deployment it made the landmark 2,000th deck landing since the completion of the refit in early 1985. Once across the Atlantic the first port of call was Virgin

'Hands to bathe' in the Mediterranean. When lowered the stern gate provided an ideal lido area.
(Official, courtesy Commodore A.J.S. Taylor)

A very full tank deck for the 'hook' operation during 'Exercise Teamwork' in Norwegian waters.
(Official, courtesy Commodore A.J.S. Taylor)

Gorda for banyan leave, which was always popular with ships of the Training Squadron. During the passage between Virgin Gorda and Bridgetown, Barbados, the landing craft were kept busy with navigation exercises for the midshipmen, which was the reason for the cruise. During recreational hours the flight deck was the venue for deck hockey and sports tournaments, and also the best sunbathing space. The visit to Barbados was marked by some unseasonal heavy rain, but this did not stop members of the ship's company making detailed studies of local bars and beaches, with the pleasure boat *Jolly Roger* taking many for swimming trips. During the visit Flag Officer Second Flotilla, Rear-Admiral W. R. S. Thomas, hoisted his flag and the Barbados Defence Minister spent a day on board. After leaving Bridgetown there were four days at sea, one of which was spent exercising with the Barbados Defence Force. The next visit, to San Juan, the capital of Puerto Rico, proved highly successful with some lavish hospitality from the large British community. For the midshipmen under training there was the unique experience of instruction in rainforest survival techniques from the Puerto Rican National Guard, whilst most members of the ship's company enjoyed a more sedate lifestyle enjoying cheap pina coladas in local bars. During the passage between San Juan and Mayport, Florida, two Sea Knight helicopters from the US Marine Corps 266 Assault Squadron were embarked for 36 hours to give the ship the opportunity of working with and operating another type of helicopter. At Mayport, whilst *Intrepid* underwent a maintenance period, the ship's company was able to take a few days' station leave and visit Disney World, Cape Canaveral and many other attractions. For the last visit of the deployment *Intrepid* steamed north to Boston, where there was a tremendous reception from the people of Massachusetts and members of the Assault Squadron were last-minute entrants in the city's marathon 'fun run'. On leaving Boston *Intrepid* set out for her eastbound crossing of the Atlantic and preparations began to convert the ship back to her amphibious role.

Arriving back in home waters at the end of June, *Intrepid* took part in Navy Days at Rosyth where she also prepared to participate in JMC 862 for which she would act as COMAW, Commodore Jeremy Larken's flagship. She also took a starring role in Portsmouth Navy Days in August, attracting over 45,000 visitors over the three days. In early September the assault ship took part in the first of two NATO exercises, 'Northern Wedding', which entailed embarking Headquarters 3 Commando Brigade in Plymouth Sound before joining seven merchant ships which had been hired by the MoD for rehearsal landings in the Cardigan Bay area. From there the amphibious force steamed north to Cape Wrath and round to Moray Firth, where they joined a large US amphibious task group. The whole force then made an 'opposed' transit of the North Sea to southern Norway where, watched by several Warsaw Pact vessels, a full-scale assault took place. There then followed a short visit to Aarhus in Denmark before the next major NATO exercise, code-named 'Bold Guard'. This time however, *Intrepid* would act as the 'enemy' for a defence exercise in northern Germany. Flying the pennant of COMAW and with Headquarters 3 Commando Brigade embarked, *Intrepid* controlled the combined RFA and merchant fleet which was taking part, with the amphibious landing itself being staged near Skenfoerd. Once the marines had re-embarked *Intrepid* returned them to Plymouth Sound before steaming to Portsmouth for a 20-

day maintenance period.

On 6 October 1986, whilst *Intrepid* lay alongside at Portsmouth, there was a change of command when Captain P. K. Haddacks RN took over from Captain Provest. For the ship herself there were just three weeks to prepare for the next deployment, a two-month trip to the Middle East to take a leading role in 'Exercise Saif Sareea' (Arabic for Swift Sword). On 23 October in Plymouth Sound, *Intrepid* embarked 260 men of 40 Commando, together with two Sea Kings and personnel from 846 Squadron, before steaming south on the first stage of her deployment to warmer climes. After calling at Gibraltar the ship steamed east for Cyprus and the opportunity to begin acclimatization exercises with the marines being landed for manoeuvres which turned out to be marked by some unseasonal heavy rain. During the ship's southbound transit of the Suez Canal over 200 sailors and marines took the opportunity to visit Cairo and the Pyramids. It was also interesting to note that the last time men of 40 Commando had been in Egypt was during the Suez Crisis of 1956. This time, however, the visit was a much happier occasion and was confined to friendly sightseeing.

After leaving the Red Sea and entering the Gulf of Aden there was a short stop at Djibouti, which allowed for more acclimatization exercises on the long sandy beaches, before *Intrepid* steamed on into the Arabian Sea to the Omani island of Masirah. Here Commodore Larken and his staff joined the ship to take command of the amphibious operations, prior to which there was a rehearsal exercise. On leaving Masirah *Intrepid* joined units of the 'Global 86' deployment, including *Illustrious*, *Nottingham* and *Andromeda*, with the RFAs *Fort Grange*, *Olmeda* and *Orangeleaf*. Also taking part were ten Omani units, making a total of 17 ships. On 26 November, watched by the Sultan of Oman, the Secretary of State for Defence, who had flown out from London, an audience of senior British and Omani officers and representatives of the world's press, a simultaneous landing by eight landing craft and six Sea King helicopters from *Intrepid* and *Illustrious* was executed at Ras Al Hadd, close to Sur on the Omani mainland. With several tons of pyrotechnics being used as battle simulation, aircraft attacks by *Illustrious'* Sea Harriers and RAF Jaguars, naval gunfire support from *Nottingham* and 260 men of 40 Commando storming the beach, the effect was quite spectacular. After securing the beachhead, 40 Commando, with support from *Intrepid's* Sea Kings, set off on a strenuous four-day exercise with elements of the Sultan of Oman's land forces. On one occasion the intense heat was broken by a most unusual 40-minute torrential rainstorm, which produced flash floods with walls of water thundering down the normally dry and scorched wadis. As the water subsided the marines went on to 'attack' more positions, prior to the main heliborne assault on a defensive position. On conclusion of the 'battle' the marines and all of their equipment were re-embarked in *Intrepid* for the passage home which, once again, was made by way of the Suez Canal, Cyprus and Gibraltar. On 19 December, after disembarking 40 Commando in Plymouth Sound, *Intrepid* returned to Portsmouth in time for Christmas, having travelled over 11,000 miles in the space of nine weeks.

Shortly before she arrived home, the Secretary of State for Defence, no doubt influenced by his visit to *Intrepid*, announced in Parliament that a contract had been placed with Swan Hunter for a feasibility study into the possibilities of extending the lives of both *Intrepid* and *Fearless*. At the same time the Ministry invited the shipbuilding industry to participate in studies of a design option for new ships which would be their eventual replacements. In the space of five years the two assault ships had moved from virtual redundancy to a leading role in Britain's naval operations.

The new year of 1987 saw *Intrepid* back in her Dartmouth Training role and having embarked a complement of midshipmen and apprentices she sailed south to the sunny Canary Islands and the port of Las Palmas. The deployment continued with a passage to the Mediterranean and the second port of call, Naples. On the first day out of the Italian port city the ship received a visit from FOF3, Vice-Admiral Sir Julian Oswald, and carried out a short amphibious exercise during which the Admiral took a hand at the wheel of the BARV and an LCVP. As the ship steamed through the Greek islands, bound for Istanbul, the midshipmen under training took the LCUs on navigation exercises with ship's company members as passengers, putting in to four small ports in the eastern Greek islands. Good weather and excellent runs ashore made it an enjoyable experience, before they rendezvoused with *Intrepid* for the visit to Istanbul and the return home by way of Gibraltar. On arrival in Plymouth Sound, with the trainees having been landed, *Intrepid* changed to her amphibious role, and in company with *Dana Anglia* steamed north to Andalsnes in Norway with Headquarters 3 Commando Brigade and elements of the Brigade Air Squadron. In the words of one marine, 'The passage north was calm for the most part, but this made little difference to *Intrepid*, which seemed to have been designed to roll in a millpond.' The main landings were carried out in Gullasfjord, with the operation being completed in 36 hours, after which *Intrepid* left for the open sea, returning to the fjord to re-embark the force. The passage back to Plymouth was not as smooth as the outward journey, with the assault ship butting her way into a Force 10 gale and heavy seas, arriving in Plymouth Sound on 30 March. There was time left for one more short exercise off the south coast before *Intrepid* returned to Portsmouth on 3 April for an extended docking period and some well-earned leave.

It was the autumn of 1987 before *Intrepid* was at sea again and during the first half of November, following

3E Mess in *Intrepid* which accommodated men of the embarked force. Conditions are cramped and a 'pusser's' suitcase makes a makeshift writing desk. *(Royal Marines Museum, Eastney, No 14/2/10 - 511)*

Intrepid and a US Navy dock landing ship in Norwegian waters. *(Royal Marines Museum, Eastney, No 14/2/10 - 504)*

The minesweepers *Brunington* (M1115) and *Kellington* (M1154) alongside *Intrepid* during exercises in Scottish waters.

(Official, courtesy Commodore A.J.S. Taylor)

post-refit trials and work-up, she took part in a major exercise which was led by the aircraft carriers *Illustrious* and *Ark Royal*. It was the first exercise in which the assault ship had been involved since the provisions of the Stockholm Conference of January that year had come into force, and carrying Headquarters 3 Commando Brigade and elements of 3 Para who had been embarked in Falmouth Bay, *Intrepid* took part in a rehearsal off Cornwall before steaming north for the Clyde. Code-named 'Purple Warrior' the exercise involved some 40 vessels, RAF Tornadoes and Phantom aircraft, with over 20,000 personnel, all witnessed by Eastern Bloc observers. For the first time since the Falklands campaign the Royal Navy had to evaluate the lessons to be learned from a large-scale, non-NATO exercise by combined forces, and flying the pennant of Commodore Jeremy Larken *Intrepid* acted as the command ship within the amphibious area. Apart from the South Atlantic Task Force the exercise saw the largest British amphibious force to be assembled since the Korean War, and the scenario commenced on 9 November off Scotland's south-west coast, with a Services Protected Evacuation of UK citizens in the face of escalating insurgency within a British Dependency. Protected and supported by over 40 ships, with air mobility provided by 40 helicopters from all three services and with both RN and RAF Harriers operating from *Ark Royal*, the amphibious force was landed at first light in a storm-lashed Firth of Clyde. On board *Intrepid* were two Red Army colonels as observers, one of whom took the helm of an LCVP; the Cold War was clearly over and a new era of cooperation had begun. *Intrepid's* embarked force joined the ship again from Loch Ryan, and after the amphibious phase of the exercise had been completed the naval force took part in a limited naval 'war', which, ironically as it would turn out, left the destroyer *Nottingham* dead in the water following 'bomb damage'. The end of the exercise on 24 November saw the 'surrender' of the enemy on the island of Arran, after which *Intrepid* returned her embarked force to Plymouth Sound.

In early 1988 *Intrepid*, flying the pennant of the new COMAW, Commodore B. W. Turner, and with two of 846 Squadron's Sea Kings as well as men of 45 Commando embarked, returned to northern waters to visit Oslo, Stavanger and Bodo. There were amphibious exercises inside the Arctic Circle, which took the assault ship to the Trondheim area, but she returned to Portsmouth for her '21st birthday party'. Six of her former commanding officers, Vice-Admiral Sir Anthony Troup, Admiral Sir James Eberle, Captain J. F. Kidd, Captain D. Morse, Rear-Admiral P. Dingemans and Captain A. Provest, all attended the event. Ceremonial Divisions were held on the flight deck, which included apprentices, the band from HMS *Sultan* and an Honour Guard formed by men of 6 Assault Squadron. The parade was inspected by Admiral Eberle and sharing the birthday honour was LMEA Glyn Mills, who was born on Saturday 11 March 1967, the day that *Intrepid* had been commissioned for the first time at John Brown's shipyard. The centrepiece was a magnificent 134lb birthday cake featuring a model of the ship which had been designed and baked on board by the galley staff. Having cut the cake Admiral Eberle and LMEA Mills proposed a toast to *Intrepid* which was joined by the ship's company and visitors.

On 18 May 1988 there was a change of command when Captain J. C. L. Wright OBE RN took over from Captain Haddacks, and *Intrepid's* next major exercise came in the early summer of 1988 when, at Rosyth, 850 men of 45 Commando embarked in the assault ship and the LSLs *Sir Percivale* and *Sir Tristram*, following which they set course for the Mediterranean. Their destination was the island of Sardinia where they linked up with units from France and Italy for 'Exercise Dragon Hammer 88', a major NATO amphibious exercise. After a brief stopover in Gibraltar where a Combined Services Review was held to honour the outgoing Chief Minister, Sir Joshua Hassan, the Task Group steamed east to rendezvous with the Allied force off Sardinia and at the same time land force commanders joined *Intrepid* to plan the campaign. After a full dress rehearsal, and in marginal weather conditions, 45 Commando was landed, with its Headquarters being augmented by *Intrepid's* internal security platoon. Then, supported by a naval gunfire bombardment the marines advanced inland for a three-day battle. On completion of the tactical phase a period of cross-training was carried out, which for some marines included fast-roping from US Navy CH46 Sea Knight helicopters and tours of USS *Iwo Jima*. After re-embarking some elements of 45 Commando, *Intrepid* sailed to Naples for a five-day informal visit where, as well as the local bars and nightclubs, visits to Rome, Pompeii and Herculaneum were arranged, as well as sporting activities with resident Italian forces. With the islands of Capri, Procida and Ischia within easy travelling distance, few members of the ship's company were left at a loose end. When the visit came to an end the assault ship steamed home by way of Gibraltar to drop the commandos at Dundee and to take part in an Operational Training Exercise off the north-west coast of Scotland. That summer, during Navy Days at Portsmouth, despite her advanced years, *Intrepid* was one of the main attractions, along with the aircraft carrier *Illustrious*, for the 80,000 visitors.

Intrepid's autumn cruise saw her continuing in her amphibious role and sailing north to Norway for 'Exercise Teamwork' during which she operated with the ferry *Bolero* and elements of 42 Commando who were involved in a 'hook' operation in the area round Tennevollen. This was followed by a nine-week training cruise to the warmer waters of the Mediterranean, and whilst the UK was experiencing a distinctly wintry nip the ship's company was able to enjoy some much warmer 'hands to bathe' sessions from *Intrepid's* sterngate which, when lowered, provided an ideal lido area. The Warrant Officers' and CPOs' mess organized a 'country fete' on the flight deck, which was well attended and raised over £4,000 for charity. In early 1989, which was to be *Intrepid's* last full year of operational service, she was back in her amphibious role and in Norwegian waters again for 'Exercise Cold Winter 89'. Over 2,000 naval personnel, as well as Royal Marines and crews from 846 Squadron, took part in the NATO manoeuvres. The men of 42 Commando and 29 Commando Artillery Regiment, together with their vehicles, ammunition and stores, were carried to Norway in *Intrepid* and *Ark Royal*, which took on an amphibious role. The exercise began in the Tromso area where *Intrepid, Alacrity* and *Beaver* linked up with forces from Norway, the USA and the Netherlands for an airborne assault. Several VIPs, including three Members of Parliament, visited the forces afloat and ashore, and one of 846 Squadron's Sea Kings assisted a local avalanche rescue group with its training. During the deployment *Intrepid* found time to call at Narvik, where there was the opportunity for a run ashore inside the Arctic Circle.

At 09.00 on Tuesday 11 April 1989, an overcast and wet day in Portsmouth, *Intrepid* embarked the men, the four-ton trucks and the Land Rovers of 40 Commando, after which the ship's company enjoyed their last run ashore in Pompey for some weeks. Next day she left harbour, embarked two of 846 Squadron's Sea Kings, and set course south for the Mediterranean. After a rough and rain-lashed crossing of the Bay of Biscay, on 15 April the assault ship steamed into a warm and sunny Gibraltar and after a pleasant weekend alongside she sailed east for Sardinia and 'Dragon Hammer 89', a NATO exercise involving British, French, Spanish, Italian and US forces. During the night of 20 April advance forces were landed on the island from *Intrepid,* and in the early hours of the next day there was a full-scale dress rehearsal involving the LCUs, LCVPs and the two Sea Kings. On completion the amphibious force, which also included three LSLs, sailed to Sardinia's south coast and the operations area at Cape Teulada. At 03.55 on 22 April the main exercise began, with assault waves of rigid raiders, LCVPs and LCUs heading in perfect formation for the beach. Also involved in the landing was the assault ship's internal security platoon who, led by Lt Chris Dyke, 'roughed it' with the marines and carried out a mass casualty exercise. The operations, which were commanded from USS *Guadalcanal,* were judged to be a success and on 1 May, after another weekend at Gibraltar, *Intrepid* sailed west for a transatlantic crossing. After 12 days at sea, out of the morning mist on 13 May loomed the luxury hotels of Fort Lauderdale, and as the ship made her way into harbour the beaches, bars, nightclubs and discos became visible to the ship's company who were manning the upper decks. During the ten-day maintenance period in the sunshine state of Florida, many members of the ship's company found their way to Disney World at Orlando, the Florida Keys, the Everglades and even more distant destinations,

Intrepid enters Aruba Harbour during her Caribbean deployment in the summer of 1991.
(Royal Marines Museum, Eastney, No 14/2/10 - 508)

and over 100 wives and girlfriends managed to fly out for some brief reunions before the ship sailed for Vieques. On arrival in Puerto Rico there was an amphibious exercise with 40 Commando using landing craft and helicopters, after which the assault ship steamed south for weapons training, when she fired her Seacat missiles and close-range guns. After re-embarking the marines *Intrepid* set course for Aruba and on 20 May, followed by her small flotilla of LCUs and LCVPs in line astern, looking like a family of ducklings following their mother, she glided into the calm clear waters of Orangestad. Here the marines exercised with their Dutch counterparts, before the ship made an overnight passage to Curacao to carry out an amphibious assault with Dutch marines and members of the Antillian Militia on beaches two miles north of Willemstad. With the embarked force back on board *Intrepid* steamed to Grenada to take part in 'Exercise Tradewind'. Over 100 marines stormed ashore through the surf, or were landed from the Sea King helicopters to 'melt' into the island's landscape, assuming the guise of 'terrorists' in order to provide training for a friendly force from Jamaica and the surrounding islands. There was time for a brief run ashore in Barbados before the ship collected her marines and aircraft to head home by way of Port of Spain, Trinidad, on the final leg of her deployment.

Following her return to Portsmouth *Intrepid* underwent a period of assisted maintenance during which, on 22 September 1989, there was a final change of command when Captain R. A. Y. Bridges RN took over for the assault ship's last 12 months of operational service. For her autumn deployment the ship reverted to her training role, and with midshipmen from Britannia Royal Naval College, young Royal Marines officers from Lympstone, Marine Engineering Course officers from the Navy's engineering college at Manadon and apprentices frm HMS *Sultan* embarked she sailed for the Mediterranean. During this period, with visits to Venice, Athens, Naples and Toulon, there was plenty of scope for culture or, perhaps, for some less refined activities. At Venice the ship was visited by HRH Princess Michael of Kent, who attended the ship's official cocktail party, and before the arrival in Naples Major Paul Irvine gave a series of lectures on the Second World War battles around Monte Casino in 1944. The embarked trainees carried out operational training and the deployment culminated in 'Exercise Nirius 89', an annual Greek exercise in the Aegean Sea which included units of the French and Spanish navies.

Intrepid's first deployment of 1990 took her once again to the cold northern waters of Norway where she operated in the Tromso area, off the Lofoten Islands and in Malangen Fjord, as part of the annual 'Cold Winter' exercise. This also involved the aircraft carrier *Invincible*, operating in an amphibious role, and under cover of darkness the amphibious fleet, which also included three LSLs and the escorts *Alacrity, Amazon* and *Hermione,* steamed into Malangen Fjord, well inside the Arctic Circle;

the LCUs and LCVPs then had a 20-mile transit to the landing point in the fjord. As the exercise progressed, early one morning *Invincible's* port anchor cable parted and, very gently, the carrier grounded on the fjord's only mud bank. Although there were no press representatives aboard, with the ship towering above the fishermen's cottages on the shoreline, the incident had potential to cause embarrassment and it was imperative that she be refloated as quickly as possible. Ship's divers from both *Invincible* and *Intrepid* were soon in the water checking whether the propellers and rudder were clear of the bottom, and whether any damage had been caused which, fortunately, was limited to superficial scratches. Later, working with the tug *Nimble,* three of *Intrepid's* LCUs succeeded in pushing the carrier clear and she was refloated. The LCU coxswains involved were rewarded with a photograph of *Invincible* and suitable liquid refreshment. To mark the occasion all three LCUs sported an *'Invincible* battle honour' in the form of the carrier's silhouette on their cockpits. The exercise ended with the usual re-embarkation and a fast passage to Portsmouth to offload the marines and to send off the first Easter leave parties.

The summer of 1990 saw *Intrepid* steaming south through a calm and sunny Bay of Biscay with men of 40 Commando embarked, and after a weekend of relaxation in Gibraltar she made her way east for the annual 'Exercise Dragon Hammer' manoeuvres. Again *Invincible* was involved, together with four other aircraft carriers, USS *Dwight D. Eisenhower* and *Saipan,* ITS *Garibaldi,* and SPS *Principe de Asturias.* In addition to the carriers the exercise also involved ten amphibious units, 20 frigates and destroyers, and eight submarines, from seven NATO countries. Sadly one of *Invincible's* Sea Harrier pilots was lost when his aircraft crashed in the sea off Sardinia, and the carrier herself was withdrawn from the exercise early with machinery problems. *Intrepid* was involved in the main amphibious landings at Cape Teulada where 40 Commando made their way ashore supported by a Spanish airborne battalion and opposed by US Marines. On her return to Portsmouth the assault ship began her final six-week assisted maintenance period.

During the period alongside *Intrepid* received a visit from the First Sea Lord, Admiral Sir Julian Oswald, who toured the ship and met members of the ship's company. Finally, in late August *Intrepid* left Portsmouth for sea trials in the Channel and for her last operational deployment. In early September, despite rumours that she was bound for the Persian Gulf and the war against Iraq, the assault ship steamed west to Plymouth Sound where she embarked elements of 40 Commando before, on 8 September, loaded to the gunwales with men and equipment, she set course north for Scapa Flow and a rendezvous with the remainder of the exercise fleet. Any doubts about her destination were quickly dispelled when, early on 11 September, led by a minesweeper, she steamed into a very misty and chilly Scapa Flow. Once at anchor there followed an intense programme of amphibious drills and rehearsals, on completion of which *Intrepid* left Scapa Flow to rendezvous with the fleet off Cape Wrath before setting course for Namsos Fjord. Having made a rough crossing of the North Sea the troops were put ashore as the landing craft, rigid raiders and the helicopters of 3 Commando Brigade Air Squadron shattered the peace of Namsos town. Four days later, after the re-embarkation, *Intrepid* and *Ambuscade* left Namsos Fjord for a two-day visit to Copenhagen. On 27 September, after this brief period of relaxation, the assault ship sailed south once again, this time for Browndown Beach in the Solent and 'Exercise Logex 90'. At first light on 28 September, elements of the Commando Logistics Regiment and supporting units were being flown ashore to Gosport's Naval Air Station, HMS *Daedalus.* With a Brigade Support Area having been established, the landing craft quickly began to offload the embarked force, also taking the opportunity to carry out compatibility trials with Stalwart amphibious vehicles and a new 14-ton truck. Both proved successful, and with her part in the exercise over the assault ship steamed up Southampton Water to Marchwood Military Port for a berthing trial at the new deep water jetty and roll-on roll-off facility, an operation which brought out large crowds of spectators on both sides of the waterway. With the trial over *Intrepid* left the Solent for a six-day port visit to Amsterdam, the finale to the ship's 23-year career.

Before paying off for the last time *Intrepid* met her sister *Fearless* for final joint manoeuvres in the Channel. On Wednesday 10 October, with her paying-off pennant flying, hr ship's company manning the upper decks, the Royal Marines Band playing and her eight landing craft following in her wake, *Intrepid* entered Portsmouth Harbour for the last time. Since recommissioning in 1985 she had steamed some 170,000 nautical miles, visiting over 70 ports and participating in 20 major exercises. Soon after her arrival in Portsmouth *Fearless* took over as the operational assault ship and *Intrepid* was paid off. Over the years which followed *Intrepid* lay in Portsmouth Dockyard's No 3 basin, providing spare parts for her sister *Fearless,* and by the end of the 1990s she had even lost her sterngate. There was mounting criticism of the fact that public money was still being spent on her and on 31 August she was officially transferred to the Disposal and Reserve Ships Organization. In early 2002, having been joined by her now redundant sister *Fearless* and having been stripped of most of her vital machinery parts, she was listed as 'For Sale or Disposal'. As this final chapter is written *Intrepid* still lies in Portsmouth Dockyard where she is being stripped of dangerous asbestos and as soon as this has been completed it is almost certain that she will make her final passage, under tow, to the shipbreaker's yard.

In January 1991 *Intrepid* and *Fearless* met at sea for the last time. *(Official, courtesy Maritime Books, Liskeard)*

Looking run-down and neglected, and minus her stern gate. *Intrepid* in Portsmouth Dockyard in December 2000, having been laid up for nine years. *(The News, Portsmouth Publishing & Printing Ltd)*

HMS *Intrepid*
Commanding Officers:

	Date Appointed:
Captain J. A. R. Troup DSC RN	2 July 1966
Captain J. H. F. Eberle RN	5 December 1968
Captain W. D. M. Staveley RN	27 November 1970
Captain J. F. Kidd RN	5 April 1972
Captain N. J. S. Hunt MVO RN	21 February 1974
Captain D. H. Morse RN	5 June 1978
Captain P. G. V. Dingemans RN	1 April 1980
Captain A. G. M. A. Provest RN	8 January 1985
Captain P. K. Haddacks RN	6 October 1986
Captain J. C. L. Wright OBE RN	18 May 1988
Captain R. A. Y. Bridges RN	22 September 1989

HMS *Intrepid*
Previous Ships

The first *Intrepid* started life as the French ship *Serieux* which was taken by the Royal Navy in 1747 off Finisterre. Having been renamed *Intrepid* she saw action with Admiral Byng at Minorca in 1756, with Admiral Hawke off Isle d' Aix in 1758 and with Boscawen off Lagos in 1759. She also won honours at Quiberon Bay in 1759 and during the Havana Expedition in 1762. She was broken up at Chatham in 1765.

Launched at Woolwich in 1770, the second *Intrepid* was a Third Rate which saw service in the Caribbean, where she won battle honours at St Kitts in 1782 and at Martinique in 1809. She also saw service in the Mediterranean and the Atlantic. Between 1817 and 1820 she was a depot ship at Devonport where she acted as a receiving ship for those who were unfortunate enough to be taken by the Press Gangs. She was sold for scrap in 1828.

The third ship of the name started life as the merchantman *Free Trade*, but was bought by the Royal Navy in 1850 and commissioned as the 342-ton sloop *Intrepid*. She took part in Captain Austin's 1850-51 expedition to the Arctic, and later Commander F. L. McClintock's expedition there in 1854, when she was abandoned in the ice. The next *Intrepid* was an 862-ton vessel built at Blackwall on the River Thames in 1855.

Two more modern ships of the name served the Royal Navy during the twentieth century, the first being an Apollo-class cruiser of 3,600 tons which was built on the Clyde in 1891. By 1906, however, she was outdated and was laid up. In 1907 she was converted to a minelayer and she served in this capacity for three years when she became a depot ship. In 1917 she was stationed at Murmansk, and in April 1918 she was sunk as a blockship at Zeebrugge.

The next *Intrepid*, which was launched in December 1936, was an I-class destroyer of 1,890 tons, built at Cowes on the Isle of Wight. During the Second World War she had a magnificent record of service, which is revealed by her battle honours. These include Atlantic 1939-41, during which time she sank *U45* off Ireland; Dunkirk 1940; Norway 1941-42; *Bismarck* Action 1941; Arctic 1941-43; Malta Convoys 1942; Sicily 1943; Salerno 1943 and Aegean 1943. She was eventually sunk on 26 September 1943 in Leros Harbour after being dive-bombed by Stuka aircraft. Whenever she was in the area, the ship's company of the assault ship *Intrepid* would remember their predecessor by laying a wreath close to the spot where she was lost.

The Apollo-class cruiser *Intrepid* which was built in 1891. In April 1918 she was sunk as a blockship at Zeebrugge.
(Maritime Photo Library, Cromer, Norfolk, No 1006)

The I-class destroyer of 1936. This photograph shows her undergoing builder's trials, before her main armament was fitted.
(Maritime Photo Library, Cromer, Norfolk, No 1958)

HMS *Intrepid*
Battle Honours

Cela va sans dire
(That goes without saying)

Lagos 1759
Quiberon Bay 1759
Havana 1762
St Kitts 1782
Martinique 1794
Zeebrugge 1918
Atlantic 1939-41
Aegean 1943

Dunkirk 1940
Norway 1941-42
Bismarck Action 1941
Arctic 1941-43
Malta Convoys 1942
Sicily 1943
Salerno 1943
Falkland Islands 1982

Acknowledgements:

My thanks to Commodore A. J. S. Taylor CBE RN for kindly contributing the Foreword to this book, also to Tony Perrett (Royal Marines Historical Society), Gosport, Hampshire, for working tirelessly to research information about both *Fearless* and *Intrepid*. Thanks also to John S. Morris, Dalgety Bay, Fife, for his superb pen and ink drawings and Derek Fox, Southsea, for providing excellent photographs from his collection.

I must also thank the following for their kind help and, in many cases, for the loan of very valuable photographs: -
Brian (Mick) Ahern, Plymouth, Devon: John Ambler, Photographic Librarian, Royal Marines Museum, Eastney, Hampshire: Kenneth Anderson, Ulster Folk & Transport Museum, Holywood, County Down: Lt Cdr D. A. Barlow RN (Rtd), Emsworth, Hampshire: Michael Cassar, Valletta, Malta: Mike Critchley and Steve Bush, Maritime Books, Liskeard, Cornwall: Admiral Sir James Eberele GCB, Lower Abbotsleigh, Totnes, Devon: George Gardner, University of Glasgow: Phil Gornall, Bolton, Lancashire: Peter Grindon, Pill, North Somerset: John E. Higgins, Aylesbury, Buckinghamshire: Lee Howard, Street, Somerset: Ron Kelbrick, Llandudno Junction, Conwy: Michael Lennon, Waterlooville, Hampshire: David Lippman, Portsmouth, Hampshire: Colin Mitchell, Wokingham, Berkshire: Laurence Nolan, Carrickfergus, County Antrim: David Parry, Photographic Archive, Imperial War Museum, London: Harry Piper, Poole, Dorset: Peter Rudwick, Portchester, Hampshire: Neil Segger, Arbroath, Angus: Jerry Shore, Assistant Curator, Fleet Air Arm Museum, Yeovilton, Somerset: E. I. Shrimpton, Rugby, Warwickshire: Ron Slater, Northwich, Cheshire: John Solway, Friends Office, National Maritime Museum, Greenwich: Ian Spashett, Folkestone, Kent: Frank Stockton, Llay, Wrexham: Adrian Vicary, Maritime Photo Library, Cromer, Norfolk: John Vitti, Altrincham, Cheshire: David White, Weymouth, Dorset: Ian Wilson, Thatcham, Berkshire. Finally, to my wife Freda and my daughter Louise for all their help and support.

Other Titles Available

HMS *Eagle* 1942-1978 £18.95

HMS *Victorious* 1937-1969 £21

Three *Ark Royals* 1938-1999 £23

Tiger, Lion and *Blake* 1942-1986 £21.50

The Illustrious & Implacable Classes of Aircraft Carrier 1940-1969 £23

HMS *Hermes* 1923 & 1959 £24

The Colossus-Class Aircraft Carriers 1944-1972 £24

HMS *Vanguard* 1944-1960 £19.95

HMS *Glory* 1945-1961 £19.95

SS *Canberra* 1957-1997 £21

(Plus £2.50 postage in UK/EU or £4.50 worldwide surface mail)

FAN PUBLICATIONS
17 Wymans Lane
Cheltenham
Glos GL51 9QA
Tel/Fax: 01242 580290
E-mail: info@fan-publications.i12.com

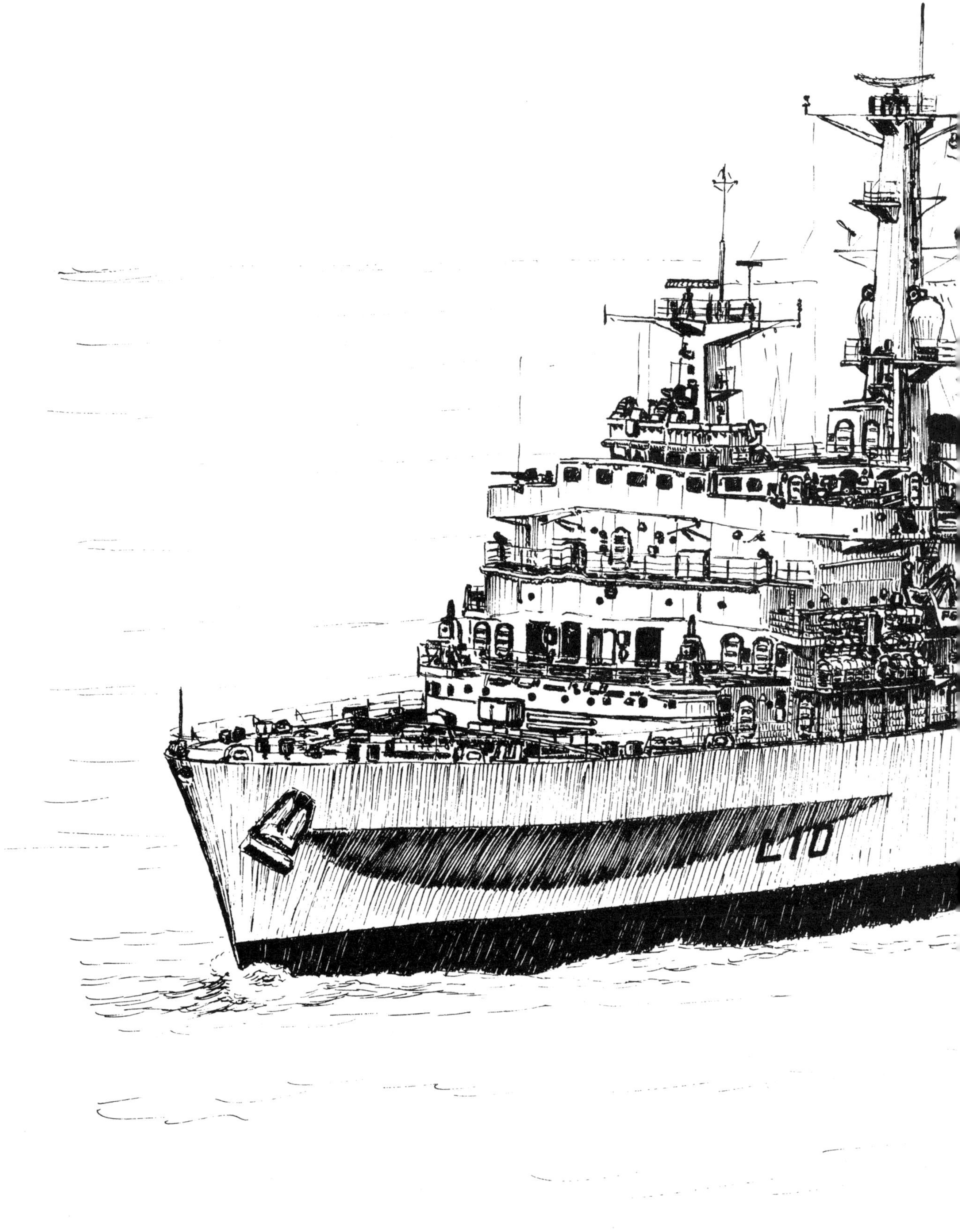
L10